WHAT'S NEW?

Recent developments included in this supplement:

- Specific dates of harassment are not necessary to prove a hostile environment; proof of ongoing conduct is sufficient (*Fernot v. Crafts Inn, Inc.*)

- Federal Rule of Evidence 412 governs the admissibility of evidence relating to the plaintiff's use of sexually oriented language in the workplace (*Sheffield v. Hilltop Sand & Gravel Co., Inc.*)

- Relatively "mild" harassment may become tortious if continued over a substantial period of time (*August v. Star Enterprise, Inc.*)

- The undermining of employee security through threats constituted quid pro quo sexual harassment (*Talada v. International Service System, Inc.*)

- Evidence of continued harassment by supervisor following dismissal was clearly relevant to the jury's assessment of damages (*Nicks v. State of Missouri*)

- Damages were awarded for intentional infliction of emotional distress when sexual harassment exacerbated a preexisting disease, which led to permanent disability (*Estate of Underwood v. National Credit Union*)

- A supervisory employee can state a claim for relief against his or her employer on basis of hostile work environment created by one or more subordinate employees (*Hanlon v. Chambers*)

- The president of the United States is not entitled to immunity during the course of the presidential term for conduct occurring before taking office (*Jones v. Clinton*)

SEXUAL HARASSMENT IN THE WORKPLACE
LAW AND PRACTICE
SECOND EDITION
VOLUME 1

1997 Cumulative Supplement No. 1 Current through July 1996
by
ALBA CONTE

*****HERE'S WHAT'S NEW INSIDE*****

- Specific dates of harassment are not necessary to prove a hostile environment, see page 102, volume 2.
- Federal Rule of Evidence 412 governs the admissibility of evidence relating to the plaintiff's use of sexually oriented language in the workplace, see page 126, volume 1.
- Relatively "mild" harassment may become tortious if continued over substantial period of time, see page 76, volume 1.
- and more, see page i for details.

---

*Insert in the pocket in the back
inside cover of the bound book.
Discard 1996 Cumulative Supplement No. 2.*

Wiley Law Publications
JOHN WILEY & SONS, INC.
New York • Chichester • Brisbane • Toronto • Singapore • Weinheim

CONTE/HARASS 2E2VST 97S1
ISBN 0-471-17587-0

Library of Congress Cataloging in Publication Data:

ISBN 0-471-01447-8 (v.1)
ISBN 0-471-01446-X (set)
ISBN 0-471-17587-0 (supplement)

Printed in the United States of America

10 9 8 7 6 5 4 3 2 1

PREFACE

Despite little media attention, the case of *Jones v. Clinton* recently reached the Eighth Circuit Court of Appeals, which held that the president was not entitled to a temporary or limited immunity during his term from civil suits alleging actionable behavior by him in his private capacity rather than in his official capacity as president. The court concluded that if the trial preliminaries of the trial itself became barriers to the effective performance of his official duties, Mr. Clinton's remedy was to move for rescheduling, additional time, or continuances. The district court must protect the president's role as chief executive without impeding Jones's right to have her claims heard without undue delay.

The saga of Bob Packwood ended with his resignation late last year. While Packwood's demise was propelled only in part by allegations of sexual harassment, it was, unfortunately, that aspect of the investigation into misconduct that received the most media exposure. Much of the alleged behavior occurred before such conduct was illegal, and although under today's standards the senator may have created a hostile environment for his employees, there is no evidence that he ever used sexual advances as leverage for employment opportunities.

On August 3, 1995, a manufacturer of women's cosmetics agreed to pay a record $1.2 million to 15 female employees who alleged they were humiliated, hounded, and sexually harassed by the company's chief executive. The Equal Employment Opportunity Commission said the agreement by the Farmingdale, New York-based Del Laboratories was the largest settlement of a sexual harassment suit ever reached by the commission. The plaintiffs were secretaries or executive assistants to the alleged harasser, and the EEOC said another 12 women had related similar charges against him. The settlement, which still must be approved by the court, provides for payment to the 15 complainants and mandatory courses for all employees and management of the company on sexual harassment issues. EEOC chairman Gilbert Casellas told a news conference that the case was important because of the size of the settlement, the seniority of the person accused, and the large number of people who came forward.

On October 28, 1994, a jury awarded $1.7 million in compensatory damages to Lt. Paula Coughlin, one of several dozen women sexually

PREFACE

assaulted during the Tailhook convention in 1991 and the first to publicly admit that she had been assaulted. On October 31, the jury ordered the Hilton Hotel, which was accused of failing to set up adequate security, to pay $5 million in punitive damages. Sexual harassment continued to plague the Navy in 1995, with several officers denied promotions and one court-martialed on charges of sexual harassment.

But the gravity of sexual harassment aside, there are still many unresolved issues in sexual harassment law: What kind of conduct constitutes "sufficiently severe and pervasive" behavior? Should the alleged harassment be analyzed through the perspective of a reasonable person or woman? Does limiting sexually oriented speech at the workplace violate the First Amendment? Has the after-acquired evidence rule been applied to sexual harassment? How sexual does conduct have to be to be considered *sexual* harassment? Should sexual harassment by female superiors be judged by the same criteria as harassment by male superiors? Does the fact that an employer harasses men as well as women preclude a finding of sexual harassment, when the conduct clearly would have been sexual harassment had it been aimed at women alone? Is harassment by members of the same sex sexual harassment under the law? Are supervisors individually liable for sexual harassment? Courts continue to grapple with these and other issues. In this supplement, courts decide questions about presidential immunity liability, favoritism, mental exams of plaintiffs, free speech, appropriate employer response, and many other topics.

Materials new in this supplement are indicated by an asterisk (*) in the left margin, throughout the supplement.

ACKNOWLEDGMENTS

Special thanks to S. Beville May for her good work, good cheer and support, and to Lisa Bogar, Summer Boslaugh, Kathe Koretsky, and Jamie Morton for their excellent paralegal skills.

Portland, Oregon   ALBA CONTE
October 1996

EMPLOYMENT LAW TITLES FROM WILEY LAW PUBLICATIONS

CHAPTER 1

SEXUALITY, SOCIAL RELATIONS, AND THE WORKPLACE

§ 1.1 Introduction

Page 1, add to footnote 2:

The United States Merit Systems Protection Board updated its 1980 and 1987 studies in an October 1995 report titled "Sexual Harassment in the Federal Workplace: Trends, Progress, and Continuing Challenges" [hereinafter MSPB 1995 report]. The study concludes that "unwanted sexual attention remains a widespread problem in the Federal sector. At the same time, however, Federal agencies have made strides in educating their workforces and raising the level of sensitivity to the issues surrounding sexual harassment." Comments of the Chair, MSPB 1995 report.

§ 1.5 The Effects

Page 12, add to footnote 58:

See also Chester v. Northwest Iowa Youth Emergency Servs. Ctr., 869 F. Supp. 700 (N.D. Iowa 1994). As a result of sexual harassment, the plaintiff alleged symptoms including anxiety attacks, headaches, sleeping difficulties, nightmares, loss of self-esteem, crying, loss of trust in males, marital stress, weight gain, depression, loss of appetite, panic disorder, a major depressive episode, and posttraumatic stress disorder.

Page 13, add to footnote 61:

See also Barnes v. Breeden, CA No. H-92-0898 (S.D. Tex. Oct. 20, 1995). The plaintiff, a female African-American attorney for the SEC, established a sexually and racially hostile working environment. The plaintiff experienced emotional distress that manifested itself in sleep-lessness, depression, nervousness, and physical symptoms such as digestive disorder, headaches, rashes, and swelling. See § **3.18.**

Page 14, add to footnote 62:

Kelly-Zurian v. Wohl Shoe Co., 22 Cal. App. 4th 397, 27 Cal. Rptr. 2d 457, 64 Fair Empl. Prac. Cas. (BNA) 603 (1994) (sexual harassment, constructive wrongful discharge, intentional infliction of emotional distress). The lower court properly entered a judgment upon a $125,000 jury verdict in favor of the plaintiff in a sexual harassment action alleging that for three years the plaintiff suffered verbal and physical harassment at the hands of her supervisor. He would come up from behind and put both his hands on her breasts, pinch her buttocks, grab her crotch and ask if she "was wet," ask her what kind of lingerie she was wearing, how was her "pussy," if she "got any last night," if she "took it in the ass," and if she "swallowed" or "gave head." 64 Fair Empl. Prac. Cas. at 605. The plaintiff resigned and suffered panic attacks consisting of anxiety, tightness in her chest, heart palpitations, sleeplessness and depression, and developed a serious drinking problem.

Page 14, add after footnote 65 reference in last paragraph:

The MSPB 1995 report discussed the monetary costs of sexual harassment:

Monetary Costs to the Government

In 1980 the Board estimated that for the 2 years preceding that year's survey, sexual harassment cost the Federal Government $189 million. For the 2 years preceding the 1987 survey, the cost of sexual harassment was estimated at $267 million. Our most recent figures, covering the 2 years preceding administration of the 1994 survey (April 1992 to April 1994), show an estimated cost to the Government of $327 million.

The 1994 estimate represents an increase over the cost figures derived from the 1987 study. However, this increase reflects inflation and the rise in salaries to a greater degree than it reflects an increase in the ill effects of harassment. Although a larger number of 1994 respondents who had experienced sexually harassing behaviors reported a decline in productivity than did our 1987 respondents, the amount of the decline was less. Further, as indicated earlier, fewer respondents reported leaving their jobs or using sick leave because of harassment than in 1987. Nevertheless, the price that employees and the Government pay in reacting to and dealing with sexual harassment is far too high.

Computing Sexual Harassment Costs. In computing the cost of sexual harassment in the Federal Government we take into account the cost of job turnover, sick leave that victims say they used as a result of the harassment, the cost of the individual productivity decreases reported by victims, and the estimated productivity lost by workgroups in which harassment occurs. These elements are generally computed separately for men and women (because their average annual salaries differ) and then are added together for a dollar total.

Our estimate of the cost of sexual harassment is conservative. Among the items we did not include are the cost of benefits paid by the Government and the cost of overtime for other workers who fill in for employees absent because of the effects of workplace harassment. Nor did we factor in the cost of dealing with informal complaints, processing formal ones, and handling litigation. A summary of the factors used to arrive at the estimate follows.

Job turnover. Based on data provided by our survey respondents regarding how sexual harassment affected them, we estimate that in the 2 years preceding the 1994 survey, sexual harassment caused 19,727 Federal employees (victims) to leave their jobs through reassignment, being fired, being transferred, or quitting. This is a decrease since the Board's last sexual harassment survey, which found that an estimated 36,647 employees had left their jobs because of their experiences with sexually harassing behaviors. Although the population represented by the survey respondents has decreased by 16 percent since 1987, the turnover decrease since 1987 is over 46 percent.

The expenses associated with replacing these employees include the cost of offering jobs to the replacements (recruitment and placement costs); the cost of background checks for new or potential employees; and the cost of training the replacements. Turnover estimates for the 1987 study conservatively set replacement costs at $1,000 per employee. Increasing that amount—again conservatively—to account for inflation, we estimate that employees who left because of harassment in the 2 years preceding the 1994 survey cost $1,250 each to replace. The price of turnover among Federal employees, then, amounted to an estimated $24.7 million during the 2-year period of the study.

This amount is 33 percent lower than the $36.7 million turnover cost for the period preceding the Board's 1987 survey. The turnover among men is down 60 percent and the turnover among women is 39 percent lower than in 1987.

SEXUALITY, SOCIAL RELATIONS

Sick leave. The emotional and physical impact that sexual harassment has on its victims comes with a high price tag for the employer as well as for the employee. About 8 percent of survey respondents who had experienced harassment reported using sick leave as a result. As with job turnover, the use of sick leave as a response to sexual harassment has shown a significant decrease since the Board's 1987 study, when 13 percent of individuals who had experienced unwanted sexual attention reported using sick leave as a result.

In arriving at the cost of harassment-related sick leave, we used responses of survey participants to calculate the total number of hours of sick leave used by men and by women Governmentwide as a result of sexual harassment. Using those estimates and the average annual adjusted basic pay for male and female Federal employees, we calculated a total sick leave cost of about $14.9 million. This represents an 87 percent drop in sick leave usage among men and a 35 percent drop for women, with a consequent 43 percent reduction since 1987 in the cost of sick leave usage resulting from sexual harassment.

Individual productivity losses. Even when the targets of sexual harassment do not find it necessary to use leave as a result of their experiences, some report that the amount or quality of their work suffers during and following the experiences. Survey respondents who had experienced harassing behaviors were asked to indicate how much, if at all, their productivity had been reduced as a result of the unwanted attention and how long the reduction continued.

Although nearly 9 out of 10 victims indicated that they suffered no reduction in productivity, or only a slight loss, the total effect on work quantity and quality and the dollar value associated with the reduction are still considerable. In determining how much the loss of productivity cost the Government, we took into account these responses along with the average annual adjusted pay for males and females, and arrived at an estimated total of $93.7 million for the 2-year period preceding the survey.

As with turnover and sick leave usage, these results reflect a lessening of the negative effects of sexual harassment since the Board's 1987 study. Although the dollar cost of individual productivity losses was higher in 1994 than in 1987 (when it was estimated to be $76.3 million), the higher figure reflects higher salaries in 1994 rather than more time lost due to the disruptive effects of sexual harassment. While in 1994 a larger percentage of respondents reported a loss of productivity, the loss wasn't as severe and didn't last as long as it did for 1987 survey respondents. We estimate that the amount of time lost due to sexual harassment has declined by about 37 percent for men and stayed about the same for women.

§ 1.5   EFFECTS

Work group productivity losses. Because sexual harassment can affect not only the individual victims but also their coworkers, supervisors, and others with whom they interact at work, work group productivity is included in our estimate of harassment's cost to the Government.

For the study period covered by the 1987 survey, the cost of work group productivity losses was estimated at over $128 million. These costs were calculated on the basis of a survey question which asked employees who had experienced unwanted sexual attention whether the unwanted attention had affected the productivity of others in their work group. Factoring in the rise in average basic pay for men and women since the last survey, we estimate the cost of work group productivity losses for the 1994 study period to be $193.8 million.

Total Cost. Our estimate of the cost of sexual harassment to the Government over the 2-year period for which victims were reporting may be summarized as follows:

Job turnover	$24.7 million
Sick leave	14.9 million
Individual productivity	93.7 million
Work group productivity	193.8 million
Total	$327.1 million

If these cost figures seem too large to have much down-to-earth meaning, it may help to equate lost time to lost money. For example, imagine an employee who's being bothered by a coworker who leers at her or makes comments full of innuendo or double entendres, or who tells jokes that are simply inappropriate in a work setting. The time this employee spends worrying about the coworker, the time she spends confiding in her office mate about the latest off-color remark, the time she spends walking the long way to the photocopier to avoid passing his desk, is all time that sexual harassment steals from all of us who pay taxes.

Adding up those minutes and multiplying by weeks and months begins to paint a picture of how costly sexual harassment is. Increase this one individual's lost time by the thousands of cases like this in a year, and the waste begins to look enormous. And this may well be a case that doesn't even come close to being considered illegal discrimination by the courts. Whether or not they're illegal, these situations are expensive.

Id. at 23–26 (footnote omitted).

CHAPTER 2

HISTORY OF SEXUAL HARASSMENT LAW

§ 2.17 —Complainant's Voluntary Participation

Page 67, add to footnote 206:

Cf. Honea v. SGS Control Servs. Inc., 859 F. Supp. 1025 (E.D. Tex. 1994). A terminated female employee stated a claim for sexual harassment but the employer's conduct was not outrageous enough to violate the plaintiff's right to be free from intentional infliction of emotional distress. When the alleged harasser was the plaintiff's supervisor, a fact issue was raised regarding whether management was on notice of the alleged incidents. The court rejected the defendant's contention that there was no evidence that the conduct was unwelcome and that on occasion the plaintiff did not wear a bra to work and that she delivered roses to her male coworkers. "Aside from the fact that Title VII does not require a woman to wear a bra in order to pursue a claim for sexual harassment," the plaintiff's deposition testimony countered the defendant's implication by explaining that she wore no bra to work because she wore coveralls, and that she gave flowers to male and female workers alike. With respect to the intentional infliction of emotional distress claim, while the plaintiff alleged that she was propositioned and that her coworkers repeatedly made sexual comments, it is well settled that even conduct that may be illegal under Title VII may not be the sort of extreme and outrageous conduct necessary to support an intentional infliction claim.

§ 2.25 —Mixed Motive Cases

Page 76, add to footnote 241:

Cram v. Lamson & Sessions Co., 49 F.3d 466 (8th Cir. 1995). See **§ 6.43.**

6

In Stacks v. Southwestern Bell Yellow Pages, Inc., 27 F.3d 1316 (8th Cir. 1994), the Eighth Circuit held that the district court improperly ruled in favor of the employer defendant, under the *Price Waterhouse* mixed-motives analysis, in a sexual harassment action by a former telephone directory sales representative, when evidence of discriminatory treatment and sexually oriented activities at company parties established a hostile environment. The mixed-motives analysis is inapplicable to a hostile work environment claim. Such a theory was designed for a challenge to an adverse employment decision in which both legitimate and illegitimate considerations played a part, and an employer could never have a legitimate reason for creating a hostile work environment. Rather, the key issue in analyzing a hostile work environment claim is whether members of one sex are exposed to disadvantageous terms or conditions of employment to which members of the other sex are not exposed. The district court erred as a matter of law by focusing on the plaintiff's private life in discounting her testimony that "closed parties," to which spouses were not invited and which took place in hotel rooms after canvasses, made her feel less than human because she had admitted that she had been seeing a married coworker. The district court also erred when it found that the company could not be held liable for an incident following a golf tournament, during which an employee put on a videotape showing him in a car with bare-breasted women sales representatives, on the basis that the incident was isolated and there was no showing of company involvement when viewed in the context of the parties following the close of a canvass and a sales meeting where a stripper performed. The videotape incident was not isolated. There was also undisputed testimony that managers from several states were present for the showing of the tape, but there was no evidence that the company ever reprimanded anyone for the incident.

§ 2.30 Retroactivity

Pages 78–79, replace entire section with:

In *Landgraf v. USI Film Products*, 114 S. Ct. 1483 (1994), a sexual harassment case, the Supreme Court held that the damages and jury trial provisions of the Civil Rights Act of 1991 are not retroactive.[243]

Pages 78–79, replace footnote 243 with:

See also Dombeck v. Milwaukee Valve Co., 40 F.3d 230 (7th Cir. 1994). A female employee was improperly given a jury trial on her sexual harassment claim when the alleged conduct arose before enactment of the Civil Rights Act of 1991. Thus, the injunction entered by the federal district judge on the basis of the jury's finding of liability was invalid, even though the findings were unimpugned and even though there was sufficient and perhaps overwhelming evidence to support the jury's verdict, and the district judge so found in denying the defendant's post-trial motion for judgment as a matter of law. But the court of appeals hesitated to say that only one reasonable conclusion was possible from the evidence or that the district judge would not have been justified in disregarding the jury's verdict. The error in submitting the plaintiff's Title VII claim to a jury could be cured by the entry of independent find-ings of fact and conclusions of law by the district judge.

Segarra v. Universidad Politecnica de Puerto Rico, 865 F. Supp. 72 (D.P.R. 1994). The court would not apply the Civil Rights Act of 1991 to a sexual harassment action by a female professor alleging that the defen-dant university dismissed her in retaliation for complaints of sexual harassment, even though the alleged sexual acts occurred before the Act's enactment date, when the discharge occurred after the date of enactment.

Page 79, delete footnotes 244 and 245.

§ 2.31 *Harris v. Forklift Systems, Inc.*

Page 82, add to footnote 253:

King v. Hillen, 21 F.3d 1572 (Fed. Cir. 1994). See **§ 6.44.**

CHAPTER 3

ELEMENTS OF SEXUAL HARASSMENT CLAIMS

§ 3.2 Implications for Employees

* *Page 87, add to footnote 6:*

Cf. Biggs v. Nicewonger Co., Inc., 897 F. Supp. 483 (D. Or. 1995). A former employee brought a Title VII action against former employer and supervisor alleging sexual harassment, retaliatory discharge, as well as an intentional infliction of emotional distress claim under Oregon law. The plaintiff moved the court for an order excluding evidence of the sexual predisposition of any victim of sexual harassment pursuant to Rule 412 of the Federal Rules of Evidence. In response to the plaintiff's sexual harassment complaint, the defendant employer had advised the plaintiff that she may have somewhat invited the problem by her mode of dress and counseled her to wear more conservative clothes. The court, applying the prohibition of Rule 412, prohibited evidence of unrelated sexual behavior or sexual predisposition. In the event that the plaintiff introduced evidence that her supervisor sexually harassed another employee, evidence of the actions taken by the company in response to the complaints of the other employee would be relevant evidence. However, specific rulings as to the admissibility of evidence could not be made at this stage in the proceedings.

The plaintiff also moved the court pursuant to Rule 609(c) of the Federal Rules of Evidence for an order excluding evidence of her prior criminal conduct or her criminal record on the grounds that her conviction for negotiating a bad check with insufficient funds in the bank had been set aside. The defendants opposed this motion on the grounds that the crime of negotiating a bad check is a crime that involves dishonesty or false statement, and an order setting aside the conviction did not preclude the defendants from using that conviction to impeach Biggs's credibility. There was no evidence in this record of a "finding of rehabilitation" or a "finding of innocence" under Rule 609(c) and thus

9

Rule 609(c) did not preclude the introduction of evidence of Biggs's criminal conviction.

Page 88, add to footnote 10:

Honea v. SGS Control Servs. Inc., 859 F. Supp. 1025 (E.D. Tex. 1994). A terminated female employee stated a claim for sexual harassment but the employer's conduct was not outrageous enough to violate the plaintiff's right to be free from intentional infliction of emotional distress. When the alleged harasser was the plaintiff's supervisor, a fact issue was raised regarding whether management was on notice of the alleged incidents. The court rejected the defendant's contention that there was no evidence that the conduct was unwelcome and that on occasion the plaintiff did not wear a bra to work and that she delivered roses to her male coworkers. "Aside from the fact that Title VII does not require a woman to wear a bra in order to pursue a claim for sexual harassment," the plaintiff's deposition testimony countered the defendant's implication by explaining that she wore no bra to work because she wore coveralls, and that she gave flowers to male and female workers alike. With respect to the intentional infliction of emotional distress claim, while the plaintiff alleged that she was propositioned and that her coworkers repeatedly made sexual comments, it is well settled that even conduct that may be illegal under Title VII may not be the sort of extreme and outrageous conduct necessary to support an intentional infliction claim.

§ 3.7   Implications for Employees

Page 93, add to footnote 25:

Dey v. Colt Constr. & Dev. Co., 28 F.3d 1446 (7th Cir. 1994) (reasonable person standard applied).

§ 3.10   The Harasser

Page 95, add to footnote 28:

Duron v. Hancock, 64 Fair Empl. Prac. Cas. (BNA) 81 (D. Kan. 1993). The court denied the defendant's motion for summary judgment in a Title IX action charging quid pro quo and hostile environment sexual harassment and intentional infliction of emotional distress when the former owners of an unincorporated hairstyling school could be found directly liable for a supervisor's alleged sexual harassment of an instructor. The former owners delegated authority to the supervisor to run the school and could fire or promote the plaintiff.

Page 95, add to footnote 31:

Caplan v. Fellheimer Eichen Braverman & Kaskey, 882 F. Supp. 1529 (E.D. Pa. 1995). A partner in a law firm was not an employer under Title VII and thus not subject to personal liability.

Page 95, add at end of section:

In *Karibian v. Columbia University*, 14 F.3d 773 (2d Cir.), *cert. denied*, 114 S. Ct. 2693 (1994), the Second Circuit held that an employer is liable for the discriminatory, abusive work environment created by a supervisor if the supervisor uses her or his actual or apparent authority to further the harassment, or if she or he was otherwise aided in accomplishing the harassment by the existence of the agency relationship.

> Our conclusion that Columbia would be liable on a hostile environment claim for the harassment alleged by Karibian follows naturally from our earlier conclusion that Karibian stated a valid claim for *quid pro quo* harassment. . . . It would be a jarring anomaly to hold that conduct which always renders an employer liable under a *quid pro quo* theory does not result in liability to the employer when the same conduct becomes so severe and pervasive as to create a discriminatory abusive work environment.

Id. at 780–81.

§ 3.12 —Coworkers

Page 97, add before "Zabkowicz" citation in footnote 37:

Ball v. Renner, 54 F.3d 664 (10th Cir. 1995). In an action by a former police dispatcher against the city and a coworker police officer under Title VII and for intentional infliction of emotional distress, alleging that over a two-month period the coworker followed her home many times, continually tried to put his arm around her, once grabbed her and tried to dance, and finally came into a dark closet with her and shut the door twice before she escaped, the coworker was not liable as an employer under Title VII when he had no supervisory authority over the plaintiff.

Page 98, add to footnote 40:

Doe v. RR Donnelley & Sons Co., 843 F. Supp. 1278 (S.D. Ind. 1994). When alleged harassers are coworkers who do not act as agents of the employer, the employer should not be held liable for the incidents of sexual harassment if it was not given the opportunity to remedy the situation (citing the first edition of this text). The court noted that its holding should not be construed to require plaintiffs to give affirmative notice to their employers or supervisors that they have been harassed in every case:

> Thus, in cases where previous complaints have been brought against a particular supervisor for sexual harassment, a company would have constructive knowledge that corrective measures are necessary; thus, inaction or a claim of ignorance would not be as persuasive as in this case, where nothing was brought to its attention and plaintiff has brought to the court's attention no prior incidents involving [her supervisor] and other female employees.

Id. at 1283 n.2. The court of appeals affirmed, Doe v. R.R. Donnelley & Sons Co., 42 F.3d 439 (7th Cir. 1994), noting that although the plaintiff could not maintain a cause of action based on her supervisor's conduct because her complaint was not timely, it had serious reservations as to whether it was appropriate for the district court to hold as a matter of law that the conduct was not actionable when it persisted for a lengthy period of time and was a pervasive aspect of the plaintiff's employment during that period. The court concluded that the plaintiff did not show that there was a sufficiently close nexus between the conduct of the supervisor at the North Plant and the later conduct of fellow employees at the South Plant to permit the characterization of a continuous violation. With respect to the conduct at the South Plant, it was not at all clear on the record that the supervisor actually witnessed the hugging of plaintiff by a coworker, and the plaintiff never reported the incident, even though she was aware of the company's sexual harassment policy, and of the company's willingness to take action, as management had responded promptly to her complaint involving heavy breathing on her voice mail by a coworker.

Page 99, add at beginning of footnote 44:

Gross v. Burggraf Const. Co., 53 F.3d 1531 (10th Cir. 1995) (truck driver);

Page 99, add to footnote 45:

Annis v. County of Westchester, 36 F.3d 251 (2d Cir. 1994) (police lieutenant).

Welsh v. City & County of S.F., 887 F. Supp. 1293 (N.D. Cal. 1995) (female police officer).

Bintner v. Burlington N., Inc., 857 F. Supp. 1484 (D. Wyo. 1994) (locomotive engineer).

Anthony v. County of Sacramento Sheriff's Dep't, 845 F. Supp. 1396 (E.D. Cal. 1994) (deputy sheriff).

See also Williams v. Marriott Corp., 864 F. Supp. 1168 (M.D. Fla. 1994) (security officer); Nelson-Cole v. Borg-Warner Sec. Corp., 881 F. Supp. 71 (D.D.C. 1995) (security officer).

§ 3.13 —Nonemployees

* *Page 102, add to footnote 61:*

Murray v. New York Univ. College of Dentistry, 57 F.3d 243 (2d Cir. 1995). A student in a dental school brought a Title IX gender discrimination action and retaliation claim against the university based on sexual harassment by a patient in dental clinic. Despite a warning by the head of the clinic to cease his offensive behavior,

> Davidson continued to importune Murray for dates and to make professions of love to her; he also began to stalk Murray, following her both at the clinic and in other parts of the College and outside of NYU. On several occasions, he followed Murray to a friend's apartment and waited outside for her. In an effort to avoid Davidson, Murray began to enter the clinic through a back door, use the stairways rather than the elevators, and alter her routes to and from the clinic.

Id. at 245. The head of the dental clinic made no further inquiry about Davidson's conduct and took no action to ensure that it had stopped. The district court held that since Davidson was not an agent of NYU or an NYU employee with supervisory authority over Murray, his conduct could not be imputed to the College unless an NYU official or agent had notice that Murray was being subjected to a hostile environment and failed to take appropriate corrective action. The court noted that when the complaint was made to the head of the clinic, he promptly responded by admonishing Davidson to stop harassing Murray. The court stated that since Murray did not allege that she or anyone else thereafter informed the head that Davidson's offensive conduct had continued, the head could reasonably have inferred that the warning had been effective, and that the initial complaint to the head could not be considered to constitute notice that the harassment continued thereafter.

The court of appeals agreed that the university could not be liable without notice of harassment, and that the university was not liable for retaliation. The court declined to apply a constructive discharge standard:

> We think it unnecessary to decide here to what extent we would apply a constructive-notice standard in cases under either Title VII or Title IX, however; for we conclude that, even assuming a broad application of that standard, and drawing all reasonable inferences in Murray's favor, the complaint fails to allege that even NYU's agents knew or should have known of the continued harassment in the present case.

Id. at 250. The plaintiff could point to only two incidents that she contended gave NYU actual or constructive notice of the harassment prior to its termination, and neither of these could support a reasonable inference that NYU had the requisite notice. The head of the clinic's response as alleged in the complaint was sufficiently calculated to end the harassment. Without an allegation that the head was ever informed that her admonition had not been heeded, there can be no inference that the head, and thereby NYU, had any notice that the harassment continued.

Nor did the court find any merit to Murray's contention that Davidson's harassment was so persistent and became so widely known at the college that NYU must have known, or in the exercise of reasonable care should have known, that Murray was subject to a discriminatorily abusive environment at the dental clinic. The complaint's allegations that "numerous" other NYU dental students knew of Davidson's misconduct, and that these students "teased" Murray about her "boyfriend," did not support the inference that any agent of NYU was also aware of the harassment. Indeed, the allegations that Murray's fellow students made light of Davidson's conduct undercuts such an inference by suggesting that even these students were unaware that Davidson's conduct was offensive and abusive.

§ 3.16   —Same Sex Advances

Page 105, add to footnote 82 following First Circuit case:

Second Circuit: Sardinia v. Dellwood Foods, Inc., 1995 WL 640502 (S.D.N.Y. 1995) (same sex sexual harassment claims are actionable under Title VII). *Cf.* Vandeventer v. Wabash Nat'l Corp., 867 F. Supp. 790 (N.D. Ind. 1994) (same sex harassment not actionable under Title VII). *Accord* Garcia v. Elf Atochem N. Am., 28 F.3d 446, 451 (5th Cir. 1994) ("[h]arassment by a male supervisor against a male subordinate does not state a claim under Title VII even though the harassment has sexual overtones").

Sixth Circuit: EEOC v. Walden Book Co., 855 F. Supp. 1100 (M.D. Tenn. 1995) (same sex harassment is actionable under Title VII):

[T]he plain meaning of the phrase in Title VII prohibiting discrimination based on sex implies that it is unlawful to discriminate against women because they are women and against men because they are men. When a homosexual supervisor is making offensive sexual advances to a subordinate of the same sex, and not doing so to employees of the opposite sex, it absolutely is a situation where, but for the subordinate's sex, [she] or he should not be subjected to that treatment.

Id. at 1103–04.

Gardinella v. General Elec. Co., 833 F. Supp. 617 (W.D. Ky. 1993). See § **6.43.**

Page 105, add to footnote 82 following "Seventh Circuit":

Baskerville v. Culligan Int'l Co., 50 F.3d 428 (7th Cir. 1995) (noting that sexual harassment of women by men is the most common kind, but the court did not exclude the possibility that sexual harassment of men by women, of men by other men, or women by other women would also be actionable in appropriate cases).

Griffith v. Keystone Steel & Wire, 887 F. Supp. 1133 (C.D. Ill. 1995). A male employee (a maintenance electrician who alleged that for several months, he was continually subjected to sexually suggestive comments and improper physical sexual contacts by a "foreman," under the supervision of or with the knowledge of management) stated a cause of action for same sex sexual harassment under Title VII:

> After considering the statute and the applicable case law, the Court holds that same-sex sexual harassment is prohibited by Title VII for several reasons. First, a recent statement by Chief Judge Posner, although dicta, indicates how the Seventh Circuit might rule on this issue [in] . . . *Baskerville v. Culligan International Co.*, 50 F.3d 428, 430 (7th Cir. 1995).
>
> Moreover, when ascertaining the intent of Congress, courts must begin with the statutory language. . . . Title VII prohibits employers from discriminating "against any individual with respect to [her or] his compensation, terms, conditions, or privileges of employment, because of such individual's race, color, religion, sex, or national origin." 42 U.S.C § 2000e-2(a)(1). It is well recognized that Title VII protects both males and females from sexual harassment in the workplace. . . . The plain language of Title VII simply does not restrict its prohibition against discrimination to employees of the opposite sex.
>
> Furthermore, while the number of male and female workers in a work environment may be relevant in assessing the impact of sexual harassment, such a showing is not essential to prevail on a sexual harassment claim. Griffith has alleged both hostile work environment and *quid pro quo* sexual harassment. . . .
>
> Griffith must ultimately establish that he was sexually harassed "because of his sex." . . . In other words, that but for the fact of his sex, Griffith would not have been the object of harassment. . . . Griffith can establish that the harassment was "based upon sex" by showing that his harasser only harassed men, and thus, did not treat women in a similar fashion. . . .
>
> Griffith's Amended Complaint alleges that he was continually subjected to sexually suggestive and derogatory comments and improper physical sexual contacts by Defendant Cutting. . . . The Amended Complaint further alleges that these acts of sexual harassment included unwelcome sexual advances, requests for sexual favors, and verbal or physical conduct of a sexual nature of Defendant Cutting which substantially interfered with Griffith's working environment and submission to which was demanded of Griffith in exchange for favorable working conditions or terms. . . . As Griffith has alleged that he was subjected to unwelcome sexual harassment because of his sex that was not directed to female employees, he states a claim under Title VII.

Id. at 1136–37 (footnotes omitted).

Tenth Circuit: Griffith v. State of Colo. Div. of Youth Servs., 17 F.3d 1323 (10th Cir. 1994). A male electrician who alleged that he was sexually harassed by a male foreman could sue individual employees under Title VII. The court looked to Seventh Circuit ADEA decisions and the law of agency, as well as the plain language of the statute, to come to this conclusion. Both Title VII and the ADEA define an *employer* to include a person acting as the agent of the employer, and the statutes do not limit the liability of the agent to only her or his official capacity. Moreover, the Civil Rights Act of 1991 expanded the available remedies to include compensatory and punitive damages that can be imposed against individual defendants.

Goeffert v. Beech Aircraft Corp., 64 Fair Empl. Cas. (BNA) 1387 (D. Kan. 1994). A gay female employee's sexual harassment claim was dismissed when the alleged conduct, four instances of sexual comments and gestures by other employees, and one incidence in which an employee flipped a piece of paper at the plaintiff, was not so pervasive that it affected a term or condition of her employment. There was no evidence that management tolerated such comments. The plaintiff did not make out a prima facie case of retaliation for complaining of coworkers' conduct when the employer articulated a legitimate reason for the plaintiff's discharge, her assault on another employee.

Page 105, add to footnote 82 following "Eleventh Circuit":

Prescott v. Independent Life & Accident Ins. Co., 878 F. Supp. 1545 (M.D. Ala. 1995); McCoy v. Johnson Controls World Servs., 878 F. Supp. 229 (S.D. Ga. 1995). A Caucasian female employee who alleged that a female coemployee sexually harassed her stated a claim for hostile work environment under Title VII but not under 42 U.S.C. § 1981.

> [W]hile *Vinson* did not directly address homosexual harassment, nothing in the Court's reasoning suggests that Title VII is limited to heterosexual harassment. . . .
>
> Furthermore, merely because McCoy was harassed by a woman instead of a man will not prevent her from establishing a *prima facie* case of sexual harassment under *Henson.*

Johnson Controls, 878 F. Supp. at 232. The court noted that the defendant did not suggest that the alleged harasser also harassed male employees.

ELEMENTS OF CLAIMS

Page 105, add to footnote 83 following "Fifth Circuit":

Garcia v. Elf Atochem N. Am., 28 F.3d 446 (5th Cir. 1994). A male employee who alleged that his male supervisor on several occasions grabbed his crotch and made sexual motions from behind the plaintiff could not bring a sexual harassment action. The court cited Giddens v. Shell Oil Co., No. 92-8533 (5th Cir. Dec. 6, 1993), in which the court previously held that harassment by a supervisor against a male subordinate does not state a claim under Title VII, even though the harassment has sexual overtones, because Title VII addresses gender discrimination.

Pritchett v. Sizeler Real Estate Management, 67 Fair Empl. Prac. Cas. (BNA) 1377 (E.D. La. 1995). The sexual harassment of a female subordinate by a female supervisor was clearly a form of gender discrimination, as the plaintiff would not have been harassed but for her sex; while sexual orientation is not protected by Title VII, it would be inappropriate to exempt homosexuals from the very laws that govern the workplace conduct of heterosexuals.

> [I]t seems discriminatory that a supervisor should be exempt from a Title VII sexual harassment claim solely because of that supervisor's sexual orientation. To deny a claim of same gender sexual harassment allows a homosexual supervisor to sexually harass his or her subordinates either on a quid pro quo basis or by creating a hostile work environment, when a heterosexual supervisor may be sued under Title VII for similar conduct. Although it is clear that Title VII does not protect a homosexual who is discriminated against based on his or her sexual orientation, here it is not the homosexual who seeks to be protected.

Id. at 1379.

Oncale v. Sundowner Offshore Servs., 67 Fair Empl. Prac. Cas. (BNA) 769 (E.D. La. 1995). A male employee's allegations of specific physical acts and verbal assaults by male coworkers and a supervisor did not state a Title VII claim for sexual harassment.

Page 105, add to footnote 83 following Fifth Circuit cases:

Eighth Circuit: Doe v. Marshalls Inc., 63 Fair Empl. Cas. (BNA) 1123 (D. Minn. 1993). Defendant's motion for summary judgment was denied in an action by a male employee who alleged that he was sexually harassed by his male supervisor on two occasions when factual disputes existed regarding, among other things, the alleged incidents of harassment, their severity and effect on the plaintiff's work environment and his personal and professional life, the adequacy of the defendant's investigation of the plaintiff's allegations, and the validity of the reasons proffered by defendants for discharging the plaintiff. "The several fact disputes in this matter preclude a finding that a reasonable jury could not, as a matter of law, find that the Plaintiff had established a hostile work environment." *Id.* at 1124. Factual disputes also precluded summary judgment on the plaintiff's retaliatory discharge claims.

Tenth Circuit: Goeffert v. Beech Aircraft Corp., 64 Fair Empl. Prac. Cas. (BNA) 1387 (D. Kan. 1994) (court declined to decide issue of whether harassment motivated by homophobic prejudice can support claim under Title VII).

District of Columbia Circuit: Ryczek v. Guest Servs., Inc., 877 F. Supp. 754 (D.D.C. 1995).

California: Mogilefsky v. Superior Court (Silver Pictures), 20 Cal. App. 4th 1409, 26 Cal. Rptr. 2d 116 (1993). A male employee who alleged that on two occasions a male supervisor demanded that the plaintiff stay overnight in his hotel suite, during which he informed the plaintiff that he would receive more money if he cooperated, ordered the plaintiff to play a pornographic film on the VCR, made lewd and lascivious comments about the film, requested that plaintiff take his clothes off, referred to the plaintiff in a profane and degrading manner, and later falsely implied to others that the plaintiff had engaged in anal sex with him, stated a claim for sexual harassment under the state antidiscrimination act. The court rejected the defendant's argument that freeing everyone from sexual remarks and conduct would "put the First Amendment right of free speech on the endangered species list," 26 Cal. Rptr. 2d at 121, or that allowing such a cause of action would make an inquiry into the sexual orientation of the male supervisor an absolute necessity.

Page 106, add at end of carryover footnote 83:

The following cases have held that same sex sexual harassment is not cognizable under Title VII:

Fourth Circuit: *Cf:* Benekris v. Johnson, 882 F. Supp. 521 (D.S.C. 1995) (same sex sexual harassment was not cognizable in an action by a male teacher, alleging that a coworker sexually harassed him during a pickup basketball game by placing his genitals against the plaintiff's buttocks and by placing his hands on the plaintiff's genitals); Hopkins v.

Baltimore Gas & Elec. Co., 871 F. Supp. 822 (D. Md. 1994) (male bisexual–male hostile environment claim was not cognizable under Title VII, but a retaliatory discharge was).

Fifth Circuit: Garcia v. Elf Atochem N. Am, 28 F.3d 446 (5th Cir. 1994) (harassment of a male subordinate by a male supervisor was not cognizable under Title VII, even if the alleged harassment had sexual overtones); Myers v. City of El Paso, 874 F. Supp. 1546 (W.D. Tex. 1995) (same sex sexual harassment not actionable under Title VII; female employee plaintiff alleged that her supervisor made comments to her about the size of her breasts and about her buttocks, hair, and clothing and touched her on a number of occasions).

Sixth Circuit: Fleenor v. Hewitt Soap Co., 67 Fair Empl. Prac. Cas. (BNA) 1625 (S.D. Ohio 1994). A male employee who alleged that his fellow male employees created a hostile environment by using suggestive and vulgar language, exposing a penis and testicles to the plaintiff, threatening to force the plaintiff to engage in oral sex, and sticking a ruler up his buttocks without his consent, did not state a claim for sexual harassment.

> When both the harasser and the victim are male, the harasser must have treated the victim in an inferior manner because of the victim's gender and, as a result, created an anti-male work environment. In his second amended complaint . . . , the Plaintiff does not allege that his work-place was other than male dominated. Indeed, with one exception, those mentioned in that pleading are male. Moreover, Plaintiff does not allege that the harassment to which he was subjected created an anti-male work environment. In addition, Plaintiff does not allege that he was harassed because he was a male or set forth factual allegations that would support such a contention; rather, he merely alleges that he "believes" he was harassed because he is a male. Therefore, as did Judge Williams in *Goluszek,* this Court concludes that a claim of male against male hostile environment, sexual harassment is not actionable under Title VII, in the absence of an allegation that an anti-male environment was created thereby.

Id. at 1628 (footnote omitted).

Seventh Circuit: Vandeventer v. Wabash Nat'l Corp., 867 F. Supp. 790 (N.D. Ind. 1994) (male-male quid pro quo and hostile environment claims not cognizable).

§ 3.16   SAME SEX ADVANCES

Page 106, add after "Accord" in footnote 84:

Ryczek v. Guest Servs., Inc., 877 F. Supp. 754 (D.D.C. 1995). In light of language in *Barnes* and *Bundy* that suggests that harassment by bisexuals would not be protected by Title VII, the parties in this action by a female employee alleging sexual harassment by her female supervisor hotly disputed the issue of the alleged harasser's sexual orientation:

> The Court is not well-prepared to resolve such a dispute.
>
> This purported issue of fact suggests a practical flaw in this Circuit's interpretation of Title VII. Assuming that the language in *Barnes* and *Bundy* is the law of this Circuit, any defendant could avoid Title VII liability for sexual harassment by claiming to be a bisexual or by harassing members of both sexes. This would appear to produce an anomalous result: a victim of sexual harassment in the District of Columbia would have a Title VII remedy in all situations except those in which the victim is harassed by a particularly unspeakable cad who harasses both men and women. In addition to this troubling possibility, the prospect of having litigants debate and juries determine the sexual orientation of Title VII defendants is a rather unpleasant one.*
>
> *One can only speculate as to what would be legally sufficient to submit the issue of a supervisor's bisexuality to a jury. Would the supervisor's sworn statement of his or her bisexuality be adequate? Would the supervisor need to introduce affirmative evidence of his [or her] liaisons with members of both sexes? Surely Congress did not anticipate that the language of Title VII would eventually produce such concerns.

Id. at 762. The court ultimately declined to rule on the issue, noting that even assuming arguendo that same sex sexual harassment was covered by Title VII, the plaintiff could not survive summary judgment in this case when the plaintiff failed to raise any genuine issue of fact that would suggest that the employer did not respond to the plaintiff's complaint in a prompt, adequate, and effective fashion.

* *Page 106, add to footnote 85:*

See also Hopkins v. Baltimore Gas and Elec. Co., 77 F.3d 745 (4th Cir. 1996). A former employee did not prove that conduct by his supervisor, including bumping into the plaintiff, placing a magnifying glass over the plaintiff's crotch, staring at the plaintiff in the bathroom, and making inappropriate sexual comments, was sufficiently severe or pervasive to create a hostile environment in an action against his former employer under Title VII alleging that his supervisor's conduct created a sexually hostile work environment and that he was retaliated against for making a complaint about the harassment. The court also concluded that while harassment directed toward an individual employee by another individual of the same gender may be actionable if it is directed at the employee "because of" the employee's gender, the plaintiff must overcome the presumption in that circumstance that the harassment was *not* "because of" that employee's gender.

> Viewed in the abstract, a prohibition of discrimination based on "sex" is broad and perhaps even undefinable. Arguably, such a prohibition might be read to preclude discrimination based on human psychological and physiological characteristics or on sexual orientation. It might also be read to prohibit all workplace sexual behavior or words and deeds having sexual content. . . .
>
> . . . The suggestion that Title VII was intended to regulate everything sexual in the workplace would undoubtedly have shocked every member of the 88th Congress, even those most vigorously supporting passage of the Act. . . .

Id. at 749. The court did not find persuasive the reasoning of the Fifth Circuit in *Garcia* and those district courts that have concluded categorically that same-gender sexual harassment can never be actionable under Title VII.

> In aligning myself with those courts that have observed that same-gender sexual harassment may be actionable under Title VII in appropriate circumstances, I conclude that such a holding is required by the statutory language, understood in its historical context and as subsequently interpreted by the Supreme Court. While it is apparent from the historical record that Congress, in prohibiting sex discrimination, meant to prohibit discrimination only on the basis of the employee's status as a man or a woman, it is also clear from the statutory language itself that only the sex of the *employee* is relevant in determining whether Title VII is implicated. Title VII imposes no gender restriction for the person effecting the discrimination; it prohibits discriminatory conduct by an "employer," regardless of the employer's gender or the gender of those whose conduct imputes liability to the employer. Thus, the requisite causation of prohibited conduct is defined only by the status of the *employee* as a man or a woman.

22

§ 3.16 SAME SEX ADVANCES

Id. at 751. So while acknowledging the viability of same sex harassment claims, the court noted that the more difficult question arises as to what proof is necessary to demonstrate that harassment is because of the employee's gender and not for some other reason, particularly when the harasser and the victim are the same gender:

> When someone sexually harasses an individual of the opposite gender, a presumption arises that the harassment is "because of" the victim's gender. This presumption is grounded on the reality that sexual conduct directed by a man, for example, toward a woman is usually undertaken because the target is female and the same conduct would not have been directed toward another male. . . . But when the harasser and the victim are the same gender, the presumption is just the opposite because such sexually suggestive conduct is usually motivated by entirely different reasons.
>
> Thus, when a male employee seeks to prove that he has been sexually harassed by a person of the same sex, he carries the burden of proving that the harassment was directed against him "because of" his sex. The principal way which this burden may be met is with proof that the harasser acted out of sexual attraction to the employee. In *McWilliams [v. Fairfax County Bd. of Supervisors,* 72 F.3d 1191, 1195 n.5 (4th Cir. 1996)], we noted that a male employee who undertakes to prove sexual harassment directed at him by another male may use evidence of the harasser's homosexuality to demonstrate that the action was directed at him because he is a man. But we cautioned that proof of such homosexuality must include more than "merely suggestive" conduct. *Id.*
>
> I recognize that conduct directed toward an employee of the same gender as the harasser can have sexual content or innuendo and, indeed, may be offensive. But unless such harassment is directed toward an employee "because of" his or her status as a man or woman, it does not implicate Title VII. I reject the notion that when a man, for example, uses sexually oriented gestures and language, or engages in sexually perverse activity to harass another man, Title VII automatically imposes liability. Such conduct may constitute a common law tort, but, without more, it does not amount to discrimination against the employee because he is a man. . . .

Id. at 752.

McWilliams v. Fairfax County Bd. of Supervisors, 72 F.3d 1191 (4th Cir. 1996). An employee did not have a Title VII claim for hostile environment based on heterosexual-male-on-heterosexual-male harassment; nor did the equal protection clause protect against invidious gender discrimination stemming from same sex harassment between heterosexual employees. McWilliams's coworkers, collectively known as the "lube boys," beset McWilliams with a variety of offensive conduct. They teased him, asked him about his sexual activities, exposed themselves to him, and taunted him with remarks such as, "The only woman you could get is one who is deaf, dumb, and blind." Once a coworker who some-times took on supervisory responsibilities placed a condom in McWilliams's food. There were also physical assaults. On at least three occasions, coworkers tied McWilliams's hands together, blindfolded him, and forced him to his knees, and during one of these incidents, a coworker placed his finger in McWilliams' mouth to simulate an oral sexual act. During another, two coworkers placed a broomstick to McWilliams' anus while a third exposed his genitals to McWilliams. On yet another occasion, Witsman entered the bus on which McWilliams was working and fondled him. The atmosphere of the all-male work-place was very sexually oriented. Copies of Playboy magazine and a variety of pornographic material were displayed in the bathrooms, and centerfold pictures as well as Snap-On-Tool calendars of scantily clad women placed in and around mechanics' tool boxes. Off-color car-toons were circulated around the workplace, and the radio was often tuned to talk shows that featured explicit sexual references. On three occasions, McWilliams complained about certain of these matters to his supervisors, and none involved incidents of physical abuse. Both McWilliams and all his alleged harassers were males, and no claim was made that any was homosexual.

As a purely semantic matter, we do not believe that in common under-standing the kind of shameful heterosexual-male-on-heterosexual-male conduct alleged here (nor comparable female-on-female conduct) is con-sidered to be "because of the [target's] 'sex.'" Perhaps "because of" the victim's known or believed prudery, or shyness, or other form of vulnera-bility to sexually-focussed speech or conduct. Perhaps "because of" the perpetrators' own sexual perversion, or obsession, or insecurity. Certainly, "because of" their vulgarity and insensitivity and meanness of spirit. But not specifically "because of" the victim's *sex*.

The difficulty of construing this causation language to reach such same sex claims and the common sense of not doing so are emphasized when the practical implications are considered. That this sort of conduct is utterly despicable by whomever experienced; that it may well rise to lev-els that adversely affect the victim's work performance; and that no employer knowingly should tolerate it are all undeniable propositions. But to interpret Title VII to reach that conduct when only heterosexual males are involved as harasser and victim would be to extend this vital statute's protections beyond intentional discrimination "because of" the offended worker's "sex" to unmanageably broad protection of the sensibilities of workers simply "in matters of sex." We cannot believe that Congress in adopting this critical causation language and the Supreme Court in interpreting it to reach discrimination by the creation of hostile workplace environments could have intended it to reach such situations. There perhaps "ought to be a law against" such puerile and repulsive workplace behavior even when it involves only heterosexual workers of the same sex, in order to protect the victims against its indignities and debilitations, but we conclude that Title VII is not that law.

Id. at 1195–96. The court specifically reserved decision on the general question whether, when all the actors involved in a Title VII claim of sex-discrimination (in any of its forms) are of the same sex, the homosexuality of any may make the claim nevertheless cognizable as one of discrimination because of the victim's sex. The dissent noted that it was too early to "write this case off to meanness and horseplay. For now there is a material factual issue whether McWilliams was discriminated against because of his sex." *Id.* at 1198 (Michael, J, dissenting).

I would simply hold that Title VII is implicated whenever a person physically abuses a coworker for sexual satisfaction or propositions or pressures a coworker out of sexual interest or desire. This can be established by an account of what the harasser did or said to the victim, and proof of the harasser's sexual orientation should not be required. . . .

I recognize that in a same sex harassment claim, evidence of sexual orientation could be relevant to either side's case. However, it should not be elevated to a required element of the plaintiff's proof. . . .

Id. The majority addressed the dissent's concern:

Though there is no allegation or proffered proof that either McWilliams or any of the "lube boys" was in fact homosexual, our dissenting brother apparently would either find that fact properly inferable from the nature of some of the harassing conduct, or consider it unnecessary to prove homosexuality-in-fact, homosexual innuendo being sufficient. And, on this basis he would reach the homosexuality issue and hold that same sex "harassment" claims may lie under Title VII where homosexuality (either in-fact or as merely suggested by conduct) is involved. With respect, we believe that were Title VII to be so interpreted, the fact of homosexuality (to include bisexuality) should be considered an essential element of the claim, to be alleged and proved. The dissent expresses concern, because of proof (and privacy?) problems, about requiring such allegation and proof, but we believe it critical and eminently fair to require it if homosexuality is to be the critical fact making same sex harassment claims cognizable under Title VII. The (ordinarily different) sexes of the relevant actors always has been an essential element of either form of Title VII sexual harassment claims. If such claims were to reach past different sex to same sex situations where homosexuality of one or the other or both of the actors is involved, that added fact would seem equally essential to the statement and proof of such a claim. If not required to be alleged, a defendant could be blindsided by proof of conduct merely suggestive of homosexuality between persons of the same sex who actually are heterosexuals. If not required to be proved, the sexual harassment claim would effectively have been extended to cover any conduct between even same sex heterosexual workers that included sufficient homosexual innuendo. For these reasons, we do not believe that the homosexual issue properly can be considered to be presented in this case.

Id. at 1195 n.5.

Page 107, add after "Cf." in footnote 87:

Prescott v. Independent Life & Accident Ins. Co., 878 F. Supp. 1545 (M.D. Ala. 1995). A male former employee who alleged that his male supervisor sexually harassed him stated a claim for quid pro quo harassment when a question of fact existed as to whether statements allegedly made to the plaintiff were properly understood to be quid pro quo harassment or whether they concerned legitimate business-related matters. The plaintiff alleged that the supervisor subjected him to numerous unwanted sexual advances, touchings, implicit threats about the plaintiff's status at the company, and implicit promises of advancement, and when the plaintiff refused to submit to the demands, the supervisor became determined to get rid of the plaintiff and contrived a false record against him as part of this scheme. The court rejected the reasoning of *Goluszek:*

> According to the court in *Goluszek,* the issue that the court should address in deciding whether Title VII prohibits homosexual sexual harassment is power. . . . That court felt that the problem that Congress sought to remedy was one in which a powerless group was disadvantaged by the dominant group. . . . Therefore the male plaintiff in *Goluszek* could not prevail because he was "a male in a male dominated environment." . . .

While this argument may be logically appealing, it is not the current state of anti-discrimination jurisprudence. If it were, a similar argument could be made when a white plaintiff attempts to sue for reverse discrimination under Title VII. That white plaintiff would have been at all times a member of the majority, a member of the "dominant" race. However, the Supreme Court "has consistently interpreted Title VII to proscribe racial discrimination in private employment against whites on the same terms as racial discrimination against nonwhites . . ." *McDonald v. Santa Fe Trail Transportation Co.*, 427 U.S. 273, 279 . . . (1976).

The language of Title VII is clear. Congress chose to use the unmodified word "sex" when referring to the discrimination that is forbidden. This is a choice of an obviously gender neutral term, just as Congress chose to prohibit discrimination based on "race," rather than discrimination against African-Americans or other specific minorities. It seems clear to the court that had Congress intended to prevent only heterosexual sexual harassment, it could have used the term "members of the opposite sex." This way Congress would have accounted for both male-female harassment and the much less frequent female-male harassment.

Therefore, Congress prohibited discrimination based on sex. This means that if a person receives discriminatory treatment from a company or a supervisor because of the employee's sex, Title VII has been violated. When a homosexual man propositions or harasses a male subordinate, but does not similarly proposition or harass female workers, the male employee has been singled out because of his gender. But for his being male, the harassment would not have occurred.

Id. at 1550 (footnotes omitted).

Page 108, add to footnote 88:

In Fox v. Sierra Development Co., 876 F. Supp. 1169 (D. Nev. 1995), a complaint by male employees against their former employer, alleging that coworkers and supervisors made homosexual references that created a hostile environment, did not allege any discriminatory hostility and thus did not state a claim under Title VII. The plaintiffs did not allege that they were discriminated against because of their gender preference. The complaint alleged that the supervisors and coworkers

in an open and notorious manner, engaged in the sexual harassment of plaintiffs by means of writing, drawing, and explicitly discussing homosexual sex acts, excrement, urine and other topics in a depraved manner which created for Plaintiffs a harmful and oppressive work environment, and which materially interfered with plaintiffs' ability to perform their work related duties.

Id. at 1172. The court did not see how this type of conduct could form the basis of a claim of sexual discrimination:

> Scatological and urinary fixations can be a source of harassment to persons not so fixated. It is a common fact of life that such topics are not the substance of polite conversation. Nevertheless, not every disturbance or annoyance can be the basis for a sexual harassment claim.

*   *   *

> The alleged conduct relating to "excrement, urine and other topics" is not sexual in nature. There is no indication this conduct involved any sexual connotations, the complaint merely alleges scatological and not copraphilial behavior. If this conduct were directed only at men, or were directed at plaintiffs because they were men, it might be actionable as gender oriented harassment . . . . However, there is no indication that this is the case. If anything, the complaint indicates the excretory and urinary references were published widely to the general employee population. Thus, there is nothing to indicate this conduct constitutes gender oriented harassment.

*   *   *

> The Court notes that the complaint is very nearly deficient in alleging conduct from which a hostile environment could reasonably be perceived. Essentially all that plaintiffs have alleged is a work environment saturated with sexual references, and that the pervasive theme of these references was homosexual. The Court declines to determine whether it is reasonable to perceive a work environment as hostile and abusive merely because a person might be uncomfortable with homosexuality. Thus the homosexual content of the alleged conduct is not relevant to determining whether the alleged conduct adequately demonstrates a hostile environment.

> The Court merely holds that given the highly charged views and attitudes about sex which are prevalent in our society, allegations of a work environment in which employees are constantly assaulted by a stream of sexual drawings, writings and discussions adequately alleges a work environment which could reasonably be perceived as hostile.

> If the Court were to stop its analysis here, it would conclude that plaintiffs' complaint does state a claim, and that Sierra's motion to dismiss

should be denied. However, the Court believes one further requirement must be considered [: that the environment must be discriminatorily hostile].

*   *   *

A work environment, saturated with sexual references, is potentially abusive or hostile to men and women in equal measure. There is nothing to indicate that men or women will feel a sexually charged atmosphere such as that present here to be abusive or hostile to them on the basis of their gender. More to the point, the complaint does not allege facts from which men, such as the plaintiffs, or women could reasonably conclude they were being intimidated, ridiculed, or insulted because they were men or women.

To the extent the work environment is alleged to be hostile or abusive it is not hostile or abusive to plaintiffs on a discriminatory basis. Plaintiffs do not perceive the work environment to be hostile to them because they are men. Plaintiffs perceive it to be hostile or abusive to them because they, like some members of society, may not be entirely at ease with sexuality in general and homosexuality in particular.

Id. at 1172–75 (footnotes omitted).

Page 108, add to footnote 91:

Mogilefsky v. Superior Court (Silver Pictures), 20 Cal. App. 4th 1409, 26 Cal. Rptr. 2d 116 (1993).

§ 3.17 —Actions by Male Victims

Page 108, add to footnote 92:

Williams v. Runyon, 881 F. Supp. 359 (N.D. Ill. 1995). A male former Postal Service employee failed to establish a prima facie case of sexual harassment when he alleged that a female supervisor came near him two or three times a day and each time would stand close enough that the plaintiff could feel her breath on his face, and that several times her hips and thighs touched his body and otherwise touched him on several occasions, and that on three occasions she asked him to come to her home to fix electrical problems and have a meal.

Jones v. Aspin, 64 Empl. Prac. Dec. (CCH) ¶ 43,005 (E.D. Pa. 1994). A male employee who alleged repeated false and malicious accusations of sexual harassment leveled against him, resulting in various emotional reputational harms, stated a claim for hostile environment sexual harassment. Under Andrews v. City of Philadelphia, 895 F.2d 1469 (3d Cir. 1990), when the allegedly offensive conduct is not overtly sexual in nature, the court is obliged to conduct a factually intensive inquiry. The court noted that given the procedural posture of this case, such an inquiry could not be made until the factual record was better developed and recognized that a man's hostile environment claim, although theoretically possible, would be much harder to plead and prove.

Goering v. Nynex Info. Resources Co., 619 N.Y.S.2d 167 (1994). A mere showing that the male plaintiff in a sexual harassment suit brought under state executive law declined offers of transfer was not evidence that the sexual harassment did not constitute a term or condition of his continued employment, in the absence of evidence that the employer took any disciplinary action against the employee who perpetrated the alleged harassment or other steps to alleviate the threat of further occurrences.

Page 108, add to footnote 93:

Anderson v. SUNY Health Science Center has been officially reported at 826 F. Supp. 625 (N.D.N.Y. 1993), *dismissed without op.*, 23 F.3d 396 (2d Cir.), *cert. denied*, 114 S. Ct. 2763 (1994).

§ 3.18 —Welcomeness of the Sexual Advance

Page 109, add to footnote 97:

Cuesta v. Texas Dep't of Criminal Justice, 805 F. Supp. 451 (W.D. Tex. 1991). The court found sexual harassment in an action by a female parole case worker against the parole officer and parole board, rejecting the defendants' claim that the plaintiff may have invited the harassment by calling the parole officer on the phone frequently, offering him a gift, and other conduct. The plaintiff denied the allegations, witnesses recalled seeing the plaintiff visibly upset after encounters with the parole officer, and the uninvited behavior, including repeatedly asking the plaintiff to have an affair or to at least hug, kiss, or put his arms around her, asking the plaintiff whether she preferred anal or vaginal sex, and suggesting that he assign her to a distant county so that they could meet away from town, was clearly beyond what was socially acceptable conduct for a supervisor. The court also concluded that the defendant board did have a working policy against sexual harassment, but that it was unclear whether a timely complaint would have provided a remedy in the plaintiff's case.

Page 113, add to footnote 106 following Fourth Circuit case:

Seventh Circuit: Carr v. Allison Gas Turbine Div., 32 F.3d 1007 (7th Cir. 1994). The district court improperly ruled in favor of the defendant former employer, in a sexual harassment action by a female tinsmith, on the bases that the plaintiff welcomed the conduct by participating in it herself, the alleged conduct had no effect on the conditions of her employment, and she did not show that the defendants failed to take appropriate responsive action. The plaintiff was the first woman to work in the tinsmith shop and her male coworkers were not happy about working with a woman, making derogatory sexual comments on a daily basis, such as "I won't work with any cunt," referring to the plaintiff in her presence as "whore," "cunt," and "split tail," painting "cunt" on her toolbox, cutting the seat out of her overalls, hiding and stealing her tools, stripping down to their underwear in her presence when changing in and out of their workclothes, exposing themselves, and making other vulgar and racist statements. But even though the coworkers' behavior was harassing, the district judge concluded that it was not actionable because it was invited by the plaintiff's use of abusive language and crude behavior, such as telling "dirty" jokes, using terms such as "dickhead" and "fuck head," once placing her hand on the thigh of a young male worker, and obliging when shown a pornographic picture and asked to point out the clitoris. A female welder at the plant testified that she considered the plaintiff vulgar and unladylike, a "tramp" because she "used the F word" and told dirty jokes. The welder also testified that she herself had no trouble with the men in the shop, although on occasion she did have to zap them with her welding arc to fend them off. The court of appeals disagreed with the trial court's assessment:

> Of course [the conduct] was unwelcome. A plaintiff's words, deeds, and deportment can cast light on whether her coworkers' treatment of her was unwelcome and should have been perceived as such by them and

their supervisors, . . . but we do not understand General Motors to be suggesting that Carr enjoyed or appeared to enjoy the campaign of harassment against her. . . . What the judge found . . . was that Carr had *provoked* the misconduct of her coworkers. Had she been ladylike, he thought, like the welder, they would have left her alone—maybe; for remember that the welder had to use her welding arc to protect herself.

Even if we ignore the question why "unladylike" behavior should provide not a vulgar response but a hostile, harassing response, and even if Carr's testimony that she talked and acted as she did in an effort to be "one of the boys" is (despite its plausibility) discounted, her words and conduct cannot be compared to those of men and used to justify their conduct and exonerate their employer. . . . The asymmetry of positions must be considered. She was one woman; they were many men. Her use of terms like "fuck head" could not be deeply threatening, or her placing a hand on the thigh of one of her macho coworkers intimidating; and it was not she who brought the pornographic picture to the "anatomy lesson." We have trouble *imagining* a situation in which male factory workers sexually harass a lone woman in *self-defense* as it were; yet that at root is General Motors' characterization of what happened here. It is incredible on the admitted facts.

Id. at 1011. The judge's alternative grounds for dismissal were that the conduct had no effect on the conditions of her employment and that the plaintiff did not show that the defendant employer failed to remedy the situation. Because the plaintiff was not seeking fees for mental anguish, it was irrelevant that her "suffering" was due to a troubled life rather than the alleged harassment. All she needed to show was that her conditions of employment were adversely affected. The dissent argued that, in ruling the way it did, the majority overruled the precedent in the Seventh Circuit concerning unwelcome sexual harassment in Reed v. Shepard, 939 F.2d 484 (7th Cir. 1991) (a decision joined in by the author of the majority opinion in this case), in which the court held that an employer could not be held liable for sexual harassment because the plaintiff was enthusiastically receptive to sexually suggestive jokes and activities.

Dey v. Colt Constr. & Dev. Co, 28 F.3d 1446 (7th Cir. 1994). The district court improperly found that a discharged employee did not show that alleged harassment by the company vice president had any subjective effect on her. The alleged conduct had not prevented the plaintiff from performing her assigned tasks, she described the work environment as "professional," she had not consulted a physician for any psychological problems related to the alleged harassment, and the conduct did not prompt the plaintiff to quit, avoid the office, or even react angrily. The district court gave weight to evidence that the plaintiff continued to voluntarily associate herself with the vice president, including asking him for legal advice on a personal matter and considering buying his car. The court of appeals disagreed: Turning her back and having nothing to do with the vice president was probably not an option if the plaintiff wished to keep her job, regardless of how offensive she may have found his behavior, and the incidents relied on by the district court, when viewed in the light most favorable to the plaintiff, simply did not establish that the plaintiff sought to maintain a close personal relationship with her superior. From an objective perspective, the fact that the plaintiff alleged only five specific incidents of sexual harassment over a period of two and a half years did not render the conduct relatively isolated when the plaintiff maintained that she was subjected to almost daily comments, gestures, and innuendoes of a sexual nature.

Page 114, add to footnote 108 following Third Circuit cases:

Fourth Circuit: *See also* Munday v. Waste Management of N. Am., Inc., 858 F. Supp. 1364 (D. Md. 1994). In an action by a female truck driver against her employer for breach of a settlement agreement for earlier charges of sexual discrimination, the court concluded that what happened to the plaintiff when she returned to work after the settlement agreement was not sexual harassment or sex discrimination but rather a pattern of retaliation designed to encourage the plaintiff to resign, as well as constructive discharge. With respect to the sexual harassment charge, the plaintiff "greatly contributed to the difficulties of which she complains by her own abrasive conduct and by her tendencies to blame her problems on others and to assume little responsibility for her own errors, as well as by her general dissatisfaction with her life." *Id.* at 1372. The court also noted that the type of employment was difficult and demanding and the entire work atmosphere could only be described "as a rather tough one." *Id.*

Page 115, add at end of carryover footnote 108:

Oregon: Ballinger v. Klamath Pac. Corp., 898 P.2d 232 (Or. Ct. App. 1995). In an action by two female former employees against their employer and supervisors, plaintiffs stated a claim for sexually hostile environment under state antidiscrimination law. Although one plaintiff joined in some of the "ribald" conduct of supervisors and joined in the telling of adult or sexual jokes, some of the sexually hostile conduct directed toward the plaintiff was unwelcome to her.

Page 115, add to footnote 110:

Fuller v. City of Oakland, Cal., 47 F.3d 1522 (9th Cir. 1995). The district court improperly ruled for the defendant city in a Title VII sexual harassment action by a female former police officer when the city failed to take any appropriate remedial steps once it learned of the sexual harassment. After the plaintiff ended a relationship with a fellow police officer, the coworker allegedly started harassing the plaintiff and was eventually transferred into a supervisor position with authority over the plaintiff. Among the acts of harassment were calling and hanging up, sometimes 25 times a day, threatening to kill himself, attempting to run the plaintiff and her new boyfriend off the road, and forcibly extracting her new unlisted phone number from her. Other officers learned of the alleged harasser's prior conduct and over the plaintiff's objections, because she feared the alleged harasser, the matter was brought to the attention of the police chief, who conducted an internal affairs investigation and offered the plaintiff an immediate transfer, which she refused. The plaintiff alleged that the harassment by the former boyfriend continued after the investigation, and she eventually resigned because of a severe stress disorder.

> Once an employer knows or should know of harassment, a remedial obligation kicks in. . . . That obligation will not be discharged until action—prompt, effective action—has been taken. Effectiveness will be measured by the twin purposes of ending the current harassment and deterring future harassment—by the same offender or others. . . . If 1) no remedy is undertaken, or 2) the remedy attempted is ineffectual, liability will attach. Our prior cases stand for the proposition that an employer's actions will not necessarily shield it from liability if harassment continues. . . . It does not follow that the employer's failure to act will be acceptable if harassment stops.
>
> Putting it another way, even if inaction through some Orwellian twist is described as a "remedy," it will fail the deterrence prong of the *Ellison* test whether or not the individual harasser has voluntarily ceased harassment. Nor can inaction fairly be said to qualify as a remedy "reasonably calculated to end the harassment." Title VII does not permit employers to stand idly by once they learn that sexual harassment has occurred. To do

so amounts to a ratification of the prior harassment. We refuse to make liability for ratification of past harassment turn on the fortuity of whether the harasser, as he did here, voluntarily elects to cease his activities, for the damage done by the employer's ratification will be the same regardless.

*   *   *

An employer whose sole action is to conclude that no harassment occurred cannot in any meaningful sense be said to have "remedied" what happened. Denial does not constitute a remedy. Nor does the fact of investigation alone suffice; an investigation is principally a way to determine whether any remedy is needed and cannot substitute for the remedy itself.

Id. at 1528–29.

Barnes v. Breeden, CA No. H-92-0898 (S.D. Tex. Oct. 20, 1995). The plaintiff, a female African-American attorney for the SEC, established that a supervising attorney [Matta] and his supervisors' malicious conduct created and perpetuated a sexually and racially hostile working environment. There was no doubt that Matta's supervisor knew of his conduct as early as 1986 but chose to duck the issue by telling the victim to try to get along with Matta. When the problems persisted and the total work environment became "unconscionably turbulent" in 1989 and 1990, Matta's supervisor continued to take the "now, now, big fellow" attitude toward Matta's illegal conduct. *Id.* at 31. The plaintiff experienced emotional distress that manifested itself in sleeplessness, depression, nervousness, and physical symptoms such as digestive disorder, headaches, rashes, and swelling. The emotional distress and physical symptoms that the plaintiff experienced were directly caused by the discriminatory conduct directed toward her by Matta and permitted by Matta's supervisors.

Kelly-Zurian v. Wohl Shoe Co., 22 Cal. App. 4th 397, 27 Cal. Rptr. 2d 457, 64 Fair Empl. Prac. Cas. (BNA) 603 (1994) (sexual harassment, constructive wrongful discharge, intentional infliction of emotional distress). The lower court properly entered a judgment upon a $125,000 jury verdict in favor of the plaintiff in a sexual harassment action alleging that for three years the plaintiff suffered verbal and physical harassment at the hands of her supervisor. He would come up from behind and put both his hands on her breasts, pinch her buttocks, grab her crotch and ask if she "was wet," ask her what kind of lingerie she was wearing, how was her "pussy," if she "got any last night," if she "took it in the ass," and if she "swallowed" or "gave head." 64 Fair Empl. Prac. Cas. at 605. The plaintiff's testimony was corroborated by other employees. When she complained, management told her that their hands were tied because the plaintiff was unwilling to confront the alleged harasser face to face, and asked her if she had any videos to corroborate her complaints. The plaintiff resigned and suffered panic attacks consisting of anxiety, tightness in her chest, heart palpitations, sleeplessness and depression, and developed a serious drinking problem.

Page 116, add to footnote 113:

Bouton v. BMW of N. Am., 29 F.3d 103, 106 n.2 (3d Cir. 1994) (discrimination must be "pervasive and regular").

Alphonse v. Omni Hotels Management Corp., 643 So. 2d 836 (La. Ct. App. 1994). The trial court properly found sexual harassment in an action by a former hotel employee who alleged that her supervisor ordered her to take meals with him at the hotel, take walks with him at lunch in the French Quarter, accompany him to hotel functions as his date, ride to and from work with him, and generally hold herself out as his "showpiece" until a point in time when his attitude changed and he began to berate her and assign her additional duties without additional pay or proper training. "Courts have consistently held that sexual harassment need not take the form of sexual advances or of other instances with sexual overtones." *Id.* at 839. The defendant did not offer any evidence to refute the allegations, and the court found the plaintiff's testimony to be credible and sufficient to establish her claims. The employer knew or should have known about the harassment because of the plaintiff's repeated attempts to report the offensive behavior. General damages of $85,000 and attorneys' fees of $16,500 were also proper.

Cf. Thompson v. Haskell Co., 65 Fair Empl. Prac. Cas. (BNA) 1088 (M.D. Fla. 1994). In an action by a discharged female marketing representative charging sexual harassment under the state human rights act, a regional manager supervisor did not create a hostile environment by placing or trying to place his arm around the plaintiff's shoulder during business conversations and by making crass comments to the plaintiff about other female employees' anatomy and clothing, and by once saying that he had sexual fantasies about his cousin. The plaintiff did not immediately complain to the supervisor's superiors, and did not confront him, although she did register contemporaneous complaints with her peers and resisted his discussions and touching, thus raising a genuine issue of material fact as to whether the conduct was unwelcome. But no sexual remarks or innuendo accompanied the touching incidents, none of the alleged sexual remarks were aimed at the plaintiff, the supervisor did not physically threaten or personally humiliate the plaintiff, and the plaintiff made subtle attempts to deter the behavior but did not directly ask him to stop the offensive conduct. There was no evidence that the alleged harassment substantially interfered with the plaintiff's employment.

In Giuliani v. Stuart Corp., 512 N.W.2d 589 (Minn. Ct. App. 1994), the fact that the plaintiff asked a supervisor to keep her confidences about the harassment a secret did not waive her claim. The persons in whom she confided recognized their legal obligation to report her allegations to company officials, but chose not to. Nor did she forfeit her claim by retaining an attorney in lieu of meeting personally with company counsel; such retention of counsel did not constitute failure to cooperate in the company's investigation of her claim. "By retaining counsel, Giuliani recognized the importance of full representation of her position in the dispute." *Id.* at 596.

§ 3.19   —Verbal or Physical Conduct

Page 122, add to footnote 144:

Hodges v. Gellerstedt, 833 F. Supp. 898 (M.D. Fla. 1993). A female employee stated claims for hostile environment and quid pro quo sexual harassment when she alleged that her supervisor offered her money and material goods for a sexual relationship and that after she refused, the harassment continued through the display of sexual literature and sexual devices in the office in her presence and the supervisor's attempts to touch her.

In re Stroh Litig., 63 Fair Empl. Prac. Cas. (BNA) 258 (D. Minn. 1993). Although there was no question as to the admissibility of the advertising and promotional material that was present within the work areas of the relevant plant, or that which was used in the course of the alleged harassment, advertising and promotional materials used by defendant employer outside the workplace were not admissible in a sexual harassment action. The court rejected the plaintiffs' argument that such materials were admissible because they tended to establish the existence of a corporate culture that demeans and objectifies women, and that the existence of such a culture explained why the alleged harassing conduct occurred and why the defendant failed to take prompt and appropriate remedial action:

> Conduct and lack of action are the questions that are at the heart of these actions. Did sexual harassment take place within the Saint Paul Plant, did defendant know or have reason to know about such conduct, and did defendant fail to take prompt remedial action? The answers to these questions do not turn on the existence of any particular corporate culture. Proof that specific acts occurred does not require proof of the reasons for the acts. Likewise, proof of inaction does not require proof of the reasons for the inaction. The conduct involved here is alleged to have taken place within the Saint Paul plant. Defendant's failure to take prompt remedial action took place at the Saint Paul plant. Defendant's general advertising strategies and their executions did not occur at the Saint Paul plant, and were not directed at the plaintiffs in their capacities as employees. Accordingly, it cannot be said that such evidence would have any tendency to make any of the issues in this case more probable than not.
>
> Assuming that the non-workplace materials were relevant, their introduction in this case would be wasteful and cumulative. Plaintiffs will introduce the material that was present in the workplace or used in the alleged harassing conduct. From that material they can make whatever appropriate arguments they deem germane to the issues in these actions. Given the real issues and the elements of the claims made here, the probative value of the non-workplace is slight and is substantially outweighed by the danger of turning an already complex trial into a forensic enigma.

Id. at 259.

Page 122, add to footnote 146:

Stair v. Lehigh Valley Carpenters Local 600, 855 F. Supp. 90 (E.D. Pa. 1994). After trial in an action by a female employee against the union for the distribution of offensive calendars, the court permanently enjoined the union from creating a hostile work environment and ordered it to adopt a statement of policy and procedures for the control of sexual harassment. Upon motion to suspend this order, the court amended the statement of policy and procedures so as to afford an offending party due process rights in union disciplinary proceedings, to require only that active union members attend sexual harassment seminars, and to give the union limited discretion to exempt attendance in cases of undue hardship. The requirement that the union host annual seminars on sexual harassment for all union members did not constitute discipline of union members within the meaning of the Labor-Management Reporting and Disclosure Act provision requiring that union members receive certain process before being disciplined. The court rejected the union's argument that the policies and procedures order was improper because there was no precedent for a finding of liability against a local union for creating a hostile work environment by its distribution of calendars when the complainant was an employee of a third-party employer and the employer's supervisory personnel displayed the calendars. "The court is bound by precedent, not the lack of precedent. This is particularly the case in evolving fields of law including the law governing sexual discrimination in the workplace." *Id.* at 91.

Page 124, add to footnote 149:

Cf. Hutchison v. Amateur Elec. Supply, Inc., 42 F.3d 1037 (7th Cir. 1994). An office manager who alleged that the owner and president of the defendant company regularly quizzed female employees about the frequency and nature of their sexual relations, engaged in numerous sexually explicit telephone conversations with his brother, leaving his office door open to ensure that the plaintiff and the other primarily female office workers would overhear his comments, and refused to stop the conversations despite complaints from the plaintiff on behalf of the staff, stated an actionable hostile environment claim. The court rejected the defendants' argument that because the president's acts would have been "equally offensive" to men or women, they cannot support a Title VII claim. "One would hope that men would be 'equally offended' by Sterman's treatment of Ms. Hutchinson and his other female employees. That conduct is egregious enough to offend the sensibilities of men as well as women cannot serve to immunize it for Title VII purposes." *Id.* at 1043. The court added:

> It blinks reality to claim that sexual conduct which demeans women by a man in a position of power, even if not directed at a specific woman victim, equally impacts male and female subordinates. This disparate effect is the discriminatory element in a hostile environment. Moreover, Sterman directed his offensive treatment strictly at women. Defendants' argument that a male worker would be equally offended by having to

brush against Sterman to pass between the file cabinets or by being pinned in by him at their desk, even if true, is irrelevant. Sterman did not force men to brush against him to get past, nor did he look them up and down and express his pleasure in their appearance.

Id. (footnote omitted).

Steiner v. Showboat Operating Co., 25 F.3d 1459 (9th Cir. 1994), *cert. denied*, 115 S. Ct. 733 (1995). A former casino employee, the first female casino "floorperson," established a prima facie case of hostile environment sexual harassment in an action alleging sexual harassment, retaliation, constructive discharge, and intentional infliction of emotional distress. She proved without contradiction that her supervisor habitually referred to her and to other female employees in a derogatory fashion, using sexual explicit and offensive terms, such as "dumb fucking broad," "cunt," and "fucking cunt." The district court improperly endorsed the defendant's argument that the supervisor's conduct was not sexual harassment because he consistently abused men and women alike, when his abuse of women was different from his abuse of men, referring to women as "dumb fucking broads" and "fucking cunts" and to men as "assholes."

> And while his abuse of men in no way related to their gender, his abuse of female employees, especially Steiner, centered on the fact that they were females. It is one thing to call a woman "worthless," and another to call her a "worthless broad."
>
> Furthermore, even if Trenkle used sexual epithets equal in intensity and in an equally degrading manner against male employees, he cannot thereby "cure" his conduct toward women. *Ellison* unequivocally directs us to consider what is offensive and hostile to a reasonable *woman.* . . .
>
> And finally, although words from a man to a man are differently received than words from a man to a woman, we do not rule out the possibility that *both* men and women working at Showboat have viable claims against Trenkle for sexual harassment.

Id. at 1463–64. The district court's misunderstanding was revealed by its perception that the plaintiff's claim was vitiated by the fact that the supervisor referred to Asians as "UFO's—ugly fucking orientals." "The fact that Trenkle may have uttered racially discriminatory slurs only suggests that he was just as insensitive in matters of race as in those of gender. It in no way excuses his conduct toward Steiner." *Id.* at 1464. The court also rejected the defendant's assertion that the plaintiff somehow welcomed the harassment because she herself talked like a "drunken sailor," when there was no suggestion in the record that the supervisor's remarks were in fact welcomed.

Johnson v. Tower Air, Inc., 149 F.R.D. 461 (E.D.N.Y. 1993). A former flight attendant trainee did not proffer evidence sufficient to support quid pro quo or hostile environment sexual harassment claims in an action charging that plaintiff's supervisor made sexual advances and brushed up against plaintiff, on another occasion grabbed his crotch and shouted derogatory comments to the plaintiff, and during a two-week period made several other offensive gestures or comments. A hostile environment was not established when, although the plaintiff's supervisor was not a pleasant person for whom to work, it was clear that he was unpleasant to each member of the crew, irrespective of their sex, and his comments, while offensive, appeared to be far more hostile and angry than sexual. "Behavior that is immature, nasty, or annoying, without more, is not actionable sexual harassment." *Id.* at 469. *Accord* Porras v. Montefiore Medical Ctr., 742 F. Supp. 120, 127 (S.D.N.Y. 1990).

Alphonse v. Omni Hotels Management Corp., 643 So. 2d 836 (La. Ct. App. 1994). The trial court properly found sexual harassment in an action by a former hotel employee who alleged that her supervisor ordered her to take meals with him at the hotel, take walks with him at lunch in the French Quarter, accompany him to hotel functions as his date, ride to and from work with him, and generally hold herself out as his "showpiece" until a point in time when his attitude changed and he began to berate her and assign her additional duties without additional pay or proper training. "Courts have consistently held that sexual harassment need not take the form of sexual advances or of other instances with sexual overtones." *Id.* at 839. The court rejected the defendant's argument that the supervisor managed by intimidation and screamed at all his employees, both male and female, when although no one witnessed the supervisor call the plaintiff a weak woman and make a comment about her menstrual cycle, the plaintiff testified that the incidents occurred, that she sought medical help because of her emotional distress, and was ultimately forced to resign because of the harassment.

The fact that discriminatory behavior is not directed at all members of plaintiff's gender is not fatal, so long as the plaintiff shows if she had been of the opposite gender, she would not have been so treated. Payne v. Children's Home Soc'y of Wash., 892 P.2d 1102 (Wash. Ct. App. 1995).

Page 124, add to footnote 150:

Cf. Kopp v. Samaritan Health Sys., Inc., 13 F.3d 264 (8th Cir. 1993). The plaintiff cardiology technician, in a sexual harassment action, survived a summary judgment motion when she alleged that over the course of a decade, a hospital cardiologist yelled at, swore at, threatened, and physically endangered employees, both male and female, but that the incidents involving women were of a more serious nature, involving actual physical contact, and that the hospital was well aware of the cardiologist's behavior. His conduct was a frequent subject of discussion at management meetings, and one employee testified that she was warned about him when she first started to work at the hospital.

Cf. Bartlett v. United States, 835 F. Supp. 1246 (E.D. Wash. 1993). Two incidents involving sexually suggestive conduct, a request by the plaintiff's supervisor to accompany him to San Francisco and share a room, and the receipt of a sexually explicit card at her home from a coworker were insufficient, as a matter of law, viewed from the eyes of a reasonable woman, to establish a sexual harassment or hostile environment claim.

Page 125, add to footnote 155:

Chiapuzio v. BLT Operating Corp. has been officially reported at 826 F. Supp. 1334 (D. Wyo. 1993).

Page 128, add to footnote 160:

Spain v. Gallegos, 26 F.3d 439 (3d Cir. 1994). An employee may demonstrate a hostile environment without showing blatant sexual misconduct.

King v. Hillen, 21 F.3d 1572 (Fed. Cir. 1994). The Merit Systems Protection Board improperly determined that the conduct of a senior civilian manager at the Army's Military Traffic Management Command toward five women, which included touching of the buttocks, thigh, and breast, suggestive comments and looks, and the telling of vulgar jokes, did not constitute sexual harassment. The Board stated that to establish sexual harassment under the EEOC Guidelines, a serious effect on the employee's psychological well-being must be shown and that it must be determined for each incident, standing alone, whether it met the criteria of sexual harassment rather than considering the effect on the workplace of the totality of the conduct. This reasoning misapplied the fact that one victim did not complain until she learned that the alleged harasser would be placed in her chain of command, and erroneously required that the factfinder establish that the conduct was of a sexual nature.

Cf. Payne v. Children's Home Soc'y of Wash., 892 P.2d 1102 (Wash. Ct. App. 1995). Offensive conduct need not be of a sexual nature to be actionable as sexual harassment, but in this hostile environment action, the plaintiff failed to show that the alleged harassment by her supervisor occurred because of her sex; the conduct the plaintiff complained of was in the nature of a personality conflict, which does not constitute harassment as a matter of law.

A record need not contain multiple allegations of sexually oriented conduct when the conduct underlying the sexual harassment claim is directed at an employee because of her gender. But if an employer is able to adequately explain his or her reasons for negative employment-related conduct, the conduct that is sexually offensive may not be able to stand alone to prove sexual harassment. For example, in Ott v. Perk Development Corp., 846 F. Supp. 266 (W.D.N.Y. 1994), a former employee who alleged constructive discharge based on sex discrimination established a prima facie case of hostile environment sexual harassment based on the placement of a pornographic magazine in her notebook by a worker whom she supervised, the inadequacy of the remedial measures taken by management when she complained, and allegedly sex-based discipline, reprimands, and less favorable evaluations and assignments. Although the *Penthouse* magazine incident may have been the only patently sexual episode complained of, the totality of the circumstances indicated that the plaintiff met her minimal prima facie burden of proof. However, the plaintiff did not meet her burden of proving that the defendant's proffered reason for his work-related actions—namely, the plaintiff's marginal work record—was pretextual. Management and work shift statistics presented by the plaintiff to provide statistical evidence of the disparity between male managers and female managers, from which it could be inferred that a discriminatory reason likely motivated the defendant's conduct, were insufficient to create a genuine issue of fact as to the credibility of, or discriminatory motive for, the defendant's stated reason for its evaluations, reprimands, or criticisms of the plaintiff's work performance.

Page 128, add to footnote 163:

Payne v. Children's Home Soc'y of Wash., 892 P.2d 1102 (Wash. Ct. App. 1995). "When gender-based harassment is not of a sexual nature, but is a term or condition of employment, it too unfairly handicaps the employee against whom it is directed and creates a barrier to sexual equality in the workplace. . . . A court-imposed requirement that the conduct be explicitly sexual to be actionable would be contrary to the purpose of RCW 49.60." *Id.* at 1105.

§ 3.20 Effect of the Harassment: *Harris v. Forklift Systems, Inc.*

Page 130, add to footnote 176:

Ward v. Johns Hopkins Univ., 861 F. Supp. 367 (D. Md. 1994). A jury could reasonably conclude that an alleged harasser's conduct interfered with the plaintiffs' ability to work or affected their psychological well-being when one plaintiff testified that every time the alleged harasser was in the office or in the copy room, he would touch her in some way, and he could not speak to her without being six inches away from her face, she had to constantly maneuver her workload to avoid the coworker, he showed up at her home late at night with beer and a gun, and as a result she suffered from migraine headaches and an inability to trust men. The other plaintiff alleged similar facts.

Sudtelgte v. Reno, 63 Fair Empl. Prac. Cas. (BNA) 1257 (W.D. Mo. 1994). A female former employee who claimed that her mental illness was due to sexual harassment did not establish a hostile environment when, although she subjectively perceived the environment to be sexually abusive, much of the plaintiff's case was based on her feeling that she was being persistently picked on.

> When the Court [in *Harris*] ruled that "Title VII bars conduct that would seriously affect a reasonable person's psychological well-being" (114 S.Ct. 371), I believe it effectively disposed of claims based on abnormal sensitivity, whether or not the sensitivity was simply unusual or produced by mental illness. This might be a different test than would be applied in standard tort law, where a tort-feasor takes the injured party as it finds him or her, but it likely comports with Congressional intent. Employers must police the environment for the benefit of the average person or "reasonable person" under the Civil Rights Act; particular disabilities may be subject to other legislative protection.

Id. at 1267.

Zvelter v. Brazilian Nat'l Superintendency of Merchant Marine, 833 F. Supp. 1089 (S.D.N.Y. 1993). The court could not say that the "buttocks-touching, leering, attempted leg-touching, and sundry comments, jokes, and suggestions," did not, as a matter of law, make out a claim for a hostile working environment. The court rejected the defendants' claim that one instance of touching the plaintiff's buttocks, a suggestion that the plaintiff wear apparel which would complement the physical appearance of her legs and a withdrawn attempt to touch her legs, three invitations to go out for cocktails, sporadic jokes, and the plaintiff's discomfort at having her legs looked at were isolated incidents that could not create a hostile environment.

§ 3.21   Quid Pro Quo Harassment

Page 130, add to footnote 177:

Doe v. R.R. Donnelley & Sons Co., 843 F. Supp. 1278 (S.D. Ind. 1994). In quid pro quo cases, an employer or supervisor requires sexual favors from an employee or subordinate to obtain a job benefit or to avoid a detriment (citing the first edition of this text). The court of appeals affirmed Doe v. R.R. Donnelley & Sons Co., 42 F.3d 439 (7th Cir. 1994), noting that although the plaintiff could not maintain a cause of action based on her supervisor's conduct because her complaint was not timely, it had serious reservations as to whether it was appropriate for the district court to hold as a matter of law that the conduct was not actionable when it persisted for a lengthy period of time and was a pervasive aspect of the plaintiff's employment during that period. The court concluded that the plaintiff did not show that there was a sufficiently close nexus between the conduct of the supervisor at the North Plant and the later conduct of fellow employees at the South Plant to permit the characterization of a continuous violation. With respect to the conduct at the South Plant, it was not at all clear on the record that the supervisor actually witnessed the hugging of plaintiff by a coworker, and the plaintiff never reported the incident, even though she was aware of the company's sexual harassment policy, and of the company's willingness to take action, as management had responded promptly to her complaint involving heavy breathing on her voice mail by a coworker.

Page 131, add to footnote 178:

Johnson v. Merry-Go-Round Enter., 67 Fair Empl. Prac. Cas. (BNA) 1456 (N.D. Ill. 1995) (employers are strictly liable for quid pro quo harassment by their employees, but the employees must have the power and opportunity to make employment-related decisions).

Thompson v. Berta Enter., Inc., 72 Wash. App. 531, 864 P.2d 983 (1994). An employer is strictly liable for quid pro quo sexual harassment perpetuated by supervisory personnel.

> Adopting this standard is sound public policy because it requires employers, who themselves have the power to hire and fire supervisory personnel to be responsible for insuring that those they cloak with apparent authority to affect terms and conditions of their employee's jobs do not abuse that authority. Therefore, it places the burden for preventing quid pro quo sexual harassment on those best situated to prevent it. We also believe this holding is consistent with the legislative mandate that RCW 49.60 be construed liberally to accomplish the purposes of the statute.

864 P.2d at 987.

Page 131, add to footnote 181:

Cf. Longmire v. Alabama State Univ., 151 F.R.D. 414 (M.D. Ala. 1992). A university employee who brought an action against the former president and the university could discover evidence of the president's other sexual activities with women at the university, but not with women at another university. The court noted that this ruling was based on the present state of the record; if the plaintiff had actual evidence, not argument, which would establish a good faith basis for the inquiry about the president's sexual activity at places other than this university and some relevance to this inquiry, the plaintiff could make an ex parte motion under seal requesting that the court allow such inquiry.

§ 3.22 Hostile Environment Harassment

Page 132, add to footnote 182:

Doe v. RR Donnelley & Sons Co., 843 F. Supp. 1278 (S.D. Ind. 1994), *aff'd*, 42 F.3d 439 (7th Cir. 1994). In a hostile environment case, no deal is sought or struck (citing the first edition of this text).

§ 3.22 HOSTILE ENVIRONMENT

* *Page 136, add to footnote 193 following "Eleventh Circuit":*

A damages award for battery does not necessarily support a finding of hostile environment. Faragher v. City of Boca Raton, 76 F.3d 1155 (11th Cir. 1996). In an action by former city lifeguards against the city and supervisors for sexual harassment under § 1983, with one plaintiff, Faragher, claiming sexual harassment under Title VII and alleging pendent state law claims against supervisors for battery, and against city for negligent retention and supervision of one supervisor, the district court properly entered judgment for the plaintiff on her § 1983 claim against supervisors, for supervisors on the second plaintiff, Ewanchew's, § 1983 claim, for the plaintiffs on their battery claims and for the city on their negligent retention claims, but improperly ruled against the city of Faragher's Title VII claim. On appeal Ewanchew argued that the district court's factual finding that she did not perceive her work environment to be abusive was inconsistent with its finding that she suffered $35,000 in damages on her battery claim. But the court of appeals found that a "finding of damages resulting from an offensive touching—even if the touching, when combined with other conduct, constitutes sexual harassment—does not necessarily mean that the victim of the touching perceived her *work environment* to be abusive." *Id.* at 1160 (emphasis by the court). Although the district court made no specific finding as to when the plaintiff suffered damages, the damages from the battery seem to have occurred some time after she resigned from her lifeguard position with the city. The plaintiff's counsel conceded that the plaintiff suffered a delayed reaction to the offensive conduct, but argued that such delayed reaction satisfies *Harris v. Forklift Systems, Inc.,* 114 S. Ct. 367 (1993). The plaintiff pointed to no evidence in the record indicating that she suffered damages from the battery before she resigned. Thus the district court reasonably could have found that Ewanchew did not view her work environment as abusive but, after resigning, suffered emotional or psychological trauma from the offensive touchings. Under *Harris,* Title VII is not violated when the victim of harassment does not perceive her work environment to be abusive at the time that she is employed.

Page 136, add to footnote 194:

Thomson v. Olson, 866 F. Supp. 1267 (D.N.D. 1994), *aff'd without op.,* 56 F.3d 69 (8th Cir. 1995). A male former employee failed to state a claim for sex discrimination when he alleged that a female coworker who was having a romantic relationship with their supervisor enjoyed preferential treatment; "this court joins in the chorus of reviewing courts in finding that preferential treatment on the basis of a consensual relationship between a supervisor and an employee is not a cognizable sex discrimination claim under Title VII." 866 F. Supp. at 1272.

Herman v. Western Fin. Corp., 254 Kan. 870, 869 P.2d 696, 64 Fair Empl. Prac. Cas. (BNA) 351 (1994). The district court properly granted summary judgment to the defendant employer in a sexual harassment action by a regional bank manager when the plaintiff claimed that an alleged affair between her supervisor and another employee affected his work performance.

> We do not believe that an actionable Title VII claim may be made simply from allegations that female employees had to take up the slack for a male supervisor who was shirking his duties while involved in a consensual affair with another supervisor.
>
> Federal courts faced with claims of hostile work environments created by an affair between noncomplaining employees have concluded that such circumstances fall short of violating Title VII.

64 Fair Empl. Prac. Cas. at 355.

* *Page 137, add to footnote 200:*

Tomka v. Seiler Corp., 66 F.3d 1295 (2d Cir. 1995). The district court improperly dismissed a female employee's claims of hostile environment sexual harassment and retaliatory discharge in violation of Title VII and New York's Human Rights Law against her former employer and three male coemployees. The plaintiff claimed that the work environment was permeated with a discriminatory animus towards women in general and that various supervisors and employees subjected her to sexual jokes, comments, and innuendoes. Specifically, Tomka lists a number of incidents that occurred at various locations to which Tomka had been assigned:

1. A senior account executive stated that he would buy a diamond bracelet for someone who would be "special" to him; while looking at the plaintiff, he then stated "I wonder if anyone in this office could be special to me?" A senior account executive [Toomey] later asked a manager who was standing with Tomka, if Tomka and the manager were sleeping together;

2. While on an inspection with the plaintiff and two other male employees a district manager grabbed plaintiff's hand and stated "Carol, when are you going to go out with me?";

3. Tomka's supervisor instructed her to accompany him to Toomey's house for dinner and to bring a bathing suit to use in Toomey's pool; upon arrival at Toomey's house, Toomey expressed disappointment that Tomka was not wearing her bathing suit because he "had been looking forward to seeing her in it";

4. A senior account executive talking on the phone with a vice president stated, with Tomka present, that "when I am not doing that I'll be in bed with Carol Tomka." Tomka said nothing and left the office from which the call had been made;

5. At a required orientation function, a manager at Tomka's table referred to a radio show that had discussed women's underwear;

6. While on an inspection with Tomka and two other male employees, a vice president turned to the two employees and stated, "[a] bunch of us were sitting around at dinner the other night and we all wondered does she fuck." Snook looked at Tomka as he made this remark, and then laughed and said, "[n]o, more appropriately does she fuck you?";

7. Unidentified male employees nicknamed Tomka "Sergeant Slaughter" and stated that she had "great legs";

8. At a business dinner, the plaintiff felt pressured to drink, vulgar comments about women were made, and the plaintiff later was raped by three workers, including the district manager.

Accepting that these assaults occurred, the court agreed with the district court that even a single incident of sexual assault sufficiently altered the conditions of the victim's employment and clearly creates an abusive work environment for purposes of Title VII liability. The district court also found that the verbal harassment was not, standing alone, enough to create an abusive working environment. The court of appeals stated:

> It is true that isolated remarks or occasional episodes of harassment will not merit relief under Title VII; in order to be actionable, the incidents of harassment must occur in concert or with a regularity that can reasonably be termed pervasive. . . . The trier of fact should consider the comments about Tomka's body, innuendoes about her sex life, and other lewd

remarks, together with the assaults, on the issue of abusive working environment.

Id. at 1305. The court noted that while there was no evidence to suggest that Tomka was physically forced to drink six glasses of wine, it would be reasonable for her to feel pressure to drink, given that all of the others were drinking. A fact finder could reasonably conclude that Seiler employees on assignment customarily met after working hours to eat and discuss business, and the district manager, as the agent of Seiler, used his apparent authority to promote this policy, which included the supplying of alcoholic drinks on the company's credit card. There was contradictory evidence in the record that the dinner was simply a social event that Tomka chose to attend and that her consumption of alcohol was likewise voluntary.

The court also found that the plaintiff met her burden of establishing a prima facie case of retaliation based on allegations that she complained of sexual harassment to her employer when she spoke to her supervisor and when she later told him she was considering legal action, the employer disadvantaged plaintiff by terminating her, and a causal connection between plaintiff's complaints and employer's actions could be inferred by the fact that the employer terminated the plaintiff a few weeks after she told the supervisor she was considering legal action.

Page 139, add to footnote 203:

See also Coleman v. Tennessee, 846 F. Supp. 582 (M.D. Tenn. 1993). In an action by an African-American female former employee against her state employer, alleging sex and race discrimination, a genuine issue of fact existed as to whether, among other things, a hostile work environment existed. The court determined that although none of the allegedly objectionable statements made to the plaintiff (such as telling her that she was not promoted because she had two problems: she was black and female) in isolation rose to the level of discriminatory sexual or racial harassment, when coupled with the plaintiff's allegations regarding discrimination in promotional opportunities, the plaintiff established a prima facie case of hostile work environment race and sex discrimination.

Page 148, add new text to end of section:

In *Jones v. Aspin*, 64 Empl. Prac. Dec. (CCH) ¶ 43,005 (E.D. Pa. 1994), a male employee who alleged repeated false and malicious accusations of sexual harassment leveled against him, resulting in various emotional reputational harms, stated a claim for hostile environment sexual harassment. The court noted that under *Andrews v. City of Philadelphia*, 895 F.2d 1469 (3d Cir. 1990), when the allegedly offensive conduct is not overtly sexual in nature, the court is obliged to conduct a factually intensive inquiry. Given the procedural posture of this case, such an inquiry could not be made until the factual record was better developed and recognized that a man's hostile environment claim, although theoretically possible, would be much harder to plead and prove.

§ 3.24   The Reasonable Woman Standard

Page 150, update Austin citation in footnote 249:

aff'd, 967 F.2d 583 (9th Cir 1992).

Page 153, text in the third line of the first full paragraph should read:

state supreme court addressed the elements . . .

Page 154, add to footnote 257:

See also Hall v. Transit Auth., 883 S.W.2d 884 (Ky. Ct. App. 1994). The trial court properly instructed the jury that an objective "reasonable female employee" standard rather than a subjective standard should be applied to the plaintiff's hostile environment claim.

§ 3.25   Quid Pro Quo and Third-Party Employees

Page 155, add to footnote 261 following Third Circuit cases:

Seventh Circuit: Piech v. Arthur Andersen & Co., 841 F. Supp. 825 (N.D. Ill. 1994). In asserting a claim that a less qualified, single female coworker was promoted to manager instead of the plaintiff, because of the "favored" female's knowledge of inappropriate male partner sexual conduct and her amorous relationship with a partner in the decisionmaking process, the plaintiff did not allege that she suffered an adverse employment decision because of her sex. The plaintiff did, however, allege that it was generally necessary for women to grant sexual favors to decisionmakers for professional advances and that because she did not grant sexual favors she was denied a promotion, fitting the classic definition of quid pro quo harassment. The plaintiff's allegations "regarding the favored female co-worker who received a promotion while involved romantically with a decision-maker may be considered simply circumstantial evidence that her employer conditioned employment benefits on the granting of sexual favors." *Id.* at 830.

Cf. Dirksen v. City of Springfield, 842 F. Supp. 1117 (C.D. Ill. 1994). A demoted female secretary for the city police department claimed that a police officer made numerous nonconsensual sexual advances toward her, which included attempts to kiss and touch her body, offensive placement of his hands on her body, forcing the placement of her hands on his body, and attempted sexual assault, during which the alleged harasser stated that if the plaintiff wanted to be promoted to his personal secretary, she had to submit to sexual intercourse with him; also, when she went on medical leave she was replaced by a worker who was having sexual relations with him. This stated a claim for quid pro quo sexual harassment, despite the defendant's argument that the plaintiff was not discriminated against on the basis of sex but because her boss allegedly favored his paramour. This was not a single instance of favoritism based on a relationship, as in *DeCintio*; the plaintiff alleged that it was generally necessary for *women* to grant sexual favors for professional advancement.

§ 3.26   Hostile Environment and Third-Party Employees

Page 155, add to footnote 263:

Cf. Ramirez v. Bravo's Holding Co., 67 Fair Empl. Prac. Cas. (BNA) 733 (D. Kan. 1995). A male supervisor could not seek damages under Title VII for alleged emotional distress arising from working in an environment that was sexually hostile toward the women he supervised when he did not allege that he was the direct object of the sexual harassment or that it was related to his gender. "In piggyback fashion he would add sort

of bystander tort action to the statutory discrimination claims of others."
Id. at 735.

* *Page 155, add to footnote 264:*

   Cf. Lyman v. Nabil's Inc., 903 F. Supp. 1443 (D. Kan. 1995). The
court refused to extend Title VII's contemplation of associational benefits to the plaintiff in a Title VII sex discrimination and retaliation action
brought by a male former employee against his former employer, alleging that discriminatory acts directed against women in his workplace
were sufficiently pervasive to seriously affect his own working environment, that the women complained to him about these offensive acts, that
the defendant's owner, Saleh, made sexual comments about the women
to Lyman, and that Saleh made Lyman transfer the women from restaurant to restaurant in retaliation for their complaints. Lyman alleges that
he suffered emotional distress as a direct and proximate result of Saleh's
alleged discriminatory acts, and that defendant retaliated against him by
firing him for his complaining about the alleged discriminatory acts, his
being supportive of women complaining of those acts, and his refusal to
cooperate in defendant's retaliation against the women. The plaintiff
argued by analogy that his situation was similar to cases in which whites
suffered "associational" injuries due to racial discrimination directed at
minorities, and asked the court to apply the reasoning of those cases to
his Title VII claim of emotional distress caused by the alleged sexually
hostile workplace for women under his supervision. The court found that
no court had extended Title VII's contemplation of associational benefits
to the type of claim Lyman alleged.

> *Hicks[v. Gates Rubber Co.,* 833 F.2d 1406 (10th Cir. 1987)] merely
> approved the use of incidents of sexual harassment directed at a woman's
> female coworkers as evidence supporting the woman's claim that such
> harassment was also directed at her. . . . The case in no way supports the
> proposition that a hostile work environment directed toward one gender
> can give rise to a Title VII claim by violating the rights of the opposite
> gender.
>
>   . . . The Act does not specifically address whether an unlawful business
> practice directed at a person in a protected class is actionable by a person
> who, although outside the protected class, is allegedly injured by the
> unlawful practice.
>
>   Neither party to this action cites any case in which a court has directly
> considered whether men have standing to sue for alleged injuries suffered

as a result of discrimination directed at women. Most courts that have considered the question seem to hold that males lack standing to sue because they are not "persons aggrieved" under Title VII when they seek redress for injuries suffered due to alleged discrimination directed at women.

Id. at 1447. The court concluded that plaintiff's complaint was sufficient with respect to his claim of retaliatory discharge. His allegations of resistance and supportiveness amounted to an allegation that he made an informal complaint, which constitutes distinct action. "[P]rotected opposition includes informal complaints expressing support of coworkers who are subjected to discriminatory employment practices." *Id.*

Page 156, add to footnote 269:

Spain v. Gallegos, 26 F.3d 439 (3d Cir. 1994). A female employee established a prima facie case of hostile environment sexual harassment with evidence of untrue rumors among her colleagues that she was having an affair with her superior. These rumors developed because coworkers saw her and her superior in private meetings, which were actually the scene of improper solicitations of loans by the superior, but which led to the fellow employees shunning her and supervisors evaluating her poorly for promotion purposes with respect to her integrity and ability to work with others. Management personnel did not take remedial action to eliminate the rumors. The district court abused its discretion in excluding the superior's alleged solicitation and acceptance of loans from the plaintiff on relevancy grounds when it was clear that the evidence of private meetings had a tendency to prove certain elements of the plaintiff's claims. In addition, the probative value of this evidence was not substantially outweighed by the danger of unfair prejudice.

Page 156, add to footnote 270:

See also O'Patka v. Menasha Corp., 878 F. Supp. 1202 (E.D. Wis. 1995). A male employee who alleged sex discrimination, sexual harassment, and intentional infliction of emotional distress based on alleged differential and unfair treatment by a male supervisor because the supervisor was involved with a female coworker did not establish a prima facie case of sexual harassment because the claim did not implicate gender and did not allege that there was widespread managerial favoritism for those who accept sexual advances, that it was necessary for women or men to grant sexual favors to management for professional advancement, and that the workplace was fraught with sexual innuendo or overtones.

§ 3.27 Constructive Discharge

Page 159, add to footnote 277:

In Al-Dabbagh v. Greenpeace Inc., 873 F. Supp. 1105 (N.D. Ill. 1994), the plaintiff's claim of constructive discharge was unnecessary to prove her Title VII claim but provided her with the potential for additional recovery—compensatory or punitive damages or both, and perhaps reinstatement or back pay "for a Title VII violation that was already complete when she suffered the rape itself." *Id.* at 1112. A female former employee stated a cause of action for sexual discrimination under Title VII against Greenpeace when she alleged that a coworker suddenly attempted to kiss her as she was preparing to leave the office at the end of the day, and then responded to her rejection of his actions by slapping her, tearing off her shirt, beating her, hitting her on the head with a radio, shocking her with a phone cord, and ultimately raping her.

Page 160, add to footnote 283:

Cuesta v. Texas Dep't of Criminal Justice, 805 F. Supp. 451 (W.D. Tex. 1991). The court found sexual harassment in an action by a female parole case worker against the parole officer and parole board. Although a reasonable person would have considered the working conditions to be intolerable because of sexual harassment, the court would not find constructive discharge because the plaintiff's resignation did not result solely from the harassment. Although the plaintiff stated that the main reason for leaving was that she perceived that her immediate supervisor acted as a go-between for the parole officer and thereby cooperated in the harassment, the court was not convinced that the plaintiff did not have other alternatives to resignation.

Page 161, add to footnote 290:

Cuesta v. Texas Dep't of Criminal Justice, 805 F. Supp. 451 (W.D. Tex. 1991).

§ 3.28 Retaliation

Page 164, add to footnote 304 following Sixth Circuit paragraph:

Henry v. Gehl Corp., 867 F. Supp. 960 (D. Kan. 1994). A genuine issue of fact existed on hostile environment, retaliatory discharge, and disparate treatment claims as well as whether the employer was liable for a hostile work environment claim when the plaintiff alleged that her office manager daily engaged in sexual banter, made sexual innuendoes about her, told crude sexual jokes, embarrassed her with comments about her body and clothes, and stood so the plaintiff was forced to brush against him. Following an incident at a bar with coworkers where the office manager put his hand on her thigh twice, plaintiff called in sick. When she eventually complained to the office manager about his conduct, she was fired immediately. The court rejected the defendants' claim that the plaintiff was terminated for poor attendance and production and not in retaliation when there was evidence that only after the office manager fired the plaintiff did he prepare and insert into the plaintiff's personnel file most of the negative comments about her performance and attendance and his secretary testified that the office manager even forged the plaintiff's signature on an employee reprimand prepared after her termination. There was a factual and legal basis for imposing liability on the employer based on agency principles when the office manager had the ultimate authority to hire and fire the plaintiff and thus exercised significant control over her conditions of employment. There were also issues of material fact regarding liability based on conduct outside the scope of delegated authority when the office manager allegedly capitalized on his authority over the plaintiff to create an intimidating and sexually charged atmosphere in which the plaintiff realized the almost certain termination facing her if she challenged the offensive conduct. The company handbook contained no alternative to taking complaints to the supervisor.

Page 164, add to footnote 305:

Davis v. Fleming Cos., 55 F.3d 1369 (8th Cir. 1995). Summary judgment in favor of the employer should not have been granted by the lower court in an action by a male employee who claimed that he was fired in retaliation for reporting the sexual harassment of another employee, in violation of Title VII and the state human rights act when material issues of fact existed regarding whether retaliation was the reason for termination. The plaintiff produced evidence that deficient performance was a pretext for his termination in that before he reported the harassment, he had never received complaints about poor job performance, and that increased scrutiny of his job performance commenced very shortly after he reported the incident. Although some memos submitted by the defendant showed that the plaintiff had some grievance about the company and that there were some complaints about his own actions, they were not so strong a showing of deficient performance as to preclude a reasonable person from inferring a retaliatory intent or pretext from the other evidence presented by the plaintiff.

Wyatt v. City of Boston, 35 F.3d 13 (1st Cir. 1994). In an action by a former teacher against a school committee and school personnel alleging that he was retaliated against for opposing what he considered to be sexual harassment and filing a complaint with the state office against discrimination, the lower court improperly dismissed the action for failure to state a claim when it was impossible to tell from the court's "cryptic" order whether it addressed the question of a prima facie case; even assuming the plaintiff's complaint demonstrated that there was cause for his alleged demotions and dismissal, he should have been given a fair opportunity to show that the defendants' reasons for their actions were pretextual.

*   Lyman v. Nabil's Inc., 903 F. Supp. 1443 (D. Kan. 1995) (see § 3.26).

Wilson v. Wayne County, 856 F. Supp. 1254 (M.D. Tenn. 1994). This Title VII sexual harassment and retaliatory discharge action was brought by a former dispatcher, the alleged victim of discrimination, and a male coworker deputy sheriff who alleged that he was fired for opposing the harassment. The court found that the female plaintiff was subjected to quid pro quo and hostile environment harassment: her supervisor lured the plaintiff into his office in the dead of night, locking off her only route of escape, fondled her, placed her hand on his crotch, and pulled her to the floor and penetrated her. The male plaintiff proved retaliation for opposing the sheriff's harassment of the female plaintiff; among the actions he took in opposition to the harassment were the following: he notified an assistant district attorney of the female plaintiff's allegations, obtained a rape detection kit, contacted a sheriff's department sergeant, took the female plaintiff to the hospital for examination, and testified before the county grand jury. The court rejected as pure pretext the sheriff's explanation that he laid off the male plaintiff because of budget restrictions when he was the only employee laid off that summer and another employee was hired within a month. The case was dismissed, however, because Title VII does not allow actions against individual defendants in their individual capacities.

Page 164, add to last paragraph of footnote 305:

Cf. Beasley v. Spiegel, Inc., 64 Empl. Prac. Dec. (CCH) ¶ 43,127 (N.D. Ill. 1993). A male employee was not discharged in retaliation for reporting an incident of sexual harassment of a female employee to his supervisor and then reporting the same incident two months later to an official of the human relations department but for poor work performance 18 to 20 months after he made his complaints.

Page 164, add to footnote 306 following "Third Circuit":

Cf. Frederick v. Reed Smith Shaw & McClay, 63 Empl. Prac. Dec. (CCH) ¶ 42,865 (E.D. Pa. 1994). Comments by a supervisor accused of sexual harassment to the media regarding the fact that the plaintiff was under psychiatric care and that she was fired from her previous employer and that the suit was to extort money did not amount to an adverse employment action and thus the statements did not make out a claim for retaliation. While the statements could be upsetting to the plaintiff, they did not transform what could be a claim for defamation into a claim for retaliation under Title VII or state law. An internal memorandum to employees denying the plaintiff's charges and assuring them that the company would defend against the charges did not constitute retaliation, but merely advised the employees about the firm's position concerning the litigation. The memorandum does not contain any statements that could be construed as malicious. "Informing one's employees about a highly publicized lawsuit involving the firm, and assuring the employees that the claims are, in its view, unfounded" did not constitute adverse employment action. *Id.* at 78,802.

CHAPTER 4

PREPARING THE SEXUAL HARASSMENT CASE

§ 4.10 —Title VII

Page 178, add to footnote 5:

Cf. Howard v. Board of Educ. Sycamore Dist., 876 F. Supp. 959 (N.D. Ill. 1995). A female former director of music and band director stated claims for hostile environment sexual harassment and retaliation when she alleged that during her employment, notes referring to the plaintiff in a sexually offensive manner were posted, a male teacher made offensive comments about a female teacher, and male students made offensive comments. The plaintiff could not maintain a claim against the Board of Education under Title VII. Absent knowledge or direct involvement by the school or educational agency, it was difficult to characterize any form of sex discrimination as an authorized program or activity of the school or educational agency. "Moreover, it is difficult to imagine that Congress intended to open schools and educational agencies to virtually unlimited liability based on the conduct of their employees." *Id.* at 974.

> In the wake of the Civil Rights Act of 1991, there are two remaining, competing schools of thought on the issue. First, courts finding the federal employment discrimination statutes to create individual liability on the part of co employees have based that stance on the inclusion of "any agents of" in the definition of employer and on the purposes of the statutes to compensate victims of discrimination and to deter future discrimination. . . . Second, courts finding the federal employment discrimination statutes not to create individual liability have explained that the "any agent of" language in the definition of employer is merely a mechanism for incorporating *respondeat superior* liability into the statutes. These courts then look to the exclusion of small employers from liability.

Id. at 970.

Page 178, add to footnote 11:

Cf. DiDonato v. A.G. Edwards & Sons, 65 Fair Empl. Prac. Cas. (BNA) 1207 (N.D. Cal. 1994). The Title VII and state tort claims of sexual harassment by a registered sales assistant in a retail stock brokerage firm were dismissed because a broad and inclusive arbitration clause in her employment application required the arbitration of such claims. The court rejected the plaintiff's claims that she did not realize or intend that claims of sexual harassment would require arbitration, that the defendant used the arbitration provision as a

> sword and club that would force [her] to submit to violations of her dignity based on gender, that she would be denied her constitutional right to a trial by jury if she is forced to arbitrate her dispute, and that requiring arbitration frustrated the policies underlying Title VII. The language of the arbitration provision belied the first argument. Were the court to accept the second and third arguments, it would essentially be holding that all arbitration agreements are unenforceable, and the fourth argument was directly contradicted by the language of the agreement. The fifth argument was expressly contradicted by case law.

§ 4.13 —Title IX

Page 182, add to footnote 48:

Ward v. Johns Hopkins Univ., 861 F. Supp. 367 (D. Md. 1994) (employees' Title IX claim would be analyzed under Title VII standards).

Dickinson v. McCarty, 65 Fair Empl. Prac. Cas. (BNA) 1508 (S.D. Fla. 1994). Parties may bring actions against institutions under Title IX, but not against employees of institutions.

Page 182, add to footnote 51:

Duron v. Hancock, 64 Fair Empl. Prac. Cas. (BNA) 81 (D. Kan. 1993). The former owners of an unincorporated hairstyling school could be found directly liable for a supervisor's alleged sexual harassment of an instructor in a Title IX action when the former owners delegated authority to the supervisor to run the school and could fire or promote the plaintiff.

§ 4.17 PENDENT STATE CLAIMS

§ 4.15 State Fair Employment Practice Laws

Page 185, add to footnote 68:

See also Sanborn v. Hunt Real Estate Corp., 65 Fair Empl. Prac. Cas. (BNA) 1305 (W.D.N.Y. 1994). A motion to strike a jury demand will be denied when a plaintiff, although not entitled to a jury under Title VII (before the Civil Rights Act of 1991), is entitled to a jury under the state law cause of action. In this action under Title VII and the state human rights law, the jury's concern would be solely with the state human rights claim and thus any likelihood of confusion would be minimal. "If necessary, any such concern could be controlled by the use of special interrogatories and a carefully prepared verdict report form." *Id.* at 1310.

§ 4.17 —Pendent or Supplemental Jurisdiction

Page 186, add to footnote 72 following First Circuit case:

Second Circuit: Sanborn v. Hunt Real Estate Corp., 65 Fair Empl. Prac. Cas. (BNA) 1305 (W.D.N.Y. 1994). The court exercised pendent jurisdiction over a state human rights law claim that arose out of the same facts and circumstances as the Title VII claim.

Page 186, add to footnote 72 following "Sixth Circuit":

Bintner v. Burlington N., Inc., 857 F. Supp. 1484 (D. Wyo. 1994).

Page 186, add to footnote 72 following Ninth Circuit cases:

Tenth Circuit: Duron v. Hancock, 64 Fair Empl. Prac. Cas. (BNA) 81 (D. Kan. 1993) (intentional infliction of emotional distress).

Page 186, add to footnote 72 following "Bell" citation in "Eleventh Circuit":

Prescott v. Independent Life & Accident Ins. Co., 878 F. Supp. 1545 (M.D. Ala. 1995). A male former employee who alleged that his male supervisor sexually harassed him stated a claim for quid pro quo harassment under Title VII. The court exercised supplemental jurisdiction over a state law claim of assault and battery.

Page 187, add to footnote 73:

Fisher v. Somerville Sch. Dist., 874 F. Supp. 448 (D. Mass. 1995) . A Title VII claim against a coworker was not viable in an action by a grade school teacher against the school district, its officials, and the coworker, alleging that the district and its officials violated the teacher's right to a workplace free of sexual harassment by failing to adequately respond to her complaints of harassment by a female coworker. The court had supplemental jurisdiction over state law claims of defamation and intentional infliction of emotional distress against the coworker, however, when the federal court had original jurisdiction over Title VII claims and one set of events gave rise to all of the asserted claims. State law claims did not predominate over Title VII claims; proof of the coworker's alleged behavior was an essential part of both the state and federal claims, and similar damages were available under the relevant state and federal law. The coworker's hope of resolving the issue solely through the less expensive procedures provided by the state commission against discrimination was blocked by the plaintiff's filing a state court lawsuit alleging the same state law claims presented here. In light of the duplicative proceedings that would otherwise be necessary, it was appropriate that the plaintiff's state law claims against the coworker be litigated with her federal and state law claims against the school district and its officials.

Gard v. Teletronics Pacing Sys., Inc., 859 F. Supp. 1349 (D. Colo. 1994) (the court would exercise supplemental jurisdiction when the same evidence would be used to prove state and federal claims).

Page 187, add to footnote 75:

Ammerman v. Sween, 54 F.3d 423 (7th Cir. 1995). An assault and battery claim against a coworker was sufficiently connected to a Title VII claim against a college by a lab instructor so as to confer supplemental jurisdiction on the district court to hear the state claim. An employer has a legal duty to take reasonable steps to discover and rectify acts of sexual harassment of its employees, and the reasonableness of the steps depends on the gravity of the harassment. Thus, the plaintiff's factual allegations regarding the extent of the harassment were highly relevant to the determination of whether appropriate remedial action had been taken by the college, for purposes of Title VII, resulting in a common nucleus of operative facts. Without reference to the facts surrounding the assault, there could have been no sexual harassment claim against the employer.

Rodriguez v. Doral Mortgage Corp., 57 F.3d 1168 (1st Cir. 1995). The district court had the authority to exercise supplemental jurisdiction over a plaintiff's state sexual harassment claim after her Title VII claim was dismissed when both claims were derived from a reservoir of common facts and both would ordinarily be heard together in a single consolidated trial:

> Because each case is bound to have its own distinctive profile, we are reluctant to impose a list of important elements. Instead, we cite two examples to illustrate the wide variety of considerations that may appropriately enter into the calculus. The running of the statute of limitations on a pendent claim, precluding the filing of a separate suit in state court, is a salient factor to be evaluated when deciding whether to retain supplemental jurisdiction. . . . Another factor to be weighed is the clarity of the law that governs a pendent claim, for a federal court may be wise to forgo the exercise of supplemental jurisdiction when the state law that undergirds the nonfederal claim is of dubious scope and application. . . .
>
> We will not attempt to single out all the elements that could potentially tip the balance here. That is grist for the district court's mill. It suffices for our purposes to remark the obvious: that although the plaintiff's Title VII claim ultimately succumbed on the merits, it was colorable when brought. Consequently, the district court's power to exercise discretionary supplemental jurisdiction over a putative [state] claim, extant at the time of trial, will remain intact on remand.

Id. at 1177.

Page 188, add to footnote 82:

Fleenor v. Hewitt Soap Co., 67 Fair Empl. Prac. Cas. (BNA) 1625 (S.D. Ohio 1994). The court declined to exercise supplemental jurisdiction when the only federal claim was dismissed, and the state law claims raised at least one novel issue of state law: does a male employee have a claim under the state antidiscrimination statute for sexual harassment arising out of allegations that male coworkers created a hostile work environment.

PREPARING THE CASE

Page 188, add to footnote 85:

Bedford v. Southeastern Pa. Trans. Auth., 867 F. Supp. 288 (E.D. Pa. 1994). In an action by a police officer for sexual harassment, retaliatory discharge, and intentional infliction of emotional distress against the transit authority and a number of individuals stemming from an incident in which a SEPTA physician during a routine medical examination allegedly and unnecessarily placed a stethoscope under the plaintiff's brassiere and pressed his pelvic area against her buttocks while examining her back, the court dismissed the intentional infliction of emotional distress claim without prejudice to plaintiff to pursue it in a state court when there was no independent jurisdictional basis for the plaintiff's claim. The court noted that if a jury were to find that in a physician-patient relationship a doctor used a physical examination intentionally and unnecessarily to thrust his pelvic area into his patient's buttocks, such conduct would be sufficiently egregious to sustain a claim for intentional infliction of emotional distress.

Page 188, add to footnote 89:

See also Douglas v. Coca-Cola Bottling Co., 855 F. Supp. 518 (D.N.H. 1994). A discharged employee who alleged that her supervisor told her he was sexually attracted to her and that he wished to have an affair with her, and that as a result of her failure to comply, he criticized her work, berated her, and soon fired her, could bring her state common law claims in federal court despite the fact that an administrative action was dismissed by the state Commission for Human Rights.

Page 189, add to footnote 94:

Chester v. Northwest Iowa Youth Emergency Servs. Ctr., 869 F. Supp. 700 (N.D. Iowa 1994) (the court would not exercise pendent jurisdiction over state claims when a Title VII claim was dismissed).

CHAPTER 5

ADMINISTRATIVE PROCEDURES

§ 5.1   Introduction

Page 192, add to footnote 6:

Arbitration may also be required under statute or collective bergaining agreement. *See, e.g.*, the following cases:

Hirras v. National R.R. Passenger Corp., 10 F.3d 1142 (5th Cir. 1994). The district court properly held that a railroad worker's Title VII sex discrimination action alleging a hostile work environment was subject to mandatory arbitration under the Railway Labor Act (RLA) when the claim was founded upon an incident of an employment relationship and thus was a minor dispute within the meaning of the RLA.

The Supreme Court vacated and remanded *Hirras*, at 114 S. Ct. 2732 (1994), in light of Hawaiian Airlines, Inc. v. Norris, 114 S. Ct. 2239 (1994), which held that the language of § 151a limits the Railway Labor Act's preemption of claims, including state law claims, to those involving the interpretation or application of a collective bargaining agreement. If the claim is brought under state law without any reference to the collective bargaining agreement, then it is not preempted. On remand, Hirras v. National R.R. Passenger Corp., 44 F.3d 278 (5th Cir. 1995), the court held that Texas does not recognize the tort of negligent infliction of emotional distress and that the state intentional infliction claim was independent of the collective bargaining agreement and thus was not preempted by the mandatory arbitration provisions of the Railway Labor Act.

> Hirras contends that the terms of the CBA are irrelevant to her state-law claim. . . . We agree. The terms of the CBA at issue in this case are not relevant to the resolution of Hirras' claim because the CBA contains no provision related to sexual harassment, much less any provision that could be interpreted to give Amtrak the right to accommodate sexual harassment or Hirras the right to work in a non-hostile environment. Hirras'

intentional infliction of emotional distress claim does not depend on an interpretation of the CBA, and thus is independent of the CBA.

Id. at 283–84 (footnotes omitted).

Agee v. Huggins, 888 F. Supp. 1573 (N.D. Ga. 1995). An employee's defamation and libel claims, based on a supervisor's accusation before two other managers that the employee had sexually harassed other staff members, could be removed to federal district court when it required interpretation of the collective bargaining agreement and was thus pre-empted by § 301 of the Labor Management Relations Act. The LMRA establishes federal jurisdiction over lawsuits for violations of contracts between employers and labor organizations without regard to the amount in controversy or citizenship of parties. In order to determine whether the supervisors were persons with authority under Georgia law, the court had to examine the scope of their actions within the context of the collective bargaining agreement.

Cf. Cole v. Appalachian Power Co., 67 Fair Empl. Prac. Cas. (BNA) 1729 (S.D. W. Va. 1995). An employer who was being sued for sexual harassment by a female employee who alleged that her supervisors and coworkers repeatedly subjected her to extremely vulgar and offensive jokes, comments, gestures, and innuendos, including the display of sexually suggestive graffiti and other material, and to unwelcome sexual advances including touching could not file a third-party complaint against the union, charging that the union violated the quoted provision of the collective bargaining agreement by permitting the alleged harassment to continue:

> All the third-party complaint of APCO alleges, viewed in the light most favorable to APCO, is that Local 978 was aware of the acts of sexual harassment charged in Cole's complaint and failed to take preventive or remedial measures or to use its influence and efforts to prevent discrimination on the basis of sex. There is no allegation that the union directed, induced, authorized or ratified any acts of sexual harassment or that any of the alleged harassers acted under express or apparent authority as a union agent. Additionally, cases imposing liability on unions for acts of their members involve affirmative or tacit encouragement or approval of conduct designed to produce a benefit for the union. Typical are the cases involving work stoppages in violation of contractual no-strike clauses. . . . No case has been found imposing such liability for the union's failure to curtail activity, such as that charged in this case, having no objective which would benefit the labor organization.

§ 5.1   INTRODUCTION

Similarly, a common sense interpretation of the contractual provision in question compels the conclusion that Local 978 cannot be held liable upon the allegations of the third-party complaint. It can hardly be questioned that creation of a proper work environment is a management responsibility and disciplining those who commit acts of sexual harassment is a management prerogative. In the contractual provision itself the union agrees to further creation of a non-discriminatory work environment in two ways: (1) it agrees not to itself discriminate; that is, not to pursue discriminatory actions or policies as a union; and (2) it promises to cooperate with the company in creating a nondiscriminatory work environment and furthering the interest of the company in this regard; that is, not to pursue union policies which interfere with efforts of management to ensure a non-discriminatory work environment. The union does not undertake in its contract with APCO to guarantee that its individual members will not on their own initiative engage in specific acts of sexual harassment. If they do, the company, in the exercise of its management prerogatives, has the right to take corrective action; the union promises not to interfere with such action, it does not undertake the contractual obligation to step in and take corrective action itself if the company fails to do so.

Id. at 1730–31.

Cherry v. Wertheim Schoder & Co., Inc., 868 F. Supp. 830 (D.S.C. 1994). Arbitration of state and federal sexual harassment claims by a former sales assistant for an investment banking firm was required by her application for registration with securities exchanges, despite the fact that she failed to pass the examination. Title VII claims were not exempt from coverage by the Federal Arbitration Act.

Cawthard v. Flagship Airlines, Inc., 863 F. Supp. 1567 (S.D. Fla. 1994). The federal district court did not have subject matter jurisdiction over whether an airline pilot who claimed that his company relied on groundless charges of sexual harassment leveled against him by two female company employees was denied his procedural rights by his employer when such a matter involved a "minor dispute" under the RLA. Claims for breach of oral contract, breach of implied covenant of fair dealing, fraudulent misrepresentation, and slander did not involve an interpretation of the collective bargaining agreement so as to require federal jurisdiction under the broad preemptive power of the RLA after the court dismissed the breach of contract claim based on the collective bargaining agreement. The case was remanded to state court.

67

ADMINISTRATIVE PROCEDURES

Bintner v. Burlington N., Inc., 857 F. Supp. 1484 (D. Wyo. 1994). A former locomotive engineer who alleged that she was required to work in an environment that included propositions for sexual favors, physical attack, verbal catcalls and vulgarity, and written comments of a sexual and perverted nature, and that the work environment demeaned women with sexual cartoons and graffiti on engines and cabooses, pictures and sexual graffiti on the walls of the defendant's facilities, specifically using the plaintiff's name and suggesting that she participated in lewd and lascivious acts was not barred by the RLA from bringing her Title VII claims; no evidence was offered that the collective bargaining agreement required employees to submit individual statutory claims to arbitration.

New Jersey Turnpike Auth. v. New Jersey Turnpike Supervisors Ass'n, 276 N.J. Super. 329, 647 A.2d 1369 (1994). In response to a demand for binding arbitration by a toll supervisors' union regarding a sexual harassment charge against a supervisor and the subsequent disciplinary action taken against him, the Public Employment Relations Commission properly held that the arbitration contemplated by the collective negotiations agreement is not preempted by the state antidiscrimination law, which protects victims of discrimination. The collective negotiations agreement sets up procedures by which the person charged with harassment may challenge his or her disciplinary penalty.

*   An employee who was precluded from bringing a sexual harassment claim because she failed to exhaust her administrative remedies was allowed to introduce evidence of sexual harassment to support the plaintiff's case for a pretextual employment decision. Hansen v. Dean Witter Reynolds Inc., 887 F. Supp. 669 (S.D.N.Y. 1995). The plaintiff asserted that she was presented with a birthday cake in the shape and color of a black man's penis. The cake bore the words, "Happy Birthday, Bitch." The plaintiff did not file a complaint or otherwise report this incident to management; indeed there was testimony by a former coworker that Hansen was so proud to receive the cake that she stored the remaining portion in her freezer and brought it to her parents' home for their July 4th barbecue.

> While food for thought, it is unnecessary to decide whether Hansen considered the cake an insult or a joke. There was evidence that she partook enthusiastically in the event, and there was testimony that she was proud of being referred to as "the bitch" and that the name was in fact a self-professed title as she considered herself "a tough cookie." The fact is that she failed to inform any supervisory personnel, and thus there is

nothing on which to base a determination that Dean Witter tolerated, prohibited, or encouraged such activity. There was, however, a similar situation that was reported to management; Dean Witter's reaction left no doubt as to its stance towards such cakes. In 1982, Ms. Jerome received a cake from coworkers "in the shape of a man's anatomy." . . . Upon being made aware of the nature of the cake, Dean Witter's chairman issued a memorandum stating that such behavior would not be tolerated and that any persons involved in such activity would be terminated. . . . In light of this response, there is hardly support that the birthday cake incident is indicative of a sanctioned hostile work environment for women at Dean Witter.

Id. at 674.

§ 5.2   Employee Actions

Page 192, add to footnote 9:

Chester v. Northwest Iowa Youth Emergency Servs. Ctr., 869 F. Supp. 700 (N.D. Iowa 1994). Title VII numerosity requirements were not met when under a state statute governing joint governmental activities, only the direct employees of the defendant juvenile detention center, rather than the employees of 11 counties that created the center, could be counted. The plaintiff did not name any of the counties, their board of supervisors or the Center's boards of supervisors, as defendants, and the latter had control over hiring and firing decisions.

§ 5.3   EEOC Actions

Page 194, add to footnote 24:

EEOC v. Horizons Hotel Corp., 831 F. Supp. 10 (D.P.R. 1993).

§ 5.6   Equitable Tolling, Waiver, and Estoppel

Page 199, add to footnote 60:

EEOC v. Wilson Metal Casket Co., 64 Fair Empl. Prac. Cas. (BNA) 1402 (6th Cir. 1994). The district court properly granted relief to a complainant in an action brought by the EEOC, despite her failure to file an EEOC charge, when a coworker had filed a virtually identical charge for the same time period and thus fell under the single filing rule.

§ 5.8 Federal Employees and Exhaustion of Administrative Remedies

Page 202, add to footnote 81:

Cf. Pacheco v. Rice, 59 Empl. Prac. Dec. (CCH) ¶ 41,671 (5th Cir. 1992). A Latino Air Force employee who was fired for sexual harassment had 30 days from the time he was told he would be terminated to consult with an EEO officer; the 30-day time limit did not begin three years later when the employee allegedly discovered that an Anglo employee had been investigated under different procedures and not fired.

> To allow plaintiffs to raise employment discrimination claims whenever they begin to suspect that their employers had illicit motives would effectively eviscerate the time limits prescribed for filing such complaints. This was not a case for equitable tolling when as a career EEO officer, the plaintiff was undoubtedly far more familiar with the procedures governing disciplinary procedures than most Air Force employees, and if he had suspected that he was being discriminated against because of his race, he easily could have complained or sought information as to how disciplinary proceedings were supposed to be handled.

§ 5.9 Continuing Violation

Page 203, add to footnote 92:

Martin v. Nannie & the Newborns, Inc., 3 F.3d 1410 (10th Cir. 1993). Although a discharged employee failed to establish a prima facie case of quid pro quo sexual harassment, a genuine issue of material fact existed as to whether there was a hostile environment in an action charging that the owner raped the plaintiff and that he and others propositioned the plaintiff, showed her lingerie and an artificial penis, and repeatedly made embarrassing comments and sexual innuendoes. In order for the doctrine of continuing violation to apply, there must be at least one instance of the discriminatory practice within the filing period, and the earlier acts must be part of a continuing policy or practice that includes the act or acts within the statutory period. It is not sufficient merely that acts outside the required time limit had a continuing effect within the statutory time allowed to bring the action. Here the plaintiff introduced facts sufficient to raise a triable issue on whether the owner and his companies engaged in a continuing course of discrimination such that the district court should consider the incidents that occurred prior to the 300-day time limitation.

> First, all the incidents alleged by the plaintiff involved sexual harassment. Second, the incidents are alleged to have occurred consistently and frequently over the course of her employment. Martin's complaint asserts that she was harassed from the beginning of her employment until she was fired and her deposition describes a fairly continuing pattern of sexual harassment. She claims that her employers allowed an atmosphere of sexual harassment to exist even after they had notice. She also claims that as a result of the harassment, and her rejection of unwelcome sexual advances, she was given unsatisfactory job reviews and was ultimately terminated. Finally, she asserts that the harassment constitutes a "continuous course of conduct." . . . The third factor of permanence is more difficult for Martin. Certainly, some of the events, including the rape, should have been reported at the time they occurred. She allowed this sexual harassment to continue for a long time before she filed a complaint with the EEOC. However, given the analysis under the first two factors, we believe that Martin has shown enough to avoid summary judgment on the statute of limitations issue.

Id. at 1416.

Shipbaugh v. Boys & Girls Clubs of Am., 883 F. Supp. 295 (N.D. Ill. 1995). A female former employee stated claims for retaliation based on sexual harassment and constructive discharge; a liberal reading of the complaint supported a continuing violation theory because the plaintiffs alleged not isolated incidents of retaliation but acts that continued from August of 1992 through April of 1994. Although the court recognized the possibility that the alleged acts were in fact not part of a continuing violation, such a determination was not appropriate on a motion to dismiss when the court found that the complaint supported the theory. The retaliatory acts included a rewritten job description, a transfer to a different department, a loss in status and conditions of employment, significant changes in duties and responsibilities, a less favorable performance evaluation, different treatment from other employees, and harassment and retaliation until she felt compelled to resign.

Ciafrei v. Bentsen, 877 F. Supp. 788 (D.R.I. 1995). A female former employee of the IRS, charging sex discrimination and sexual harassment, alleged a continuing violation when she alleged that she was denied desk audits, involving the review of her work to determine whether she was eligible for a promotion, was subjected to offensive remarks by her supervisors, and was singled out for written sick leave warning, and that those acts stemmed from animosity by the supervisors because of her size and "unfeminine" appearance.

Cf. Koelsch v. Beltone Elec. Corp., 65 Empl. Prac. Dec. (CCH) ¶ 80,706 (N.D. Ill. 1994). A female employee alleged that in late 1988 she reported to the defendant personnel department that during a company meeting in the executive conference room, Lawrence Posen, defendant's president, took off his shoe and underneath the table, ran his foot along the plaintiff's leg. She moved to get away from him, but he continued stroking until she was forced to get up and leave the table. On the following day, she told Posen she was disappointed and that she did not want him to do it again. Thereafter, Posen would, from time to time, comment on the plaintiff's attractiveness. In April or May 1990, the plaintiff reported to Bill Lucas, her supervisor at the time, that during a plant tour with two other female Beltone employees, Posen grabbed the plaintiff's buttocks while the group was in a dark, soundproof room. Posen denied that either the 1988 or the 1990 event occurred. The court concluded that even though the alleged incidents were similar in type, they were insufficiently permanent to trigger the plaintiff's awareness of the need to assert her rights, and the two-year gap between the incidents negated the plaintiff's contention that the incidents were continuous or connected, and thus the plaintiff's sexual harassment claims were time-barred under Title VII. The court analyzed the case in light of the decision in Berry v. Board of Supervisors of L.S.U., 715 F.2d 971 (5th Cir. 1983), which developed three factors that a court should consider to determine whether separate incidents are related enough to constitute a continuing violation: "(1) subject matter—whether the violations constitute the same type of discrimination, (2) frequency, and (3) permanence—whether the nature of the violations should trigger an employee's awareness of the need to assert her rights." *Id.* ¶ 80,709. The court noted that first, all of the incidents, including the discharge and the provision of false information, allegedly stemmed from sexual harassment. Second, although the plaintiff asserted that acts of sexual harassment occurred throughout her employment, her deposition testimony is to the contrary; over a year and a half passed between the last incident of alleged sexual harassment when Posen the invited plaintiff for dinner in June of 1990 and the plaintiff's termination on November 15, 1991. Thus, the court concluded that the plaintiff did not present sufficient evidence to create a genuine issue of fact that the alleged incidents of sexual harassment were frequent and continuous. Finally, the court could not conclude that the two incidents of alleged physical contact—the leg rubbing and the grabbing—were sufficiently permanent so as to trigger the plaintiff's awareness of the need to assert her rights.

Barb v. Miles, Inc., 861 F. Supp. 356 (W.D. Pa. 1994) (continuing violation found).

Price v. Public Serv. Co., 850 F. Supp. 934 (D. Colo. 1994). Material issues of fact existed regarding whether the employer engaged in a continuing course of discrimination, in an action by an employee alleging crude language, suggestive behavior, inappropriate touching, nude pictures, and sexual pranks by coworkers. The Tenth Circuit adopted a three-part inquiry to determine whether the continuing violation exception may be invoked. A court should examine (1) whether the acts alleged involve the same type of violation, (2) whether the acts are recurring or isolated, and (3) whether the acts have the degree of permanence such that the employee is on notice of the duty to assert her or his rights. Martin v. Nannie & the Newborns, Inc., 3 F.3d 1410, 1415 (10th Cir. 1993). In *Price*, although the plaintiff could not remember the specific dates of any incidents, she alleged many acts involving the same type of sexual harassment, and such acts occurred consistently and frequently over the course of her employment. Her claim could therefore survive a motion for summary judgment, but because she allowed the alleged conduct to continue for 14 years before filing a complaint, despite the fact that she had filed a sex discrimination charge 10 years earlier, the court would evaluate these factors in light of the evidence as it developed at trial.

Anthony v. County of Sacramento, Sheriff's Dep't, 845 F. Supp. 1396 (E.D. Cal. 1994) (continuing violation found).

Caprio v. American Airlines, Inc., 848 F. Supp. 1528 (M.D. Fla. 1994). Portions of the plaintiff's affidavit alleging conduct that standing alone would be barred by the statute of limitations would not be stricken when although the majority of the relevant conduct was barred by the statute, some conduct allegedly occurred subsequent to the cutoff date. However, the court rejected the plaintiff's contention that the statute of limitations on her tort claims should be tolled during the pendency of her charge before the EEOC; the fact that a plaintiff filed a claim with the EEOC does not mean that Florida's statute of limitations period should be tolled.

Dirksen v. City of Springfield, 842 F. Supp. 1117 (C.D. Ill. 1994). Particular allegations of sexual harassment were not time-barred when the plaintiff alleged a continuing violation.

Bates v. Humana Inc., 63 Fair Empl. Prac. Cas. (BNA) 327 (W.D. Tex. 1993). The court found a continuing violation despite the defendant's contention that all harassment ended when it transferred the plaintiff's first supervisor more than 300 days before she filed her EEOC charge. The plaintiff pointed to statements made during the 300-day period by several male supervisory employees, including the executive director, and the executive director admitted that sexual remarks were constantly being made in the office.

Page 203, add to footnote 93:

Giuliani v. Stuart Corp., 512 N.W.2d 589 (Minn. Ct. App. 1994). The trial court properly found that a property manager had been sexually harassed in violation of the state human rights act by her supervisor, who was vice president of the defendant real estate management firm. The plaintiff's claim was not barred by the statute of limitations when she alleged a series of events that had an adverse impact on her career. The trial court deemed these events manifestations of the alleged harasser's warning that he did not take rejection well and the retaliatory conduct flowed directly from the original sexual harassment. Some of this conduct fell well within the statute of limitations period and established a continuing violation of the state human rights act.

Page 205, add to footnote 99:

Ficek v. Griffith Lab. Inc., 67 Fair Empl. Prac. Cas. (BNA) 1396 (N.D. Ill. 1995). Thirty-six incidents of sexual harassment amounted to a hostile environment; acts of coworker harassment included comments about the plaintiff's "big booty," a sexual assault during which a coworker tried to remove the plaintiff's panty hose in the parking lot of a bar, comments about her underwear showing through her white uniform, calling her a "lazy bitch," masturbation gestures being made, comments telling her to bend over to show her a "real man," running into her with a forklift, and graffiti in the men's room. The plaintiff sometimes broke into tears when she heard the remarks, and she felt humiliated. The acts constituted a continuing violation when although they occurred both prior to and during the 300-day period before plaintiff's filing of the EEOC charge, they were all similar in that they had the single objective of belittling the plaintiff. The fact that the plaintiff did not hear every remark or see the graffiti firsthand did not make it any less forceful in creating a hostile environment.

Cf. Crighton v. Schuylkill County, 882 F. Supp. 411 (E.D. Pa. 1995). In a § 1983 action by county employees, charging sexual harassment by a supervisor, plaintiffs sufficiently alleged a continuing violation. All alleged incidents involved sexual harassment or the defendants' failure to act, harassing incidents were alleged throughout the period 1989 to 1993, and the harassment did not cause a discrete event such as a lost job or a denied promotion and thus did not trigger a duty for the plaintiffs to assert their rights arising from that deprivation.

See also Coleman v. Tennessee, 846 F. Supp. 582 (M.D. Tenn. 1993). An action by an African-American female former employer against her state employer, alleging sex and race discrimination, was not barred by the statute of limitations. She alleged facts suggesting that the employer engaged in a pattern of discriminatory conduct against her, based on her exposure to racist jokes, advice that she was not getting promoted because she was African-American and a woman, and the administrators' failure to support her after she requested their intervention.

Page 205, add to footnote 100:

Koelsch v. Beltone Elect. Corp., 46 F.3d 705 (7th Cir. 1995). A former employee failed to prove hostile environment sexual harassment even under the continuing violation theory or retaliation. The alleged harasser's conduct, while offensive, was composed of two seemingly isolated incidents, one involving the stroking of the plaintiff's leg during a company meeting, and the other, the grabbing of her buttocks in a sound-proof room during a plant tour, after which he kept his distance from the plaintiff. The plaintiff's amorphous allegations of an atmosphere of sexually suggestive joking carry no weight in the totality of circumstances analysis because the record was completely "barren of so much as a sliver of substantiation." *Id.* at 708. Even viewing the evidence in the light most favorable to the plaintiff, evidence showed that the company required significant downsizing to remain profitable, and the plaintiff's position and one other were the most easily eliminated.

*   August v. Star Enter., Inc., 899 F. Supp. 1540 (E.D. La. 1995). Relatively "mild" harassment may become tortious if continued over a substantial period of time. A genuine issue of material fact existed as to whether the alleged sexual harassment constituted a continuing violation in an action alleging that the plaintiff's supervisor had boasted about how he had made former females in his division cry and that on innumerable occasions he reduced her to tears. He also allegedly frequently referred to her as "worthless, useless" and suggested that she might lose her job, and regularly humiliated August by offensively uttering in the presence of other supervisors and coworkers that she did not know her job. As a result of this and other regularly abusive verbal and highly offensive speech and conduct, the plaintiff was constantly crying and started wearing dark glasses to disguise this from the supervisor. The harassment ultimately led to sleeplessness, overeating, and other mental distresses. During this period, the plaintiff met with the alleged harasser and a human resources person, where she was told to take off the dark glasses and to stop addressing her superior as "sir" because it sounded sarcastic.

*   *Cf.* Burrell v. City Univ. of New York, 894 F. Supp. 750 (S.D.N.Y. 1995). Alleged instances of sexual harassment did not constitute a continuing violation in a Title VII sexual harassment and retaliatory termination action by a university employee against the university and dean, claiming conduct that allegedly began on plaintiff's first day of employment. The dean, Roman, requested Burrell's home telephone number for his private address book; Burrell thought the request odd because Roman had telephoned her at home once before, in order to offer her the job. She informed Roman that her telephone number was unlisted in order to avoid receiving annoying calls, but after Roman explained that he did not usually call employees at home except in emergency situations, Burrell gave Roman her number. He then began making comments to Burrell at work, such as: "I like your style," "you are a class act," and "we communicate so well with each other." Roman asked Burrell whether a person in a picture on her desk was her brother, and she informed him that the photograph was of her fiancé. From then on Roman made it a habit, when walking past Burrell's desk, to knock the picture over and ask Burrell whether she wanted him to pick it up. On St. Valentine's Day, Roman had flowers and chocolates delivered to

Burrell's home, and at a meeting with Roman a few days later Burrell said, "I guess I should say 'thank you' for the flowers?" Roman replied, "You said that as if you did not appreciate them." Burrell explained that the gift made her very uncomfortable because it might cause tension between her and her financé and asked Roman not to send packages to her home in the future, to which Roman responded, "[Y]ou should relax; there is nothing wrong with being a little bit vulnerable; there is no reason to always be on the defensive." About two weeks after this conversation, Roman had a $177 leather writing portfolio delievered to Burrell's home with a note that said "Just to help you get it together. Stan Roman." *Id.* at 754. Roman began calling Burrell at home, frequently to invite her to dinner, and once to apologize for being demanding on Burrell in the office. Roman explained that he could not let it appear to others in the workplace that he liked Burrell but that she was very special to him, and went on to tell her about his three failed marriages and various extramarital relationships. He also told her that he "slept around" a lot, and once implied that he would like her to talk to her on the phone while he masturbated. When she refused one of his many dinner invitations, he reminded her that he could withdraw his support for her at work at any time. After the plaintiff signed a one-year renewal contract, Roman became openly critical of her work and once told her that "the road is filled with carcasses of people who have held this job before you." *Id.* at 755. She was eventually terminated by the university, ostensibly on grounds related to her immigration status.

The plaintiff filed her complaint 359 days after the date of the last act of harassment alleged against Roman and 245 days after her allegedly retaliatory termination. The court found the plaintiff's sexual harassment claim to be time barred. "The incidents alleged by the plaintiff although reprehensible if true, do not amount to a specific "policy or practice" as required under *Cornwell v. Robinson,* 23 F.3d 694, 695, 704 (2d Cir.1994)." *Id.* at 759. The court concluded that while "the minimally required characteristics of a "policy or practice" have not been established, the Second Circuit requires something more than a pattern of related actions by one individual directed against another individual over a period of five months." *Id.*

The plaintiff did present evidence that would support an inference that she was terminated in retaliation either for making her initial complaint to CUNY's Affirmative Action Office or for refusing to accede to Roman's sexual advances.

ADMINISTRATIVE PROCEDURES

Frederick v. Reed Smith Shaw & McClay, 63 Empl. Prac. Dec. (CCH) ¶ 42,864 (E.D. Pa. 1994). There must be some sexually harassing conduct within the limitations period in order for a claim to survive, and not merely that the effect of the conduct is felt within the limitations period. The court rejected the defendant's claim that in order for there to be a continuing violation, the plaintiff is required to show a company-wide policy of discrimination.

> [A] plaintiff in a hostile environment claim should not *always* be required to show company-wide discrimination in order to prove a continuing violation. Conduct that forms the basis of a hostile environment claim takes many different forms. It includes instances where there is company-wide harassment, and also instances where one individual creates a hostile environment by harassing another individual without the company even being aware of it, as is the case in this law suit. As such, because a hostile work environment claim does not necessarily involve company conduct, a plaintiff may prove a continuing violation theory by showing either a series of related acts taken against a single individual or a companywide policy of discrimination. . . .

Id. at 78,789.

Russell v. City of Overland Police Dep't, 838 F. Supp. 1350 (E.D. Mo. 1993). A former employee who alleged sexual harassment and discrimination that started before but continued into the period after enactment of the Civil Rights Act of 1991 stated a continuing violation and thus was entitled to a jury trial on all of her claims. The plaintiff could also seek punitive damages. A claim of conspiracy under 42 U.S.C. § 1985 was dismissed because the plaintiff's complaint lacked material facts demonstrating an agreement reached by the defendants and because allegations of a conspiracy to violate Title VII will not support a claim under § 1985(3).

Stein v. Chessie Computer Serv., 65 Fair Empl. Prac. Cas. (BNA) 1220 (D. Md. 1994). A female employee did not establish sexual harassment when conduct that occurred during the limitations period included only comments by a supervisor regarding how far up plaintiff's stocking butterfly appliques went, her transfer to another department where her former harasser worked, and two instances in which her supervisor brushed his leg or arm against her in a sexually suggestive manner. These incidents were isolated and not severe and pervasive, and thus the plaintiff could not rely on the continuing violation theory to challenge

§ 5.9 CONTINUING VIOLATION

conduct occurring outside the statutory period. "For Stein to rely solely on her past interaction with Schultz as a basis for her claim that her transfer to Tech Services constituted sexual harassment within the limitations period is precisely the attempt to convert the effects of past discrimination into an actionable claim against which the continuing violation theory counsels." *Id.* at 1222.

Sanchez v. Alvarado, 65 Fair Empl. Prac. Cas. (BNA) 1211 (D.P.R. 1992). A sexual harassment action brought under 42 U.S.C. § 1983, which was filed more than one year after the plaintiff gave notice of her resignation, was barred by Puerto Rico's one-year personal injury statute of limitations. The continuing violation theory was not applicable when the plaintiff did not allege any specific violations occurring after she gave notice that she was leaving work because of the stressful environment of sexual harassment and her employer's failure to take action regarding her complaints.

Cook v. Applied Data, 66 Fair Empl. Prac. Cas. (BNA) 395 (D.N.J. 1989). Allegations of sexual harassment by a supervisor, which occurred two years before the plaintiff filed her complaint, were time-barred despite the plaintiff's claim that the hostile and oppressive work environment engendered by the supervisor's sexual harassment survived the cut-off date, an argument akin to the "continuing violation" doctrine. This assertion was "nothing more" than an effects argument, and it is well settled that the present effects of past discrimination do not toll the statute of limitations.

Page 205, add at end of section:

In *Desrosiers v. Great Atlantic & Pacific Tea Co.*, 885 F. Supp. 308 (D. Mass. 1995), the continuing violation doctrine did not save a former employee plaintiff's sexual harassment claims from being time-barred. Under the continuing violation standard, as set forth in *Sabree v. United Brotherhood of Carpenters & Joiners*, 921 F.2d 396, 399 (1st Cir. 1990), causal relationship by itself is not enough; the critical inquiry is whether the plaintiff knew or should have known that she was being discriminated against when the untimely act occurred. If the plaintiff was aware of the discrimination, she cannot avoid the statute of limitations. Here the plaintiff repeatedly complained and reported the sexual harassment to her supervisor, and thus she had a duty to assert her rights as to the violations in a timely manner. The "thematic" relationship between the

alleged harassment and later retaliation and termination was not sufficient to make out a continuing violation on the facts of this case.

§ 5.10   Contents of the Charge

Page 206, add to footnote 106:

Griffith v. State of Colo. Div. of Youth Servs., 17 F.3d 1323 (10th Cir.
1994). A male electrician who alleged that he was sexually harassed by a
male foreman could allege quid pro quo sexual harassment in his complaint, even though he did not specify this type of harassment in his
EEOC charge, when he did state facts relating to repeated acts of alleged
sexual harassment and the complaint contained these same factual assertions and alleged sexual harassment in violation of his Title VII rights.

Prizevoits v. Indiana Bell Tel. Co., 882 F. Supp. 787 (S.D. Ind. 1995).
A plaintiff's EEOC charge, which refers only to her termination from
Bell, was not reasonably related to an allegation in her complaint of sex-
ual harassment by a supervisor.

Evans v. Technologies Applications & Servs. Co., 875 F. Supp. 1115
(D. Md. 1995). The plaintiff's sexual harassment allegations did not reasonably proceed from or relate to her original charge of failure to
promote.

Riley v. Technical & Management Servs. Corp., 872 F. Supp. 1454
(D. Md. 1995) *affd,* 79 F.3d 1141 (4th Cir. 1996). Sexual harassment and
retaliation claims by female employees against their former employer
were beyond the scope of their EEOC charge of sex discrimination and
thus were barred.

Sanborn v. Hunt Real Estate Corp., 65 Fair Empl. Prac. Cas. (BNA)
1305 (W.D.N.Y. 1994). This action was brought by a former employee
charging sex discrimination and retaliatory discharge. Her affidavit, stating that she had confronted a supervisor and warned him that she was
planning to tell the employer's owner about conduct by the supervisor
that she considered to be sexual harassment, created a genuine issue of
fact as to whether she had confronted the supervisor, despite the contention that the plaintiff had alleged in her EEOC charge and complaint
only that she had been a witness to sexual harassment, because her claim
of confrontation was directly related to her claim that she was fired
because of her knowledge of the sexual harassment of a coworker. A
factual issue also existed regarding whether she engaged in a protected

activity when she observed the supervisor sexually harassing the coworker and the supervisor allegedly told her not to say anything about the incident. No deposition had been taken of the plaintiff.

Page 207, add to footnote 108:

Cheek v. Western & S. Life Ins., 31 F.3d 497 (7th Cir. 1994). A female former employee's claim of sexual harassment was barred when, in her EEOC charge, she alleged only that the staff manager had intimidated her and in her EEOC affidavit claimed that he treated her in a hostile, inferior, and unprofessional manner regarding the payment of clients' insurance premiums. There was nothing in the charge or affidavit to support a claim of a sexually hostile environment. The only reference in the EEOC filings to anything that might have been considered sexual harassment was a comment by a supervisor (included in an amendment to the original charge) that if the plaintiff did not make it in this business she had a husband to fall back on; the court doubted that such comments rose to the level of sexual harassment. Such a comment did not clarify or amplify the original charge.

Whitehead v. AM Int'l, 65 Fair Empl. Prac. Cas. (BNA) 1369 (N.D. Ill. 1994). A former employee could not litigate a claim of sexual harassment when, in her EEOC charge, she used the word "harassment" only to characterize conduct including verbal reprimands and alleged unprofessional conduct by a supervisor, rather than sexual advances or other gender discrimination.

Baltzer v. City of Sun Prairie Police Dep't, 725 F. Supp. 1008 (W.D. Wis. 1989) (allegations of discriminatory restrictions on pregnant police officers not reasonably related to administrative charge of sexual harassment and hostile environment).

Page 207, add to footnote 111:

A court may look at the sophistication of the named plaintiff in determining whether the complaint was properly framed. *See* Miller v. United States Fidelity & Guar., 65 Fair Empl. Prac. Cas. (BNA) 593 (D. Md. 1994). A discharged female human resources manager's failure to include sexual harassment in her EEOC charge alleging gender discrimination barred that claim, despite the facts that she had proceeded pro se and claimed that she had told the EEOC interviewer that she had been sexually harassed. By virtue of her experience in human resources, she was not a lay complainant; she admitted familiarity with the nuances of employment discrimination claims and had ongoing contact with the EEOC.

* *Page 207, add to footnote 113:*

McKinnon v. Kwong Wah Restaurant, 83 F.3d 498 (1st Cir. 1996). To avoid waiver, a defendant must assert all affirmative defenses in the answer. *See* Fed. R. Civ. P. 8(a). The defendants in this case, through their default, waived their right to raise the issue that they were not named in the complaint to the commission.

§ 5.17   EEOC Suits

Page 216, add to footnote 188:

Cf. Loveridge v. Fred Meyer, Inc., 125 Wash. 2d 759, 887 P.2d 898 (1995). A consent decree in an EEOC action against an employer did not bar a subsequent state court action by a female former employee. The trial court improperly dismissed the action on the basis that the former employee's claims were barred by res judicata. Although the defendant had earlier insisted that it would not settle the case unless the plaintiff's claims were dismissed, no agreement was obtained from her to that effect, and the defendant obtained an agreement only with the EEOC. Because the plaintiff did not exercise control or participate in the litigation, she was thus not in privity with the EEOC and should not have been bound by the terms of the consent decree. The consent decree was based solely on the injunctive relief sought by the EEOC, expressly stated that the defendant did not admit any Title VII violation, and awarded no monetary compensation or other benefits to the plaintiff.

§ 5.18   Right-to-Sue Letter

Page 218, add to footnote 205:

Hansen v. Dean Witter Reynolds Inc., 887 F. Supp. 669 (S.D.N.Y. 1995). A female former employee failed to exhaust her administrative remedies and was thus precluded from pursuing a hostile work environment sexual harassment claim against her employer when the employee never obtained a right-to-sue letter on this issue, as it was not included in her EEOC complaint. The court, however, heard testimony on the issue as part of plaintiff's case in chief of sex discrimination because the law allows such testimony as evidence of a discriminatory atmosphere on the part of the defendant that could be used to support plaintiff's case for a pretextual employment decision. The court would have been more concerned about prejudice had the case been a jury trial, and might have ruled differently.

CHAPTER 6

TRYING THE SEXUAL HARASSMENT CASE

§ 6.3   Venue and Jurisdiction

Page 226, add to footnote 8:

Cf. Arno v. Club Med Inc., 22 F.3d 1464 (9th Cir. 1994). An employer has no obligation under Title VII to provide a remedy where the complained-of conduct is not covered by the statute. Here the underlying conduct, an alleged rape, did not violate Title VII because it occurred outside the territorial United States before the Civil Rights Act of 1991 took effect; thus the employer, though callous, was not required to investigate or take remedial action in response to the plaintiff's complaints.

§ 6.4   Plaintiffs

Page 227, add to footnote 15:

Stetka v. Hunt Real Estate Corp., 859 F. Supp. 661 (W.D.N.Y. 1994). A former real estate agent was an independent contractor for purposes of Title VII and the state human rights law. Even though the company provided her with a desk and office supplies, expected her to serve floor time answering phones and talking to new prospects, and also required her to attend weekly sales meetings and house tours, she scheduled her own hours, marketed her own listings, was expected to develop her own business leads, and had no taxes deducted from her commissions, which she did not receive until a property was sold. She received a Form 1099 at the end of the year and paid for her own licensing and multiple listing services fees.

Johnson v. Board of County Comm'rs, 859 F. Supp. 438 (D. Colo. 1994). In a sexual harassment action by two female dispatchers and one deputy sheriff against the board of county commissioners and the former sheriff, the "personal staff" exception to Title VII did not apply, because the board failed to show how the plaintiffs had intimate employment relationships with the sheriff. The mere fact that the sheriff had the exclusive power to hire and fire the plaintiffs did not establish the intimate and personal employment relationship necessary between an elected official and her or his personal staff. Moreover, there was no indication that the plaintiffs represented the sheriff in the eyes of the public, and the board failed to establish the plaintiffs' positions within the sheriff's chain of command.

Page 227, add to footnote 16:

Breen v. Hunt Real Estate Corp., 65 Fair Empl. Prac. Cas. (BNA) 1392 (W.D.N.Y. 1994). Despite the fact that the plaintiff was given an office, had her contracts reviewed by the branch office manager, was scheduled for floor time by the agency manager, and was required to attend sales meetings and to spend two to four hours per week in the agency office, a former real estate agent who alleged that she was continually sexually harassed by the agency vice president was an independent contractor and not an employee under Title VII and state human rights law. She was not paid a salary or draw but only a commission for each sale which she closed; her time was generally unstructured; she set up her own meetings, brought in her own business, developed her own leads, and marketed herself as an independent agent.

* *Page 228, add at end of section:*

In *Doe v. Bell Atlantic Bus. Sys. Services, Inc.,* 162 F.R.D. 418 (D. Mass. 1995), a female former employee who brought an action under Title VII and state law charging sexual harassment against her employer and supervisor moved to prosecute the action under a pseudonym. The court denied the motion, noting that courts have allowed plaintiffs to proceed anonymously in cases involving social stigmatization, real danger of physical harm, or where the injury litigated against would occur as a result of the disclosure of plaintiff's identity; economic harm or mere embarrassment are not sufficient to override the strong public interest in disclosure. Parties have been allowed to proceed anonymously because of privacy interests often involve abortion, mental illness, personal safety, homosexuality, transsexuality and out-of-wedlock or abandoned children in welfare cases. Plaintiffs alleging sexual harassment generally have not been allowed to proceed anonymously:

While the plaintiff in this action does not fall into a traditional category of litigants allowed to proceed anonymously, her motion presents a sympathetic argument. First, plaintiff alleges the following factual circumstances:

1) She was sexually assaulted by the defendant Mark Bowse.

2) As a result of that assault, she is now concerned that she may be infected with the HIV virus.

3) Plaintiff and her husband both come from traditional Chinese families and if the fact that plaintiff was sexually assaulted were to become known to the general public she would suffer intense embarrassment and shame within her community.

4) Plaintiff and her husband have not told their families of the attack.

5) As a result of the attack, plaintiff has become "despondent, reclusive and, at times suicidal . . . unable to work . . . a virtual prisoner in her home . . . out of fear that Bowse would try to spy on her." Complaint, ¶ 29.

Second, plaintiff submits, in support of her motion, that the Commonwealth of Massachusetts has a strong public policy in favor of protecting the privacy of rape victims. She cites several state statutes that allow for confidentiality with respect to the identity of rape victims and reports prepared by police officers, doctors, and counselors regarding rape victims. . . .

Id. at 421. The court concluded that in the civil context, "the plaintiff instigates the action, and, except in the most exceptional cases, must be prepared to proceed on the public record. The Court is cognizant of the defendants' concerns, and finds that it would be fundamentally unfair to allow plaintiff to make such serious allegations against them without standing, as they must, in a public forum." *Id.* at 422.

§ 6.5 Defendants

Page 228, add to footnote 19:

Cf. Thomason v. Prudential Ins. Co. of Am., 866 F. Supp. 1329 (D. Kan. 1994). Alleged harasser insurance agent was an independent contractor, rather than an employee of the company.

§ 6.5 DEFENDANTS

Page 228, add to footnote 22:

* A corporate client was not an employer for purposes of Title VII in King v. Dalton, 895 F. Supp. 831 (E.D. Va. 1995). A worker who was employed by a government contractor brought a Title VII sexual harassment action against the Secretary of the Navy and a Navy employee. The plaintiff alleged that the Navy employee in charge of planning and executing the project frequently made sexually explicit and demeaning remarks to her, touched her inappropriately or positioned himself in close proximity to her, commented on her physical appearance, and leered at her. He also suggested that she accompany him on certain business trips, which he indicated were at least partly for pleasure. When she again made it clear that she was uncomfortable working directly with Lovett and would not tolerate his demeaning behavior, she was removed from the project and demoted to a less desirable and less responsible position.

Although control is the most important individual factor in determining whether an employment relationship exists, the totality of circumstances must be considered. And, in this regard, it is important to recognize that all clients maintain some degree of control over the work of a hired independent contractor, although there is clearly a continuum. At one end of the continuum is the traditional employer/employee relationship, where a company hires a salaried employee, such as an engineer or secretary, to work full-time, and the company controls his or her assigned projects, workplace, and schedule. At the polar opposite end of the continuum is the standard client/independent contractor relationship, such as the association between an automobile owner who drops her vehicle off with the auto mechanic in the morning and picks it up when the work is completed in the afternoon. There, while the automobile owner maintains some control over the results to be accomplished, she maintains virtually no control over the details of how the work is performed. The auto mechanic is plainly an independent contractor, and the vehicle owner her client.

Somewhere in the middle of this continuum, but closer to the employer/employee end, may be found the temporary secretary hired by a company for a period of several months. While the company does not pay his wages and is not a permanent employer, it maintains such exclusive control over the temporary secretary's work assignments and so integrates him into its work environment that it could, in certain circumstances, be considered his employer. Also in the middle of this continuum, but tending toward the opposite pole, is the corporation that hires a law firm for representation in litigation. There, the client is involved much more intimately with decisionmaking and performance issues, yet a law firm attorney working with a client is nonetheless an independent contractor and not an employee of the client corporation.

King's relationship with the Navy seems quite similar to this last example. Like Lovett, the client may meet frequently with firm lawyers to discuss litigation strategy and even delegate particular matters to be researched. Similarly, if the litigation is large and complex, a firm associate may find herself spending all of her time on that one client's project. Moreover, if the client were dissatisfied with her work, it may request that another of the firm's attorneys take over the litigation. Such a request, of course, may adversely affect the attorney's career and chances for advancement at the firm. Or, if a client representative were to make inappropriate sexual advances toward the attorney and she complained to firm management, the firm might be reluctant to upset a lucrative client and therefore decide, inappropriately perhaps, to remove her from the project rather than to confront the client concerning the offending client employee. Notwithstanding the client's frequent interaction with the firm associate, its control over the work she receives, and its indirect influence over her success at the firm, the corporation client in that instance would simply not be the attorney's employer for Title VII purposes. There, as here, the totality of the circumstances points persuasively toward the conclusion that the client has not so transcended the bounds of client-contractor relationship as to become her employer.

Id. at 842. With respect to the alleged harasser's personal liability, the court noted that courts that have considered this issue have uniformly held that individual federal employees may not be sued for employment discrimination under Title VII.

Gallardo v. Board of County Comm'rs, 881 F. Supp. 525 (D. Kan. 1995). The city was not liable for alleged sexual harassment by a deputy sheriff who provided the city with law enforcement pursuant to a special agreement, and thus neither an employer-employee nor a principal-agent relationship existed between them for purposes of an action by a dispatcher in the county sheriff's office.

In Johnson v. Board of County Comm'rs, 859 F. Supp. 438 (D. Colo. 1994), a sexual harassment action by two female dispatchers and one deputy sheriff against the board of county commissioners and the former sheriff, the relationship between the employer and the alleged harasser was somewhat attenuated. The board was an employer under Title VII, despite its claim that the sheriff was responsible for hiring and the board had no power to control his conduct, because the board allocated funds to the sheriff's department and thus had control over the plaintiffs' working conditions. The court noted that given the intent of the statute to protect employees, its compass must be liberally construed to achieve that purpose. Nor would a damages award intrude upon the state function of establishing an autonomous sheriff's department in violation of the Tenth Amendment doctrine of state immunity. In *EEOC v. Wyoming*, 460 U.S. 226 (1983), the Supreme Court held that the extension of the Age Discrimination in Employment Act to cover state and local governments was a valid exercise of Congress's power under the commerce clause and was not precluded by the constraints of the Tenth Amendment. The defendant failed to articulate how an award of damages would fall within requirements which must be satisfied to show that congressional commerce-power legislation is invalid.

Page 228, add at end of first paragraph:

But in *Van Osdol v. Vogt*, 65 Fair Empl. Prac. Cas. (BNA) 1558 (Colo. Ct. App. 1994), the court held that the First Amendment barred the adjudication of a female minister's claim that her license to open a new church was revoked by a church after she reported sexual harassment of female church employees by a senior minister. The plaintiff admitted that proof of retaliation required the showing of a causal connection to her opposition to illegal discrimination, forcing the trial court to inquire into the good faith of the position asserted by the church officers in revoking the plaintiff's license. The court also rejected the plaintiff's contention that public policy warranted reinstatement of her Title VII claim because to deny it would chill the eradication of unlawful discrimination against nonministerial employees within religious institutions; the overwhelming majority of case law prevents secular courts from inquiry into a church's motivation in rejecting or terminating a minister. Had the plaintiff been an employee other than a minister, the result might have been different.

Page 228, add to footnote 24:

DeAngelis v. El Paso Mun. Police Officers Ass'n, 51 F.3d 591 (5th Cir. 1995). A female police officer brought a sexual harassment and retaliation action against her union as a result of anonymous comments in the union's newsletter directed toward her and female officers in general. The district court improperly found a hostile environment and retaliation when, although there were four printed derogatory references to the officer at irregular intervals in two and one-half years, 10 out of 30 columns over the course of 2¹/₂ years did make anti-female remarks. The appellate court diminished the impact of these comments, however, noting the lack of sexual advances and the plaintiff's ability to rise within the ranks:

> A claim for a sexually hostile working environment is not a trivial matter. Its purpose is to level the playing field for women who work by preventing others from impairing their ability to compete on an equal basis with men. One must always bear this ultimate goal in mind. A hostile environment claim embodies a series of criteria that express extremely insensitive conduct against women, conduct so egregious as to alter the conditions of employment and destroy their equal opportunity in the workplace. Any lesser standard of liability, couched in terms of conduct that sporadically wounds or offends but does not hinder a female employee's performance, would not serve the goal of equality. In fact, a less onerous standard of liability would attempt to insulate women from everyday insults as if they remained models of Victorian reticence. A lesser standard of liability would mandate not equality but preference for women: it would create incentives for employers to bend over backwards in women's favor for fear of lawsuits. Now that most American women are working outside the home, in a broad range of occupations and with ever-increasing responsibility, it seems perverse to claim that they need the protection of a preferential standards. The careful, heightened phrasing of a hostile environment claim, enforceable where working conditions have palpably deteriorated because of sexually hostile conduct, aims to enforce equality, not preference.

Id. at 593. This opinion appears to miss the point of a hostile environment. The chronic nature of the misogynistic comments, even at the ratio of one to three issues of the newsletter is what rendered it insidious. A woman is not necessarily offended by conduct she has confronted over the course of a lifetime. Repeated insults in a work environment become the workers' reality.

*   E.E.O.C. v. Regency Architectural Metals Corp., 896 F. Supp. 260 (D. Conn. 1995) (see **§ 6.44**).

Yerdon v. Teamsters Local 1149, 886 F. Supp. 226 (N.D.N.Y. 1995). A union did not discriminate or retaliate against a secretary whom it discharged and from whom it withdrew union membership in violation of Title VII, the state human rights law, or the Labor Management Reporting and Disclosure Act. In order to find the union liable in its capacity as a labor organization under Title VII, a plaintiff must allege that she or he was discriminated against in her or his capacity as a union member rather than as an employee. Here, despite the court's admonition, the plaintiff did not add any specific allegations that dealt with her capacity as a union member. The allegations only referred to the plaintiff's employment relationship. With respect to the Title VII retaliation claim, while the plaintiff did allege that she was removed from a political action committee, this action took place a year prior to her protected activity, and thus the removal could not have been in retaliation for the charges.

Purnell v. Dieso, 67 Fair Empl. Prac. Cas. (BNA) 1422 (S.D.N.Y. 1995). A female African-American former local union business agent stated a claim against the union under Title VII and § 1981, despite the fact that the alleged harasser was an employee of the international union who was acting as the local's administrator, when she also claimed that others harassed her, that union management created a hostile environment, and that four officers intentionally sexually and racially harassed her, causing her emotional distress. Thus, the plaintiff made clear that parties under the control of the Local engaged in racial and sex discrimination, and under Title VII and § 1981 the Local could be liable for the acts of employees or officers under its control.

Page 228, add to footnote 25:

Prudential Insurance Co. of Am. v. Lai, 42 F.3d 1299 (9th Cir. 1994). In an action by an employer to compel arbitration of employees' sexual harassment and discrimination claims, the district court improperly granted the employer's motion, when in signing a securities exchange registration form, the employees did not knowingly forgo their statutory remedies, and thus the arbitration agreement was not binding. When applying for positions as sales representatives, the plaintiffs were required to sign U-4 forms containing agreements to arbitrate any dispute, claim, or controversy that is required to be arbitrated under the rules, constitutions, or bylaws of the organizations with which they register. The issue before the court of appeals was not whether employees may ever agree to arbitrate statutory employment claims, as they can, but whether these particular employees entered into such a binding arbitration agreement, thereby waiving statutory court remedies otherwise available.

[The] Congressional concern that Title VII disputes be arbitrated only "where appropriate," and only when such a procedure was knowingly accepted, reflects our public policy of protecting victims of sexual discrimination and harassment through the provisions of Title VII and analogous state statutes. . . . This is a policy that is at least as strong as our public policy in favor of arbitration. Although the Supreme Court has pointed out that plaintiffs who arbitrate their statutory claims do not "forego the substantive rights afforded by the statute," . . . the remedies and procedural protections available in the arbitral forum can differ significantly from those contemplated by the legislature. In the sexual harassment context, these procedural protections may be particularly significant. Thus, we conclude that a Title VII plaintiff may only be forced to forego her statutory remedies and arbitrate her claims if she knowingly agreed to submit such disputes to arbitration. . . .

In this case, even assuming that appellants were aware of the nature of the U-4 form, they could not have understood that in signing it, they were agreeing to arbitrate sexual discrimination suits. The U-4 form did not purport to describe the types of disputes that were to be subject to arbitration. Moreover, even if appellants had signed a contract containing the NASD arbitration clause, it would not put them on notice that they were bound to arbitrate Title VII claims. That provision did not even refer to employment disputes. . . . Our decision does not rest exclusively upon the precise language of the clause in the U-4 manual, for it is clear and undisputed on this record that the employment contract with Prudential that plaintiffs executed did not describe any disputes the parties agreed to arbitrate.

Id. at 1305 (footnote omitted).

Gary v. Washington Metro. Area Transit Auth., 866 F. Supp. 78 (D.D.C. 1995). In a Title VII action by an employee of the Washington Metropolitan Area Transit Authority, alleging that the transit authority retaliated against her and constructively discharged her because of her sexual harassment complaints, the court held that Title VII actions can be subject to compulsory arbitration, but the plaintiff's claims were not subject to compulsory arbitration under the transit authority compact. In Gilmer v. Interstate/Johnson Lane Corp., 500 U.S. 20 (1991), the Supreme Court held that in certain circumstances, statutory claims could be subject to binding, compulsory arbitration. The Court placed the burden on the plaintiff to show that Congress, in enacting the statute under which the plaintiff brought his claims, intended to preclude arbitration of claims under the ADEA. Lower courts have extended this holding to

Title VII claims. The question here was whether under the circumstances of the case, the plaintiff's Title VII claims could be subject to compulsory arbitration under the state transit authority compact. Unlike the line of cases under Alexander v. Gardner-Denver Co., 415 U.S. 36 (1975), which held that the compulsory arbitration clause of a collective bargaining agreement would not preclude a suit to enforce the Fair Labor Standards Act or a § 1983 claim, this claim does not involve a compulsory arbitration clause in a collective bargaining agreement. Nor did it involve a compulsory arbitration clause in an agreement signed by an employee as in *Gilmore.* The compact contained an arbitration clause mandated by Congress. In consenting to the compact, Congress did not intend to preclude one class of employees—those who worked for the transit authority—from filing Title VII claims in federal court. The compact provided that only those labor disputes where collective bargaining does not result in agreement are to be submitted to arbitration, while the relevant Title VII claim had not been submitted to arbitration.

Foster v. Richardson, 843 F. Supp. 625 (D. Hawaii 1994). A terminated employee's state law claims for sexual harassment and wrongful discharge did not depend on any right or duty stemming from the collective bargaining agreement. The right to be free of discrimination is a nonnegotiable right that is fully independent of a collective bargaining agreement between the union and the employer. Nor was the plaintiff's retaliatory discharge claim based on Hawaii law preempted by § 301 of the LRA, which governs actions for violation of contract between the employer and union.

Stair v. Lehigh Valley Carpenters Local 600, 855 F. Supp. 90 (E.D. Pa. 1994). After trial in an action by a female employee against the union for the distribution of offensive calendars, the court permanently enjoined the union from creating a hostile work environment and ordered it to adopt a statement of policy and procedures for the control of sexual harassment. Upon motion to suspend this order, the court amended the statement of policy and procedures so as to afford an offending party due process rights in union disciplinary proceedings, to require only that active union members attend sexual harassment seminars, and to give the union limited discretion to exempt attendance in cases of undue hardship. The requirement that the union host annual seminars on sexual harassment for all union members did not constitute discipline of union members within the meaning of the Labor-Management Reporting and Disclosure Act provision requiring that union members receive certain process before being disciplined. The court rejected the union's argument that the policies and procedures order was improper because there was no precedent for a finding of liability against a local union for creating a hostile work environment by its distribution of calendars when the complainant was an employee of a third-party employer and the employer's supervisory personnel displayed the calendars. "The court is bound by precedent, not the lack of precedent. This is particularly the case in evolving fields of law including the law governing sexual discrimination in the workplace." *Id.* at 91.

Page 228, add to footnote 26:

Cf. Cole v. Appalachian Power Co., 67 Fair Empl. Prac. Cas. (BNA) 1729 (S.D. W. Va. 1995). An employer who was being sued for sexual harassment by a female employee who alleged that her supervisors and coworkers repeatedly subjected her to extremely vulgar and offensive jokes, comments, gestures and innuendos, including the display of sexually suggestive graffiti and other material, and to unwelcome sexual advances including touching could not file a third-party complaint against the union, charging that the union violated the quoted provision of the collective bargaining agreement by permitting the alleged harassment to continue:

> All the third-party complaint of APCO alleges, viewed in the light most favorable to APCO, is that Local 978 was aware of the acts of sexual harassment charged in Cole's complaint and failed to take preventive or remedial measures or to use its influence and efforts to prevent discrimination on the basis of sex. There is no allegation that the union directed, induced, authorized or ratified any acts of sexual harassment or that any of the alleged harassers acted under express or apparent authority as a union agent. Additionally, cases imposing liability on unions for acts of their members involve affirmative or tacit encouragement or approval of conduct designed to produce a benefit for the union. Typical are the cases involving work stoppages in violation of contractual no-strike clauses. . . . No case has been found imposing such liability for the union's failure to curtail activity, such as that charged in this case, having no objective which would benefit the labor organization.
>
> Similarly, a common sense interpretation of the contractual provision in question compels the conclusion that Local 978 cannot be held liable upon the allegations of the third-party complaint. It can hardly be ques-

tioned that creation of a proper work environment is a management responsibility and disciplining those who commit acts of sexual harassment is a management prerogative. In the contractual provision itself the union agrees to further creation of a non-discriminatory work environment in two ways: (1) it agrees not to itself discriminate; that is, not to pursue discriminatory actions or policies as a union; and (2) it promises to cooperate with the company in creating a nondiscriminatory work environment and furthering the interest of the company in this regard; that is, not to pursue union policies which interfere with efforts of management to ensure a non-discriminatory work environment. The union does not undertake in its contract with APCO to guarantee that its individual members will not on their own initiative engage in specific acts of sexual harassment. If they do, the company, in the exercise of its management prerogatives, has the right to take corrective action; the union promises not to interfere with such action, it does not undertake the contractual obligation to step in and take corrective action itself if the company fails to do so.

Id. at 1730–31.

Durko v. OI-NEG TV Prods., Inc., 870 F. Supp. 1268 (M.D. Pa. 1994). In an action by a female union member against her employer and union under Title VII and the state human relations act, material issues of fact existed as to whether she had been subjected to a hostile work environment and whether she had requested action by the union in the matter. The court found untenable the union's contention that the employer bears the responsibility for taking appropriate action in response to sexual harassment complaints.

Page 228, add to footnote 29:

The federal courts are divided on the issue of personal liability under Title VII, especially involving supervisors. Some courts have held supervisors individually liable as agents of the employer. *See, e.g.*, Paroline v. Unisys Corp., 879 F.2d 100 (4th Cir. 1989), *vacated in part*, 900 F.2d 27 (4th Cir. 1990); Jones v. Continental Corp., 789 F.2d 1225 (6th Cir. 1986); Herring v. F.N. Thompson, Inc., 866 F. Supp. 264 (W.D.N.C. 1994) (employees who fit the statutory definition of employer, such as those with supervisory authority over a fellow employee, may be held personally liable for violations of Title VII).

Prescott v. Independent Life & Accident Ins. Co., 878 F. Supp. 1545 (M.D. Ala. 1995). Under Busby v. City of Orlando, 931 F.2d 764 (11th Cir. 1991), a Title VII suit may not be brought against a person in her or his individual capacity, but if the alleged harasser is an agent of the employer, a suit may be brought against the harasser in her or his official capacity. Here, in an action by a male former employee who alleged that his male supervisor sexually harassed him, the supervisor, as a district manager, was an employer/agent under Title VII, but as the employer was named as a defendant, to proceed against the supervisor in his official capacity would be redundant.

Douglas v. Coca-Cola Bottling Co., 855 F. Supp. 518 (D.N.H. 1994). A discharged employee who alleged that her supervisor told her he was sexually attracted to her and that he wished to have an affair with her, and that as a result of her failure to comply, he criticized her work, berated her, and soon fired her, could bring suit against her supervisor individually when he had the authority to hire, fire, and affect the terms of her employment.

Dreisbach v. Cummins Diesel Engines, Inc., 848 F. Supp. 593 (E.D. Pa. 1994). A supervisor could be held liable under Title VII as an agent of the employer. Janopoulos v. Walner & Assocs., 835 F. Supp. 459 (N.D. Ill. 1993); Lamirande v. Resolution Trust Corp., 834 F. Supp. 526 (D.N.H. 1993); Raiser v. O'Shaughnessy, 830 F. Supp. 1134 (N.D. Ill. 1993); Vakharia v. Swedish Covenant Hosp., 824 F. Supp. 769 (N.D. Ill. 1993); Wilson v. Gillis Advertising Co., 65 Fair Empl. Prac. Cas. (BNA) 1715 (N.D. Ala. 1993); Bridges v. Eastman Kodak Co., 800 F. Supp. 1172 (S.D.N.Y. 1992); Sandoval v. Pagano, 763 F. Supp. 1087 (D. Colo. 1991).

Cf. Straka v. Francis, 867 F. Supp. 767 (N.D. Ill. 1994). The court declined to hold that employees are per se immune from all personal liability resulting from their individual discriminatory conduct or omissions under Title VII or ADEA claims. Here the defendant supervisors had sufficient "appearance of authority" necessary to impute liability to the employer entity, and thus the individual defendants were not necessary parties to the Title VII or ADEA actions because the full measure of available relief was generally available against the remaining corporate defendant.

Other courts have held that supervisors are not agents of corporate employers and so cannot be personally liable under Title VII. *See, e.g.,* Grant v. Lone Star Co., 21 F.3d 649 (5th Cir. 1994). The district court improperly held a private sector employee's superior individually liable for sexual harassment when he was not her employer for purposes of Title VII. The district court found that the plaintiff was subjected to frequent sexual harassment, including sexually explicit jokes and cartoons, comments about her body, clothing, and personal appearance, lewd comments, and suggestive noises, all of which has the effect of making her the center of male attention because of her sex. Sexually explicit language, jokes, and remarks were directed at other female employees at her office. Pictures of nude women, including an employee, were posted on the office walls and were passed around among employees, including supervisors. With the approval of the supervisor, visitors were permitted to make sexually explicit jokes at sales meetings. The plaintiff was subjected to crude, hostile, and intimidating remarks that were belittling to women in general, and to her in particular. The district court also found that the supervisor participated in these activities and that the behavior of the supervisor and other defendants had the effect of creating a hostile work environment that affected a term or condition of the plaintiff's employment, in violation of Title VII. The district court held that the supervisor was liable for sexual harassment not as an employer, but personally, because he participated directly and engaged in acts in addition to condoning and encouraging the acts of other workers that contributed to a hostile environment. The court ordered him to pay back pay and attorneys' fees and expenses. The court of appeals reversed, finding no reason to limit the rationale of cases involving public employees to that realm of disputes. The plaintiff presented no persuasive argument why Congress would not have intended to protect private employees, as well, from individual Title VII liability.

Sauers v. Salt Lake County, 1 F.3d 1122 (10th Cir. 1993); Miller v. Maxwell's Int'l, 991 F.2d 583 (9th Cir. 1993); Busby v. City of Orlando, 931 F.2d 764 (11th Cir. 1991) (per curiam); Harvey v. Blacke, 913 F.2d * 226 (5th Cir. 1990); Winston v. Hardee's Food Systems, Inc., 903 F. Supp. 1151 (W.D. Ky. 1995) (a store manager could not be held individually liable in a sexual harassment action alleging sexual jokes, remarks and gestures, unwanted touching and groping of plaintiff's breasts and other parts of her body, and physical intimidation. "The 1991 amendments reveal no intent by Congress to expand liability to include agents in their individual capacity." *Id.* at 1155).

See also Ascolese v. Southeastern Pa. Transp. Auth., 902 F. Supp. 533 (E.D. Pa. 1995) (an employee of the public transportation authority could not maintain a Title VII action against "employee-agents" of employer, i.e. those employees operating at a significant policy-making level, who allegedly participated in their individual capacities in employer's decision to take adverse action against employee. In the provision of Civil Rights Act of 1991 regarding the sliding scale of maximum awards, Congress failed to mention liability of parties that did not have employees, and this failure indicated that Congress did not contemplate that employee-agents would not be liable for such damages) Thanning v. Gulotta, 898 F. Supp. 134 (E.D.N.Y. 1995) (a former medical examiner alleging that her supervisor touched and fondled her and made inquiries into her sexual and social life, stated a claim for intentional infliction of emotional distress against her supervisor. When the plaintiff did not respond, he insulted her. These insults, sometimes within earshot of her coworkers, went "beyond all possible bounds of decency" and were "utterly intolerable in a civilized community." Individual liabililty under Title VII was not appropriate. "The purpose of the agent provision is to provide a mechanism for imposing respondeat superior liability on employers for the acts of their employees. The provision allows a plaintiff to bring a suit against her employer and the accused supervisor, in his *official* capacity." *Id.* at 139); Parsons v. Nationwide Mut. Ins. Co., 889 F. Supp. 465 (M.D. Fla. 1995) (female former employees failed to state a claim for sexual harassment and retaliation against their supervisor when he was not functioning as their employer); Redman v. Lima City Sch. Dist. Bd. of Educ., 889 F. Supp. 288 (N.D. Ohio 1995) (no individual liability under Title VII); Lynam v. Foot First Podiatry Ctrs., P.C., 886 F. Supp. 1443 (N.D. Ill. 1995) (supervisors could not be held liable in their individual capacity under Title VII); Nelson-Cole v. Borg-Warner Sec. Corp., 881 F. Supp. 71 (D.D.C. 1995) (supervisor was not an employer for purposes of Title VII when the plaintiff did not show how her supervisor exercised significant control over her; the only authority the supervisor had over the plaintiff was the assignment of duties); Lane v. David P. Jacobson & Co., 880 F. Supp. 1091 (E.D. Va. 1995) (the Fourth Circuit does not support individual liability for agents of employers under Title VII); Bremiller v. Cleveland Psychiatric Inst., 879 F. Supp. 762 (N.D. Ohio 1995) (there is no individual liability under Title VII); Hudson v. Soft Sheen Prods., Inc., 873 F. Supp. 132 (N.D. Ill. 1995) (the Civil Rights Act of 1991 did not expand Title VII liability to include individuals in their individual capacity: "It is unclear whether individual liability is necessary to eradicate discrimination. Those who claim that it is necessary must realize that individuals already face deterrents. For example, they risk the loss of employment status, defense fees, and social approval. On the other hand, those who claim that individual liability is unnecessary must realize that, despite the deterrents, individuals still discriminate. Is Title VII too young or too weak? That sounds like a question for the legislature, not the courts, to answer." *Id.* at 136); Ballou v. University of Kan. Medical Ctr., 871 F. Supp. 1384 (D. Kan. 1994) (individuals not liable for discrimination under Title VII or state antidiscrimination act); Thomson v. Olson, 866 F. Supp. 1267 (D.N.D. 1994), *aff'd without op.*, 56 F.3d 69 (8th Cir. 1995) (a Title VII claim may not be brought against a supervisory employee in her or his individual capacity); Engle v. Barton County Memorial Hosp., 864 F. Supp. 118 (W.D. Mo. 1994). A hospital administrator could not be held individually liable for alleged sexual harassment in an action by employees against a hospital and the administrator; the new civil rights act did not change the fundamental definition of employer. The court noted that violations of Title VII will not go unchecked in the absence of individual liability as employers themselves are liable. Dickinson v. McCarty, 65 Fair Empl. Prac. Cas. (BNA) 1508 (S.D. Fla. 1994); Williams v. Rothman Furniture Stores, 65 Fair Empl. Prac. Cas. (BNA) 1507 (E.D. Mo. 1994); Jaskowski v. Rodman & Renshaw, 813 F. Supp. 1359 (N.D. Ill. 1993); Loury v. Clark, 843 F. Supp. 228 (E.D. Ky. 1994); Johnson v. Northern Ind. Pub. Serv. Comm'n, 844 F. Supp. 466 (N.D. Ind. 1994); Dirksen v. City of Springfield, 842 F. Supp. 1117 (C.D. Ill. 1994); Wilson v. Wayne County, 856 F. Supp. 1254 (M.D. Tenn. 1994); Roos v. Smith, 837 F. Supp. 803 (S.D. Miss. 1993); Henry v. E.G.&G. Mo. Metals Shaping Co., 837 F. Supp. 312 (E.D. Mo. 1993); Stafford v. Missouri, 835 F. Supp. 1136 (W.D. Mo. 1993); Pelech v. Klaff-Joss Ltd. Partnership, 828 F. Supp. 525 (N.D. Ill. 1993); Pommier v. Edelstein, 816 F. Supp. 476 (N.D. Ill. 1993); Jenkins v. City of Grenada, 813 F. Supp. 443 (N.D. Miss. 1993); Weiss v. Coca-Cola Bottling Co., 772 F. Supp. 407 (N.D. Ill. 1991); Robinson v. Jacksonville Shipyards, 760 F. Supp. 1486 (M.D. Fla. 1991); Davis v. State Dep't of Health, 744 F. Supp. 756 (S.D. Miss. 1990); Bradley v. Consolidated Edison Co., 657 F. Supp. 197 (S.D.N.Y. 1987).

See Accordino v. Langman Constr., 65 Fair Empl. Prac. Cas. (BNA) 1379 (S.D. Iowa 1994) for a holding that supervisors may not personally be held liable under Title VII:

> Before the Civil Rights Act of 1991, many courts holding against personal liability of supervisors noted that the remedies under Title VII—backpay and reinstatement—were of a nature that was appropriate only to employers, not supervisors or co-workers. . . . The 1991 amendments, however, added compensatory and punitive damages in 42 U.S.C.

TRYING THE CASE

§ 1881a, leading some district courts to conclude that Congress had created personal liability for supervisory personnel. *E.g., Vakharia v. Swedish Covenant Hosp.*, 824 F. Supp. 769, 784–86 . . . (N.D. Ill. 1993); *Bridges v. Eastman Kodak Co.*, 800 F. Supp. 1172, 1179–80 . . . (S.D.N.Y. 1992). The significant changes in 1991 render most pre-1991 cases inapposite on this question.

* * *

Despite the 1991 changes in remedies, the overall structure of the workplace discrimination laws remains focused on employing entities. Section 2000e still exempts employers with fewer than fifteen employees; new section 1981a includes damage limits scaled to the size of the employer's workforce. The term "employer" must be interpreted in the context of this structure. It is implausible that this structure, which purposefully excludes or limits the liability exposure of small businesses, would simultaneously allow recovery against individuals who are employed by a covered employer, such as supervisors.

District courts that have found supervisors personally liable have stressed the need to interpret broadly the definition of employer to best effect the purposes of Title VII. *See Lamirande v. Resolution Trust Corp.*, 834 F. Supp. 526, 527–28 . . . (N.D. Ill. 1993). Plaintiff argues that, as a matter of policy, an individual who engages in acts like those alleged in this case should properly be held responsible, that failing to do so diminishes the deterrence of sexism and racism at work. . . . This broad goal is not, however, fully implemented in the law as it stands today. Broadening the sweep of Title VII is a task for Congress, not the courts. . . . I agree with and follow the weight of authority finding no personal liability for individual supervisors in the current language of Title VII.

Id. at 1380–81 (footnote omitted).

In Ball v. Renner, 54 F.3d 664 (10th Cir. 1995), the court noted that some courts of appeal have sent somewhat mixed or evolving signals:

[I]n the Fifth Circuit, contrast *Hamilton v. Rodgers*, 791 F.2d 439, 442–43 (5th Cir.1986) (holding supervisors in charge of staffing and assignments liable) with the later decisions in *Harvey v. Blake*, 913 F.2d 226, 227–28 (5th Cir.1990) (holding that a municipal supervisor could be sued in official capacity only) and *Grant v. Lone Star Co.*, 21 F.3d 649, 651–52 (5th Cir.1994) (extending that principle to the branch manager of a private employer); and in the Eleventh Circuit, contrast *Cross v. Alabama*, No. 92-7005, 1994 WL 424303, . . . (11th Cir. Aug. 30), petition for rehearing en banc pending (imposing individual liability) with *Busby v. City of*

Orlando, 931 F.2d 764, 772 (11th Cir. 1991) (per curiam) (holding a superior officer not individually liable); and see also *Quillen v. American Tobacco Co.,* 874 F.Supp. 1285, 1296 (M.D.Ala.1995) (suggesting that *Cross* "made a sharp departure from past precedent").

Id. at 666–67. In this action by a former police dispatcher against the city and a coworker police officer under Title VII and for intentional infliction of emotional distress, alleging that over a two-month period the coworker followed her home many times, continually tried to put his arm around her, once grabbed her and tried to dance, and finally came into a dark closet with her and shut the door twice before she escaped, the coworker was not liable as an employer under Title VII when he had no supervisory authority over the plaintiff. The court noted that all courts that "give a downstream interpretation to the 'agent' phrase distinguish between coworkers and supervisors' managers in order to limit liability to those who wield employer-like authority." *Id.* at 667.

*   *Cf.* Parsons v. Nationwide Mut. Ins. Co., 889 F. Supp. 465 (M.D. Fla. 1995). Former employees of an insurance company brought an action against their supervisor, alleging sexual harassment and retaliation in violation of Title VII and state law claims of intentional infliction of emotional distress and defamation. The supervisor alleged orally published "rude and offensive speculations" about the plaintiffs sexual practices, gave detailed accounts of his own sexual exploits, made unwelcome sexually suggestive comments to the plaintiffs and generally created a sexually graphic and offensive work environment. Each of the plaintiffs was discharged after the occurrence of the alleged events. The court found that the supervisor was not functioning as an employer of the plaintiffs when he allegedly harassed and retaliated against them. It had only been plead that the supervisor maintained some form of supervisory control over the plaintiffs, a fact which in and of itself did not lead to the conclusion that Walker was an "employer" under the guidelines of Title VII. The court made no finding as to whether the supervisor was functioning as an "agent" of Nationwide during his alleged misconduct.

Cf. Humpreys v. Medical Towers, Ltd., 893 F. Supp. 672 (S.D. Tex. 1995). A former building manager brought suit alleging claims for intentional infliction of emotional distress, violations of Title VII and violations of the Texas Commission on Human Rights Act (TCHRA), including sexual harassment, sex discrimination, and retaliation. The court found that a fact issue existed as to whether the defendants failed to take prompt remedial action after receiving actual notice of her complaint of sexual harassment, as required to establish employer liability. The plaintiff claimed that the company president, Lawson, was liable because he was acting within the course and scope of his employment as president and as Humphreys's supervisor. Individual employees, however, even those functioning in a management capacity, cannot be held personally liable under Title VII. The fact that the president controlled the operations of MTL, Humphreys's employer, and was the sole shareholder and president of Diva, the managing and general partner of MTL, was insufficient, standing alone, to impose individual liability upon him under Title VII. With respect to liability as a limited partner, however, summary judgment was inappropriate because fact issues exist as to whether Lawson conducted himself as a general partner of MTL.

An argument can be made that the 1991 amendment to Title VII strengthens the notion that individuals may be sued in their individual capacity because it allows for punitive damages. *See* Jendusa v. Cancer Treatment Ctrs. of Am., Inc., 868 F. Supp. 1006 (N.D. Ill. 1994).

Several courts noted that Congress exempted small businesses from coverage by Title VII because it perceived that such businesses would be unable to cope with the centralized regulations created by bureaucracies such as the EEOC and extended this reasoning to the exclusion of supervisors from liability under Title VII. *Barb v. Miles, Inc.*, 861 F. Supp. 356 (W.D. Pa. 1994) (a supervisor could not be held individually liable under Title VII).

Page 229, add to footnote 30:

Cook v. Applied Data, 66 Fair Empl. Prac. Cas. (BNA) 395 (D.N.J. 1989). The court could not accept as a blanket rule that a high-level supervisor is automatically relieved of Title VII liability merely because he or she serves management functions in a different department from that in which the plaintiff works:

> Instead, the facts and circumstances surrounding the alleged Title VII violation must be fleshed out in each case to determine whether the supervisor was in a position to exert influence over personnel decisions with regard to plaintiff. This may be demonstrated by showing that the supervisor in question, while not directly overseeing plaintiff's work, had the power to evaluate job performance, recommend personnel actions or otherwise influence decisions concerning plaintiff's employment. If the supervisor does possess such authority, then that supervisor controls some

aspect of [plaintiff's] compensation, terms, condition, or privileges of employment" and, thus, qualifies as a proper Title VII defendants. *See Spirit [v. Teachers Insurance & Annuity Ass'n*, 475 F. Supp. 1298, 1308 (S.D.N.Y. 1979), *aff'd in relevant part*, 691 F.2d 1054 (2d Cir. 1982)].

Id. at 403. Here, Title VII claims against one supervisor were dismissed because there was no evidence that he was responsible for evaluating the plaintiff's work performance or had the authority to grant or deny promotions or increased compensation on her behalf.

Cf. Stefanski v. R.A. Zahetner & Assocs., 855 F. Supp. 1030 (E.D. Wis. 1994)(individual defendants may be sued under Title VII only in their official capacities as agents of employer).

Page 230, add to footnote 38:

Dreisbach v. Cummins Diesel Engines, Inc., 848 F. Supp. 593 (E.D. Pa. 1994). The district court did not have subject matter jurisdiction over executives and a related corporation in a sexual harassment suit when such parties were not named in the administrative charge, and the plaintiff failed to prove any of the factors that would have allowed her to proceed against those parties without having named them.

Cook v. Applied Data, 66 Fair Empl. Prac. Cas. (BNA) 395 (D.N.J. 1989). The plaintiff was not barred from proceeding with a civil suit against individual defendants because she did not specifically identify them in the initial charge to the EEOC. For the purpose of giving notice to the EEOC, it was irrelevant that the plaintiff did not provide the details of the alleged discriminatory conduct or the persons responsible until she submitted her factual affidavit.

Page 230, add to footnote 39:

Henry v. E.G.&G. Mo. Metals Shaping Co., 65 Fair Empl. Prac. Cas. (BNA) 600 (E.D. Mo. 1993). A former employee who failed to name her supervisor in his individual capacity in her EEOC charge was not barred from suing him when there was a clear identity of interest between him and the employer. The charges clearly named the supervisor as the source of the harassment and claimed that she was later terminated because she complained of his harassment. The defendant supervisor provided no evidence that he was unaware of her EEOC charges or that she had specifically named him as the person harassing her in her charges. Nor did he provide any evidence that he was not given the opportunity to participate in any conciliation proceedings.

Page 230, add to footnote 40:

Bridges v. Eastman Kodak, 822 F. Supp. 1020 (S.D.N.Y. 1993). Female plaintiffs in a sexual harassment action could sue their supervisor, despite the fact that they did not name him in their EEOC charge, when he was on notice that the charges described him as the harasser, an agency relationship existed between him and his corporate employer, and he was not harmed by the EEOC's failure to contact him. The supervisor admitted in his brief that the EEOC investigation of the plaintiffs' allegations prior to its issuance of a right-to-sue letter was perfunctory.

Page 230, add to footnote 41:

Bridges v. Eastman Kodak, 822 F. Supp. 1020 (S.D.N.Y. 1993).

Ball v. City of Cheyenne, 64 Fair Empl. Prac. Cas. (BNA) 286 (D. Wyo. 1993). The failure to name the alleged harasser in the formal EEOC charge deprived him of notice that he, as an individual, was a target of the EEOC investigation and further deprived him of the opportunity to participate in conciliation efforts:

> Clearly, plaintiff knew the identity of "the harasser" when she completed and signed the formal discrimination charge. Just as clearly, Renner's personal liability for the charges asserted against him in this lawsuit are sufficiently different from those asserted against the City of Cheyenne that he should have had the opportunity to participate in conciliation efforts before finding himself a named defendant in this lawsuit.The Court finds that Renner was prejudiced by the lost opportunity to participate in the conciliation efforts and further finds that there is no indication that Renner, as the unnamed party, ever represented to the plaintiff that for the purposes of pursuing these complaints, she should proceed solely against the Police Department.

Id. at 293.

Page 231, add to footnote 44:

Bridges v. Eastman Kodak, 822 F. Supp. 1020 (S.D.N.Y. 1993).

§ 6.6   Intervention

Page 231, add to footnote 49:

See also Mullins v. City of Griffin, 886 F. Supp. 21 (N.D. Ga. 1995). The court granted a newspaper's motion to intervene in a sexual harassment action for the limited purpose of modifying a court order of dismissal so that the parties would not be required to keep the settlement agreement confidential, and found that the order of confidentiality in this case was unjustified.

EEOC v. Domino's Pizza, Inc., 870 F. Supp. 655 (D. Md. 1994). An employee who alleged that she became suicidal and eventually suffered a nervous breakdown as a result of sexual advances by her supervisor could intervene in an EEOC action brought on her behalf against the employer, but the relation back doctrine could not be applied to allow the employee to add new tort claims that were time-barred when the employee could have pursued those claims independently of the EEOC.

§ 6.7   Class Action Litigation

Page 232, add to footnote 59:

A class of female employees was certified in Bremiller v. Cleveland Psychiatric Inst., 879 F. Supp. 762 (N.D. Ohio 1995), an action charging sexual harassment and retaliation against a psychiatric institution, alleging that the male employees subjected the plaintiffs to verbal threats, physical intimidation, sexual jokes, and unwanted touching and groping and that although nurses constantly reported this behavior to their supervisors and the female acting CEO, no one took any action to stop the harassment.

§ 6.8   —Rule 23(a)

Page 234, add to footnote 69:

Bremiller v. Cleveland Psychiatric Inst., 879 F. Supp. 762 (N.D. Ohio 1995). Plaintiff brought an action charging sexual harassment and retaliation against a psychiatric institution, alleging that the male employees subjected the class of plaintiffs to verbal threats, physical intimidation, sexual jokes, and unwanted touching and groping and that although nurses constantly reported this behavior to their supervisors and the female acting CEO, no one took any action to stop the harassment. The numerosity requirement was met when the putative class consisted of at least the 260 women currently employed at the institute, the plaintiff's allegations suggested that the atmosphere at the workplace may have intimidated many of the putative class members into not coming forward, and the complaint requested prospective relief that would cover all current and future female employees.

Page 235, add to footnote 77:

In Bremiller v. Cleveland Psychiatric Inst., 879 F. Supp. 762 (N.D. Ohio 1995), the named plaintiff charged sexual harassment and retaliation against a psychiatric institution, alleging that the male employees subjected the plaintiffs to verbal threats, physical intimidation, sexual jokes, and unwanted touching and groping and that although nurses constantly reported this behavior to their supervisors and the female acting CEO, no one took any action to stop the harassment. The fact that the named plaintiff had additional claims that appeared to apply only to her did not defeat the commonality requirement.

Page 237, add to footnote 87:

In Bremiller v. Cleveland Psychiatric Inst., 879 F. Supp. 762 (N.D. Ohio 1995), the action charged sexual harassment and retaliation against a psychiatric institution, alleging that the male employees subjected the plaintiffs to verbal threats, physical intimidation, sexual jokes, and unwanted touching and groping and that although nurses constantly reported this behavior to their supervisors and the female acting CEO, no one took any action to stop the harassment. The adequacy of representation was met when the plaintiff and unnamed class members shared common interests in eliminating the pervasive sexual harassment to which their male colleagues allegedly perpetually subjected them:

> Plaintiff's and the putative class' interests diverge only in that those putative class members currently employed at CPI presumably want to remain employed there. Whereas, plaintiff, having been terminated, does not share that interest. Yet, the lack of shared interest in this one regard does not prevent plaintiff from fairly and adequately representing the putative class. Furthermore, plaintiff's advocacy to date demonstrates a vigorous

prosecution of the action on behalf of the class. Finally, as detailed in her brief, plaintiff's counsel appears qualified.

Id. at 797. The class also met all the requirements of Rule 23(b).

§ 6.18   Drafting the Complaint

Page 248, add to footnote 149 following Fourth Circuit case:

Cf. Miller v. United States Fidelity & Guar., 65 Fair Empl. Prac. Cas. (BNA) 593 (D. Md. 1994).

Page 248, add to footnote 149 following "Seventh Circuit":

Cheek v. Western & S. Life Ins., 31 F.3d 497 (7th Cir. 1994); Baltzer v. City of Sun Prairie Police Dep't, 725 F. Supp. 1008 (W.D. Wis. 1989).

Page 248, add to footnote 149:

Bridges v. Eastman Kodak, 822 F. Supp. 1020 (S.D.N.Y. 1993). Female employees who alleged a hostile environment in their EEOC charge could sue their supervisor for quid pro quo harassment when both types of sexual harassment stemmed from the same set of facts alleged in the EEOC charges. "In actuality, the two sexual harassment theories are not distinguishable on the basis of the sexual conduct alleged." *Id.* at 1026. The EEOC charges alleged that the supervisor was abusive almost daily, used foul and offensive language, and treated the complainants in a violent manner, referring to them and other women as "bitches."

§ 6.24   Federal Employment Action Allegations

Page 254, add to footnote 172:

Carlson v. United States Dep't of Health & Human Servs., 879 F. Supp. 545 (D. Md. 1995). Title VII provided the exclusive remedy for discrimination claims in federal employment, and thus Fifth Amendment and Administrative Procedure Act claims had to be dismissed.

Ciafrei v. Bentsen, 877 F. Supp. 788 (D.R.I. 1995). Title VII is the exclusive remedy for the redress of federal employment discrimination and preempts other discrimination laws, such as state antidiscrimination acts.

§ 6.25   Amendments to Pleadings

* *Page 255, add to footnote 178:*

Potts v. Boeing Co., 162 F.R.D. 651 (D. Kan. 1995). The untimely filing of plaintiff's motion for leave to file an amended complaint, seeking to add a Title VII sexual harassment claim, warranted denial of the motion when the plaintiff provided no explanation for the failure to file the motion within the time specified in the scheduling order, failed to ask for additional time to file, and was aware of the facts upon which the amendment was based for some time prior to filing, and prior to the deadline for filing motions to amend.

Page 255, add to footnote 179:

*   Schofield v. Trustees of Univ. of Pa., 894 F. Supp. 194 (E.D. Pa. 1995). On an employee's motion to amend a Title VII complaint to add claims of negligent retention and violations of Pennsylvania Human Relations Act, the district court held that the university would suffer no prejudice if employee were allowed to add negligent retention claim, and the addition of PHRA claim would not be futile, since complaint alleged discriminatory conduct occurring within limitations period. The court rejected the defendant's argument that the plaintiff's failure to offer any reasonable explanation as to why she waited until one month prior to trial to submit the instant motion precludes the attempted amendment, that the PHRA claim was barred by the applicable limitations period, and therefore futile, and that it would be severely prejudiced if the negligent retention claim goes forward, because its counsel has not retained an expert to contrast the propriety of its actions with community norms. "The issue the University asserts will emerge fresh from the amended complaint and is not germane to a negligent retention claim. As a result, we find its argument regarding the need for an expert to be without merit." *Id.* at 196.

United States Equal Employment Opportunity Comm'n v. Clayton Residential Home, Inc., 874 F. Supp. 212 (N.D. Ill. 1995). In an action by the EEOC, alleging that a class of female employees were subjected to a hostile environment, the EEOC was able to amend the complaint to clarify that in addition to the plaintiff female employee, another female employee was constructively discharged. Allowing an amendment to the complaint would not require that discovery be reopened or that the trial be delayed, and the defendant had not demonstrated that there was any bad faith or dilatory motive behind the EEOC's request to amend or that any undue prejudice to itself would result.

Page 255, add to footnote 180:

Cf. Clemmer v. Enron Corp., 882 F. Supp. 606 (S.D. Tex. 1995). An employee who brought an action alleging age discrimination could not amend her complaint to add claims for violation of the ADA, reverse discrimination, sexual harassment, and violation of the Rehabilitation Act when the alleged conduct occurred before the enactment of the ADA, she did not exhaust her administrative remedies under Title VII, and she did not state facts that would support a claim under the Rehabilitation Act.

§ 6.26 Motions

Page 256, add to footnote 190 following "For examples of cases that survived motions for summary judgment, see":

Morgan v. Ford, 6 F.3d 750 (11th Cir. 1993), *cert. denied*, 114 S. Ct. 2708 (1994). Material issues of fact existed as to whether a supervisor of a correctional officer had made work conditions intolerable, precluding summary judgment. The plaintiff alleged that soon after she came to work, her supervisor asked her out on a date and, when she refused, stated that she "had not had a real man until she had him." *Id.* at 752. He then began to spend long periods, up to three or four hours at a time, at the plaintiff's work station and would scrutinize the minutiae of her work and engage her in unwanted conversation. The harassment resumed during a second period of supervision.

TRYING THE CASE

§ 6.27 Discovery

* *Page 258, add to footnote 193:*

Biggs v. Nicewonger Co., Inc., 163 F.R.D. 607 (D. Or. 1995). The fact that an employer had had a prior opportunity to depose a former employee in her sexual harassment suit did not bar a subsequent deposition on the issue of her prior criminal conviction, if any. The district court ruled that the evidence could be used for impeachment purposes, when the prior conviction was "set aside" under state law, and no record of conviction was otherwise available. The employer's failure to comply with a local rule requiring it to confer precluded it from deposing the employee in her sexual harassment suit as to her employment history since her first deposition.

Page 258, add to footnote 194:

* Cole v. Appalachian Power Co., 903 F. Supp. 975 (S.D. W.Va. 1995). An employer filed a motion for a protective order that would prohibit employee's counsel from interviewing certain of its other employees, and an employee filed a motion to clarify the status of employees. The court concluded that *ex parte* interviews of the following five classes of an organization's employees were inappropriate:

1. Officials of the organization (those having a managerial responsibility);

2. Other persons whose act or omission in connection with the matter may be imputed to the organization for purposes of civil or criminal liability (those who have the legal power to bind the organization in the matter);

3. Those who are responsible for implementing the advice of the organization's lawyers;

4. Any members of the organization whose own interests are directly at stake in a representation (i.e., any person who is independently represented by counsel directly or indirectly by membership in a class, partnership, joint venture, or trust);

5. An agent or servant whose statement concerns a matter within the scope of the agency or employment, which statement was made during the existence of the relationship and which is offered

against the organization as an admission. However, *ex parte* interviews of employees who are "mere witnesses" to an event for which the organization is sued (i.e., holders of factual information), are permitted.

Id. at 979.

Carter-Herman v. City of Phila., 897 F. Supp. 899 (E.D. Pa. 1995). A female police officer and female police sergeant sued the city, the police commissioner, and other police officers of various ranks for sexual harassment and retaliation. The plaintiffs' counsel sought to interview nonparty police officers without the presence of anyone representing the defendants. The district court held that there could be no *ex parte* communications with any current employee or member of the police department having managerial responsibility, and plaintiffs' counsel could interview without prior notice or consent from defendants' counsel non-managerial members or employees.

> We do not accept the notion that every city employee is automatically a represented party simply by virtue of his or her employment without any initiative on the part of the employee to obtain legal help from the City. Otherwise an organization could thwart the purpose of [state professional conduct] Rule 4.2 simply by unilaterally pronouncing its representation of all its employees. On the other hand, even assuming the merits of plaintiffs' arguments about the difficulty in obtaining evidence without *ex parte* contacts, we cannot permit communications which violate the intent of Rule 4.2. The Rule with its Comment allows plaintiffs' counsel to contact and interview *ex parte* only those employees of the Philadelphia Police Department who do not have "managerial responsibility."

Id. at 903. The court ordered that plaintiffs' counsel before conducting any interview would have to advise the interviewee of:

1.   counsel's representative capacity;
2.   counsel's reasons for seeking the interview;
3.   the interviewee's right to refuse to be interviewed; and
4.   the interviewee's right to have his or her own counsel present.

Id. at 904.

Ex parte communications with former employees of defendants were permissible with limitations in an action by current and former female

firefighters for sex discrimination, sexual harassment, intentional infliction of emotional distress, and invasion of privacy, but ex parte communications with current employees would not be permitted. Lang v. Reedy
Creek Improvement Dist. & Walt Disney World Co., 888 F. Supp. 1143
(M.D. Fla. 1995).

> Access to an organizational party's employees should be regulated on the
> basis of balancing of interests affected in the particular case. . . . Proof of
> wrongdoing, and especially of discrimination, is difficult to establish, and
> Plaintiffs must be afforded the opportunities to discover all factual infor-
> mation pertinent to their case. *Goff v. Wheaton Industries*, 145 F.R.D.
> 351, 356, n. 3 (D.N.J. 1992). The *Goff* court favored flexibility in the dis-
> covery process, a position without which this Court concurs. The ability
> to informally interview former employees of the Defendants would mate-
> rially assist Plaintiffs' preparation of their case at both the summary judg-
> ment and trial stages and reduce the costs of litigation for both parties.

Id. at 1148. The court issued the following guidelines for ex parte communications with former employees:

1. Upon contacting any former employee, Plaintiffs' counsel shall
   immediately identify herself as the attorney representing Plaintiffs in
   the instant suit and specify the purpose of the contact.

2. Plaintiffs' counsel shall ascertain whether the former employee is
   associated with either Defendant or is represented by counsel. If so,
   the contact must terminate immediately.

3. Plaintiffs' counsel shall advise the former employee that (a) participation in the interview is not mandatory and that (b) he or she may
   choose not to participate or to participate only in the presence of personal counsel or counsel for the Defendants. Counsel must immediately terminate the interview of the former employee if she or he does
   not wish to participate.

4. Plaintiffs' counsel shall advice the former employee to avoid disclosure of privileged materials. In the course of the interview, Plaintiffs'
   counsel shall not attempt to solicit privileged information and shall
   terminate the conversation should it appear that the interviewee may
   reveal privileged matters.

5. Plaintiffs shall create and preserve a list of all former employees contacted and the date(s) of contact(s) and shall maintain and preserve
   any and all statements or notes resulting from such contacts, whether
   by phone or in person. Defendants are entitled to review the lists and

notes within seven (7) days of demand subject to the protections of work product.

6. Should the Defendants have reason to believe that a violation of either the ethical rules or this Court's Order has occurred, the Defendants shall file an appropriate motion with this court. Appropriate sanctions or remedial measures will be imposed if a violation is found by the Court. If the violation is revealed at trial, the Defendants shall make such motion in open Court, and the Court will take the matter under advisement at that time.

Id. at 1148–49. With respect to communications with current employees, the court noted that it would be difficult to conceive of a scenario in which the plaintiffs could contact current employees other than the husband of one plaintiff without risking violation of the ethical rules and the representation the plaintiffs had made to the court. However, if the plaintiffs provided to the court and the defendant the names of the current employees they wished to contact, the court would be willing to reconsider its decision on an employee-by-empoyee basis after the defendants had adequate time to respond.

Page 259, add to footnote 199:

In Ward v. Maritz Inc., 156 F.R.D. 592 (D.N.J. 1994), the district court granted a defendant employer's motion to compel the production of tape recordings of the plaintiff's telephone conversations with non-party witnesses, to which the witnesses did not consent. The plaintiff had secretly recorded the conversations immediately after consultation with her attorneys and denied to at least one of these persons that she was recording their conversations. The court found that regardless of whether the conduct violated the state rules of professional conduct, the secret tape recording vitiated the work product rule, and the court did not find any special circumstances that could have overcome the finding of vitiation. In this case, the concerns of fairness and safeguarding the adversary process required the production of the tape recordings. Without such production, the plaintiff unilaterally maintained the ability to use the secretly recorded statements for discovery purposes and for impeachment purposes at trial. Fundamental fairness required that the defense be afforded the opportunity, if Maritz so desired, to use the statements to impeach the credibility of the witnesses, a capability that rested solely with the plaintiff at this point.

Page 260, add to footnote 201:

See also Ryall v. Appleton Elec., 153 F.R.D. 660 (D. Colo. 1994). An employer was not required to produce written notes that its chief employment counsel took during interviews of the alleged harasser and the complainant's husband, because the notes were protected by Fed. R. Civ. P. 26(b)(3); the investigation began in response to contact by the complainant's attorney indicating that litigation was imminent. A better option would be to bar the employer from introducing the contents of the privileged interviews or notes to establish its defense.

Page 260, add to footnote 202:

Ballou v. University of Kan. Medical Ctr., 159 F.R.D. 558 (D. Kan. 1994) (a single letter to opposing counsel did not establish a good-faith effort to confer or reasonably attempt to resolve discovery disputes).

§ 6.28   Protective Orders

Page 261, add to footnote 205:

Schofield v. Trustees of Univ. of Pa., 161 F.R.D. 302 (E.D. Pa. 1995). An employee who filed a racial and sexual harassment complaint against her employer was not entitled to a protective order to restrict access to her medical records, the deposition transcripts of psychologists and physicians, and her own deposition testimony relating to her medical condition so that only university counsel and no more than two of the university's representatives would receive the information when such an order was too restrictive. The university was a large and complex institution, employing over 20,000 people, and the responsibility for making decisions regarding the steps to take in defending the action was shared among a number of persons and departments, and thus it was unreasonable to "compel Defendant to steer its way through this litigation with only two persons at the helm." *Id.* at 304. The court was not unsympathetic to the plaintiff's concerns that the distribution of the medical records to other university employees, many of whom were her friends and coworkers, would result in extreme embarrassment to her, and strongly encouraged the parties to negotiate an agreement that properly balanced the plaintiff's concerns for privacy with the defendant's need for flexibility in defending its case. For now, however, the court would deny the plaintiff's motion as unduly hampering the defendant's ability to defend the action.

See also Roberts v. Americable Int'l Inc., 883 F. Supp. 499 (E.D. Cal. 1995). When a sexual harassment suit was removed to federal court, the former employee plaintiff moved to compel the deposition of the former supervisor, and the latter moved to stay his deposition and for a protective order. The district court held that federal law, which allows a party to intercept a conversation, not California law, which prohibits such interception without the consent of all the parties, would apply to determine whether tape recordings of conversations between the employee and her supervisor would be admissible. The interest of justice required that the supervisor be allowed to review the tapes before his deposition. The tapes were not protected by the attorney-client privilege or the work product doctrine. The plaintiff acquired all the tapes in a less than forthright manner, albeit within federal law. Finally, the plaintiff's privacy rights would not be violated by asking her to produce the tapes in discovery.

> It must seem odd, even to Roberts, that the surreptitious recording of the conversations of her supervisor . . . and other employees, which certainly impinges upon *their* privacy rights, violated the privacy rights of the person doing the recording when that person is asked to produce the tapes in discovery. Roberts has not asserted that she does not plan to use the tapes in this litigation; it is clear that she does. Roberts does not assert that she spoke of some highly confidential, private material at the time she was recording . . . employees. Even if she did, any conceivable balancing process would require the tapes to be produced in light of the fact that very probative evidence is purportedly contained on the tapes, and Roberts intends to utilize the tapes in this litigation.

Id. at 506.

Page 261, add to footnote 206:

Welsh v. City & County of S.F., 887 F. Supp. 1293 (N.D. Cal. 1995). The court granted in part a motion by the defendant municipal employer and police chief for a protective order to prevent the disclosure to the public of tapes and transcripts of witnesses interviewed during the investigation of sexual harassment charges by a female police officer; only the transcripts would be disclosed to the public. The court rejected the defendants' arguments that individual witnesses had privacy rights that precluded disclosure of all the materials because California law protects their interests, the defendants relied on assurances of confidentiality, the disclosure of the materials would have a chilling effect on witnesses in future police commission investigations, and the police chief still had legitimate privacy interests even though he was a public figure. The relevant California statutes do not create privacy interests on the part of individual witnesses or officers because they were not enacted to protect such interests, witness reliance was misplaced in light of the limited protection offered by the California Penal and Evidence Codes, and there is no empirical data suggesting that the possibility of disclosure would reduce the candor of officers who contribute to internal affairs investigations. Disclosure of the transcripts of the tapes would ensure public access to the information contained in the tapes. The plaintiff presented no reason to believe that the transcripts were inaccurate and would be able to verify the accuracy of the transcripts with the tapes to be produced by the defendants.

> Consequently, public disclosure of the tapes serves no public interest. On the other hand, the ability to edit and present the words spoken on the tapes in a context other than the questions and answers themselves provides a potential for biased presentation of the information and for invasion of the privacy of the speaker. Balancing the interests, then, favors issuance of a protective order against public disclosure of the tapes themselves.

Id. at 1302.

See also Shoney's, Inc. v. Lewis, 875 S.W.2d 514 (Ky. 1994). The trial court improperly declined to disqualify the sexual harassment plaintiff's attorney for violating a court rule prohibiting communication with persons represented by counsel when he took statements from two of the employer's senior management employees without consent of or notice to the law firm representing the employer. Suppression of the statements was also appropriate. "We recognize the disqualification of a party's counsel and suppression of information obtained by that counsel is a drastic remedy and the decisions of the courts below reflect a proper reticence. Nevertheless, in circumstances such as these, with the integrity of the adversarial process at stake, we must make every effort to prevent harm to the civil justice system." *Id.* at 516–17.

§ 6.31   Evidentiary Issues

Page 262, add to footnote 214:

Lonsdorf v. Seefeldt, 47 F.3d 893 (7th Cir. 1995). An employee of the Wisconsin Department of Revenue who brought a § 1983 sexual harassment action against a department agent was entitled to relief from judgment in the form of a new trial under Fed. R. Civ. P. 60(b)(3) when she alleged that a document proffered by the agent at trial had been altered. The district court applied an incorrect standard in denying the plaintiff's claim on the grounds that the plaintiff had failed to discover the misrepresentation in a diligent and timely fashion:

> The evidence in the record does not support a finding that Lonsdorf had failed to discover the misrepresentation in a timely fashion, nor does it demonstrate that Lonsdorf is merely attempting to relitigate the case. To the contrary, the record reflects that during discovery many documents were produced, and Lonsdorf had not previously realized that a falsified document existed. Moreover, Rule 60(b)(3) does not refer to timeliness in discovering the fraud, but only that the motion be made within a reasonable time. Indeed, in litigation the burden is on the attorney who discovers client dishonesty to take corrective action. . . . A litigant, however, should not be required to assume that falsified documents are being produced by an opposing party.
>
> It is patently obvious that Seefeldt benefitted from the use of a fraudulently altered document and Lonsdorf suffered an injustice. Fed.R.Civ.P. 60(b)(3) provides an escape valve to protect the fairness and integrity of litigation in federal courts. . . . It must be noted, however, that the responsibility for altering the training schedule has not been established on this appeal. Seefeldt's appellate brief merely mentions the issue of misrepresentation, allotting one page of a fifty-page brief to the gravamen of this appeal. Although Seefeldt's trial counsel did not represent Seefeldt on appeal, no indication of unethical conduct on the part of Seefeldt's counsel exists. Indeed, at oral argument Lonsdorf's attorney expressed his view that Seefeldt's trial counsel at all times has conducted himself in an upright and completely ethical fashion. The inference exists that Seefeldt bears sole responsibility for presenting the altered copy.

Id. at 898 (footnotes omitted).

The after-acquired evidence rule has been asserted by defendants in a number of recent decisions in an effort to avoid liability for sexual harassment or retaliation. *See, e.g.,* Wehr v. Ryan's Family Steak

Houses, Inc., 49 F.3d 1150 (6th Cir. 1995). A male restaurant manager who successfully alleged that he was fired in retaliation for reporting sexual harassment by other managers was properly awarded $2,000 in back pay, but remand was necessary to determine whether the plaintiff was entitled to reinstatement in light of after-acquired evidence that the plaintiff had lied about his employment background and medical history on his resume. The after-acquired evidence rule did not bar the award of back pay.

Prescott v. Independent Life & Accident Ins. Co., 878 F. Supp. 1545 (M.D. Ala. 1995). A male former employee who alleged that his male supervisor sexually harassed him stated a claim for quid pro quo harassment. The court rejected the defendant's claims that recovery to the plaintiff should be denied or limited under the after-acquired evidence rule because it learned during the course of preparing for this action that the plaintiff lied on his application for employment, and thus it would not have hired him had this information been known. The defendant did not show without dispute that it would not have hired the plaintiff had it known the circumstances behind his having left his previous position.

Quillen v. American Tobacco Co., 874 F. Supp. 1285 (M.D. Ala. 1995). Fact issues existed as to whether after-acquired evidence of alleged falsifications by the employee would preclude prospective relief. The plaintiff had complained to management that her supervisor [Knight] had sexually harassed her. The company held several meetings and determined that Knight had indeed harassed the plaintiff. As a result, Knight was demoted to the position of sales representative, he was suspended without pay for one week, and his salary was cut 25 percent. Knight was reassigned to a sales zone that, according to the defendant, did not overlap with the plaintiff's. The plaintiff claimed that following Knight's demotion, the workplace at American Tobacco remained hostile and that, as a result of the incident with Knight, she began to have difficulties with several of her assigned customers: one of the company's agents told a customer that the plaintiff had "set up" Knight on her sexual harassment complaint. The plaintiff alleged that she requested to be transferred to another sales district in order to escape the problem, but that the defendant company refused. The plaintiff also stated that she was forced to attend a meeting at which Knight was present, despite her having informed the company that she could not bear to be in the same room with Knight, and that the previous harassment by Knight, combined with the "gossip and hostility" from her customers and the failure of American Tobacco to take adequate steps to alleviate the situation, created and perpetuated a hostile work environment. During their investigation, the defendants alleged that they learned that the plaintiff had falsified reports that she had made to the company concerning customer calls and that the falsification of reports was their legitimate and nondiscriminatory reason for terminating the plaintiff. The plaintiff admitted that she falsified reports and also admitted that this was not the first time that she had done so. However, the plaintiff disputed that this was the reason for her termination because Knight allegedly also had falsified reports in the past, American Tobacco knew this, and still retained Knight in its employ. The defendant also alleged that during the course of discovery, they acquired information that the plaintiff had lied on her application for employment. The plaintiff apparently misrepresented her reasons for leaving two previous positions. In both cases, the plaintiff stated that she left those jobs because she relocated her residence, when in fact, the plaintiff had been fired from both positions. According to the defendant, this information should preclude recovery by the plaintiff in that she would not have been hired but for her misrepresentation. Because she would not have been hired, she suffered no damages in losing the job. In a recent opinion, the Eleventh Circuit ruled that after-acquired information may be used to preclude prospective relief to a particular plaintiff. Turnes v. AmSouth Bank, 36 F.3d 1057, 1062 (11th Cir. 1994). Therefore, according to the recent decision by the Supreme Court, as well as Eleventh Circuit precedent, where an employer can show the plaintiff would not have been hired, or would have been terminated, if the employer had possessed the after-acquired information, prospective relief such as reinstatement or front pay is inappropriate. The court concluded, however, that this was a question of fact. If the employer would not have fired her, or would still have hired her, even with the knowledge it later acquired, the defendant could not use the information as a defense to prospective relief. The burden of proof was on the defendant. In this case, the defendant American Tobacco had not shown that it would not have hired the plaintiff had it known that she was fired from two previous jobs. According to the plaintiff, the defendant had other employees who had been hired or retained despite the fact that they were terminated from previous positions. Therefore, a jury could decide that honesty on the employment application was not in fact as important as the defendant contended.

Miller v. Bircham, Inc., 874 F. Supp. 337 (D. Kan. 1995). A material issue of fact existed as to whether an employer intentionally discriminated and retaliated against a female former employee in an action involving after-acquired evidence regarding the employee's alleged failure to list on her job application a previous employer from whom she had stolen that would have resulted in the employee's termination. In light of McKennon v. Nashville Banner Publishing Co., 115 S. Ct. 879 (1995), which held that barring all relief to an employee who engaged in misconduct is inconsistent with the scheme developed in antidiscrimination statutes, the court ruled that any alleged misrepresentation or omission on the plaintiff's work application, even if it would have caused her unlawful dismissal, was not a complete defense to or bar to all relief from the plaintiff's claims of intentional discrimination under Title VII. Evidence of wrongdoing would be relevant to the court's determination of the appropriate equitable relief to be accorded should the jury return a verdict in favor of the plaintiff.

McCarthy v. Fall Corp., 625 S.2d 296 (Sup. Ct. 1995). After-acquired evidence of the plaintiff employee's fraud was relevant to a determination of damages and other remedies if and when a violation by the employer is found but did not entitle the employer to judgment as a matter of law.

Page 262, add to footnote 215:

Spain v. Gallegos, 26 F.3d 439 (3d Cir. 1994). An investigator in an EEOC office made a prima facie showing of hostile environment, despite atypical allegations that she was the subject of false rumors that she was having a sexual relationship with a supervisor and had gained influence over him as a result of their relationship, when in fact her private meeting with the supervisor allegedly resulted from the supervisor's improper solicitation of funds from the plaintiff, a practice that lasted for several years. The district court abused its discretion in ruling that evidence concerning meetings between the plaintiff and her supervisor and the resulting rumors was inadmissible on grounds of relevance under Rule 401 and prejudice under Rule 403; it was clear that such evidence would prove certain elements of the plaintiff's claims. The court rejected the EEOC's argument that the district court properly excluded evidence of the loans under Rule 403 because evidence of the supervisor's questionable conduct would be highly likely to distract the jury from focusing on the claim of sexual harassment and would cause the factfinder to find a Title VII violation out of a desire to punish the supervisor for his unethical conduct. The probative value of the evidence was not substantially outweighed by the danger of unfair prejudice, as the dispute concerned not whether there were loans, but rather the motivation for them and their frequency.

§ 6.32 Ordering Examinations

Page 264, add to footnote 222:

See also Bridges v. Eastman Kodak, 64 Fair Empl. Prac. Cas. (BNA) 1100 (S.D.N.Y. 1993). Mental anguish may be relevant to a plaintiff's sexual harassment claims under state antidiscrimination law, as a plaintiff may be entitled to compensatory damages for mental suffering under that statute. But in this sexual harassment action, in which the plaintiffs alleged that the supervisor was abusive almost daily, used foul and offensive language, and treated the complainants in a violent manner, referring to them and other women as "bitches," there was no adequate basis to support a court order requiring mental examinations of the plaintiffs under Fed. R. Civ. P. 35(a). Although the plaintiffs admitted to having undergone psychological counseling, they did not claim that their mental injury was ongoing or that they ever suffered from a psychiatric disorder. Had the plaintiffs asserted the existence of an ongoing mental illness, there might have been a sufficient basis to allow the defendants' request on the grounds that the plaintiffs' mental condition was in controversy, but the plaintiffs alleged past, not present, pain and suffering. Defendants were entitled, however, to inquire into the plaintiffs' psychological histories under Fed. R. Civ. P. 26(b):

> Although having to answer questions about their personal histories is to some extent an intrusion [on] their privacy, and may in fact inhibit some plaintiffs from proceeding with their claims, such an inquiry is warranted since plaintiffs are seeking compensation for their mental anguish. . . . Moreover, since plaintiffs seek to prove that they have suffered emotional distress as a result of their sexual harassment through their testimony and the testimony of their therapists, defense counsel has a right to inquire into plaintiffs' pasts for the purpose of showing that their emotional distress was caused at least in part by events and circumstances that were not job related. . . . Indeed, as far as the testimony of their therapists is concerned, defendants must be allowed to inquire into all relevant

information upon which the therapists' opinion is based, not necessarily only information directly related to their employment.

64 Fair Empl. Prac. Cas. at 1104–05. The court admonished the defendants not to engage in a "fishing expedition by inquiring into matters totally irrelevant to the issue of emotional distress. In other words, the scope of the inquiry must be limited to whether, and to what extent, the alleged harassment caused plaintiffs to suffer emotional harm." *Id.* at 1105 (footnote omitted).

Page 264, add to footnote 223:

Jansen v. Packaging Corp., 66 Fair Empl. Prac. Cas. (BNA) 557 (N.D. Ill. 1994). A former employee alleged that she had suffered and continued to suffer ongoing emotional distress due to alleged sexual harassment and retaliation by her former supervisor. She thus placed her mental condition in controversy and confirmed the existence of good cause under Fed. R. Civ. P. 35(a) for the defendant employer's motion for a psychological examination:

> Indeed, in this instance the existence of the "good cause" component is doubly clear, for Jansen has not limited her claim by asserting that she suffered such harms only in the past—not only has she claimed continuing harm up to and including the present in her deposition . . . , but her attorney has confirmed that fact when questioned by this Court on the issue. That being so, any doubt that might exist as to an expert's ability to gauge a prior mental state by means of a current examination could not serve as the basis for denying Packaging access to such an examination.

Id. at 557. The court designated an independent expert, rejecting the defendant's claim that it should designate the expert in order to level the playing field; that principle was really inapplicable in this situation, when the plaintiff's only professional witness in this area was expected to be her own treating physician rather than an expert in the field of mental health, and the defendant itself had argued that the plaintiff had been unwilling to discuss with her own doctor the subjects on which she was proposed to be interrogated by the defendant's expert.

Page 265, add to footnote 224:

Thompson v. Haskell Co., 65 Fair Empl. Prac. Cas. (BNA) 1088 (M.D. Fla. 1994). An employer could discover a female former employee's psychological records when she alleged that, as a result of sexual harassment by her supervisor, she was reduced to a severely depressed emotional state and her employment was terminated when she did not acquiesce to the supervisor's advances. Her emotional and mental state, documented by a psychologist 10 days after her discharge, was thus highly probative with respect to her allegations. No other comparable report was prepared during the weeks following the plaintiff's discharge.

See also Bridges v. Eastman Kodak, 64 Fair Empl. Prac. Cas. (BNA) 1100 (S.D.N.Y. 1993).

Page 265, add to footnote 228:

Cf. Covell v. CNG Transmission Corp., 863 F. Supp. 202 (M.D. Pa. 1994). In an action under Title VII and the state human relations act for sexual harassment, the plaintiff did not waive the psychiatrist-patient privilege entirely by disclosing some records. Because reports concerning the plaintiff's mental condition could be relevant to her credibility and subjective perceptions of her work environment, the court directed that copies of the records be submitted for *in camera* review by the court for the purpose of weighing the value of information contained therein for purposes of impeaching the credibility of the plaintiff's testimony and rebutting her claim that she subjectively perceived a hostile work environment.

Lantz v. Superior Court of Kern County, 34 Cal. Rptr. 2d 358 (Ct. App. 1994). In a sexual harassment action by a female deputy sheriff, the county was a subpoenaing party under a statute requiring that the subpoenaing party who seeks to obtain personal records of a "consumer" in a civil action must attempt to notify the consumer. The plaintiff's right to privacy was not adequately protected by the lower court when the court used the wrong standard for determining whether medical records are properly discoverable.

§ 6.33   Plaintiff's Sexual History

Page 266, add to footnote 232:

* *Cf.* Bottomly v. Leucadia Nat'l, 163 F.R.D. 617 (D. Utah 1995). On a defendant employer's motion to reconsider an order that allowed it limited discovery of the psychological records of an employee who brought

a sexual harassment suit against it, the court held that the employer would not be allowed to full disclosure of the records when a full personality inventory of the plaintiff's character, unrelated to her psychological or emotional condition and causation, was irrelevant to her lawsuit. In making the prior order, the court concluded that without further showing, other information about plaintiff's psychological circumstance or history would not be reasonably likely to lead to admissible evidence and that there was no justification for ordering discovery relating to any diagnosis or treatment involving third persons because of privacy interests of both third persons and plaintiff. Although the plaintiff waived her privacy claims as to those matters that are related to causation and damages as to her claim by putting her psychological and emotional condition in issue, she did not waive privacy interests on matters that are unrelated to the case or not calculated to lead to admissible evidence. The court noted that although expert testimony is not required to prove psychological or physical damage under Title VII, it is admissible as probative of damages and causation and defendants must be given an opportunity to rebut the plaintiff's evidence, and if legitimate, make an attribution of psychological damage to another exclusive cause. However, matter that is not related to causation and extent of damage, but which merely goes to the plaintiff's character, is outside of proper bounds of discovery.

> Matters that are remote to what an expert may legitimately use for foundation for an expert opinion but which may be helpful in a clinical treatment mode or for a psychoanalytic personality analysis are too broad and intrusive and not needed for an expert opinion in the issues. A clinical whole person approach is not especially functional in the legal context of the case and is unjustifiably intrusive. A full personality inventory is not necessary for an expert witness to address the relevant issues of damages and causation. Although, there is a confidentiality order in place, because of the parties involved, the nature of the accusations, and the unusual bitterness with which the parties have confronted each other in this case, as well as media publicity the case has received, the court should exercise its discretion to assure that unnecessary invasion of the privacy interests of all parties and other persons does not occur.

Id. at 620. The victim of sexual harassment is to be treated no differently on damages than any other tort victim. If the victim was vulnerable and psychologically feeble, the harasser must accept the condition of the

124

person who was subjected to the improper conduct. The defendant cannot seek a limitation on damages if the harasser's conduct was a substantial cause of the psychological or emotional distress of the victim. The harasser's conduct need not have been the sole or exclusive cause of the plaintiff's damage.

> Therefore, the use of other psychological or emotional distress that a plaintiff suffered at other times will have only limited worth for defendants if the plaintiff's present or relevant condition was substantially caused by the defendant's conduct. The experts for plaintiff in this case need *not* proclaim that defendant's conduct is the sole cause of her distress, only a substantial cause. Defendants, to be exonerated from damages on this element if the substantive conduct of liability were found, would have to show that the plaintiff's psychological or emotional condition was not substantially related to defendant's misconduct. Thus, causation is a critical factor to this case, but a full personality inventory of plaintiff's character as such, unrelated to her psychological or emotional condition and causation is not relevant. It may well be confusing to a jury if there is a causative relationship between defendant's conduct and plaintiff's emotional distress if unrelated psychological evidence is received.

Id. The expert's opinion must be founded on what an expert in the discipline would reasonably rely on given the issues in the case. It was the court's responsibility to insure that the discoverable matter was calculated or likely to lead to admissible evidence and if the material was not related or necessary to the legitimate scope of relevant expert opinion, the court would not permit discovery. The court would review the unredacted records *in camera* to determine if there has been compliance with the court's order. "The defendant's request for all records, regardless of time and circumstance, would not be granted. The records to be disclosed must be reasonably calculated to lead to admissible evidence. Defendant's request goes beyond that standard." *Id.* at 621–22.

Kelly-Zurian v. Wohl Shoe Co., 22 Cal. App. 4th 397, 27 Cal. Rptr. 2d 457, 64 Fair Empl. Prac. Cas. (BNA) 603 (1994) (sexual harassment, constructive wrongful discharge, intentional infliction of emotional distress). The lower court properly entered a judgment upon a $125,000 jury verdict in favor of the plaintiff in a sexual harassment action alleging that for three years the plaintiff suffered verbal and physical harassment at the hands of her supervisor. He would come up from behind and put both his hands on her breasts, pinch her buttocks, grab her crotch and ask if she "was wet," ask her what kind of lingerie she was wearing, how was her "pussy," if she "got any last night," if she "took it in the ass," and if she "swallowed" or "gave head." 64 Fair Empl. Prac. Cas. at 605. The lower court properly excluded evidence regarding the viewing of X-rated movies by the plaintiff and her husband, her abortions, and her prior sexual history and sexual conduct with individuals other than the supervisor and other of defendant's employees.

Page 266, add to footnote 235:

Longmire v. Alabama State Univ., 151 F.R.D. 414 (M.D. Ala. 1992). Courts need to be particularly vigilant in controlling discovery in sexual harassment cases. The court rejected the defendant's argument that, under Rule 404(b), he should be allowed to inquire into the plaintiff's sexual history because evidence of any prior instance in which the plaintiff may have been engaged in sexual relationships with individuals with authority over her (resulting in the plaintiff accepting money or favors from such individuals after they were placed in a compromising position) would be relevant to the plaintiff's motive, plan, or scheme in this case. Such discovery involved facts remote in time or place to the relevant working environment. The court noted that this ruling was based on the present state of the record; if the defendant had actual evidence, not argument, which would establish a good faith basis for the inquiry about the plaintiff's past sexual activity and some relevance to this inquiry, the defendant could make an ex parte motion under seal requesting that the court allow such inquiry. Because the president claimed that he had been defamed by the plaintiff's statement that he tried to rape her, counsel for the plaintiff could ask the president about any incidents where he was alleged to have assaulted other females or to have attempted to force them to have sex with him against their wills. If the president intended to offer evidence of his general good character, then counsel for the plaintiff could ask questions about any extramarital affair that the president may have had while he was at either university.

* *Page 267, add at end of section:*

The Advisory Committee's Note to the 1994 amendments explicitly states that Rule 412 applies "in any civil case in which a person claims to be the victim of sexual misconduct, such as actions for sexual battery or sexual harassment." In *Sheffield v. Hilltop Sand & Gravel Co., Inc.*, 895 F. Supp. 105 (E.D. Va. 1995), the plaintiff, a female waitperson charging that the restaurant manager, Bambery, repeatedly made sexually suggestive comments and gestures that were directed towards her, sought to exclude evidence regarding her purported reaction to, and participation in, sexually explicit discussions with her coworkers. Her complaint alleged that Bambery would place a food item such as a hot dog, cucumber, or roll of ground beef between his legs and make offensive remarks. The plaintiff claimed that when she complained about the treatment she received from Bambery, she was told that she was lucky to have her job, and that when she reacted negatively to Bambery's sexually suggestive actions, Bambery assigned her extra duty or criticized her work. The district court held that whether the employee's discussions were admissible was governed by the "rape shield law," and where the employer violated the "rape shield law" by failing to place under seal its statement of facts describing evidence of discussions, the employer would be sanctioned by excluding testimony of employees other than the alleged harasser regarding such alleged discussions.

In its argument that Rule 412 was inapplicable to plaintiff's present motion in limine, the defendant contended that the proffered evidence concerned the extent to which the plaintiff was involved in sexually explicit discussions in the workplace, and that such evidence did not seek to prove that the plaintiff engaged in certain "sexual behavior," or that she had a "predisposition" to participate in such conduct; rather, such evidence indicated only that Bambery's actions towards the plaintiff were not "unwelcome."

> Most of the evidence that the defendant seeks to introduce is testimony that the plaintiff described to coworkers her sexual relations with her husband. Clearly, such evidence implies that the plaintiff engaged in sexual intercourse or other physical conduct. Moreover, the defendant proffers testimony that the plaintiff, in addition to discussing her sex life, used "vulgar" language in the workplace. Evidence relating to the plaintiff's speech is certainly evidence offered to prove an alleged victim's "sexual predisposition." The Court therefore finds that the disputed evidence endeavors to establish the plaintiff's sexual behavior and her predisposition to engage in such conduct. Accordingly, Rule 412 must govern the admissibility of such evidence.

Id. at 108. Rule 412's application to the present motions was consistent with Congress' intention that the rule be invoked in sexual harassment cases.

The defendant seeks to introduce the testimony of James Bambery and of several other Pilot's Wharf employees that the plaintiff frequently participated in sexually provocative discussions and activities that took place at the restaurant. The plaintiff acknowledges that Bambery's testimony is admissible because it goes toward the issue of whether the plaintiff "welcomed" his sexually suggestive antics. The plaintiff moves, however, to exclude the other employees' testimony. According to the plaintiff, such evidence is irrelevant to this lawsuit, which concerns only the relationship between the plaintiff and Bambery, and would unfairly prejudice the plaintiff.

Id. at 109. While such evidence might be relevant, the court instead sanctioned the defendant for its "callous disregard of the procedural safeguards articulated in Rule 412(c)." *Id.*

. . . The defendant thoughtlessly filed the motion, along with a statement of facts that described with particularity the evidence it sought to introduce, without requesting that these documents be placed under seal. These sensitive materials automatically became a matter of public record, such that anyone could disseminate the contents of defendant's motion—and invade the plaintiff's privacy—before the Court could determine whether the evidence was admissible in the first place.

Id. Thus, while the court would permit Bambery to testify that the plaintiff participated in sexually provocative discussions and activities in the workplace, it would exclude all other testimony on the issue. The plaintiff had narrowly tailored her amended complaint so that it focused solely upon her dealings with Bambery, and thus the exclusion of the other employees' testimony would not deprive the defendant of a fair trial. The court warned the plaintiff that this ruling would not protect her if she opened the door to such evidence by stating unequivocally that she never engaged in such conduct at work. If the plaintiff raised this matter in her case-in-chief, the court would have no choice but to allow the defendant to put on evidence rebutting the plaintiff's contentions.

§ 6.34   Evidence of Sexual Harassment of Other Employees

Page 267, add to footnote 243:

Heyne v. Caruso, 69 F.3d 1475 (9th Cir. 1995). The district court improperly excluded testimony concerning the employer's alleged harassment of other female employees on the ground that it was not probative of quid pro quo sexual harassment when such evidence was relevant and admissible to prove discriminatory intent. The plaintiff waitress alleged that the restaurant owner [Caruso] came to the trailer park where she lived, entered her mobile home, and propositioned her for sex. When the plaintiff told him that she was not interested, he left. The plaintiff had been previously warned that if she were late for work again, she would be terminated. She was late again on the morning after Caruso came to her home, and she was fired. Prior to trial, Caruso filed a motion in limine seeking to exclude evidence of his alleged sexual harassment of other female employees on the basis that such evidence was not probative of quid pro quo sexual harassment. The district court granted Caruso's motion and prevented the plaintiff from offering testimony regarding Caruso's alleged harassment of other female employees, reasoning that such testimony, while relevant to a hostile work environment claim, was more prejudicial than probative of a quid pro quo sexual harassment claim.

> It is clear that an employer's conduct tending to demonstrate hostility towards a certain group is both relevant and admissible where the employer's general hostility towards that group is the true reason behind firing an employee who is a member of that group. . . . Recognizing that "[t]here will seldom be 'eyewitness' testimony as to the employer's mental processes," *United States Postal Serv. Bd. of Governors v. Aikens,* 460 U.S. 711, 716 . . . (1983), the Supreme Court held that evidence of the employer's discriminatory attitude *in general* is relevant and admissible to prove race discrimination.

*   *   *

[W]e recently held that evidence of an employer's sexual harassment of female employees other than the plaintiff and evidence of the employer's

disparaging remarks about women in general were relevant to a discriminatory discharge claim which alleged that the plaintiff's discharge was
motivated by the employer's general feeling of hostility towards women.
EEOC v. Farmer Bros. Co., 31 F.3d 891, 897–98 (9th Cir. 1994).

In light of these cases, we evaluate the propriety of introducing in evidence the employer's alleged sexual harassment of employees other than
the plaintiff to prove the employer's motive behind firing the plaintiff in a
quid pro quo sexual harassment claim. At the outset, we note that
Caruso's alleged harassment of other female employees cannot be used to
prove that Caruso propositioned Heyne on the night before she was fired.
See Fed.R.Evid. 404(b) ("Evidence of other crimes, wrongs, or acts is not
admissible to prove the character of a person in order to show action in
conformity therewith.").

Evidence of Caruso's sexual harassment of other female workers may
be used, however, to prove his motive or intent in discharging Heyne. *See
id.* The sexual harassment of others, if shown to have occurred, is relevant
and probative of Caruso's general attitude of disrespect toward his female
employees, and his sexual objectification of them. That attitude is relevant
to the question of Caruso's motive for discharging Heyne. . . .

* * *

There is no unfair prejudice, however, if the jury were to believe that an
employer's sexual harassment of other female employees made it more
likely that an employer viewed his female workers as sexual objects, and
that, in turn, convinced the jury that an employer was more likely to fire
an employee in retaliation for her refusal of his sexual advances. There is
a direct link between the issue before the jury—the employer's motive
behind firing the plaintiff—and the factor on which the jury's decision is
based—the employer's harassment of other female employees.

The district court can limit the potential unfair prejudice that may result
if the jury allows the employer's sexual harassment of other female
employees to influence its decision on whether the employer sexually
propositioned the employee. The district court may provide safeguards,
such as a limiting jury instruction to the effect that the sexual harassment
testimony is to considered only for the determination of the employer's
motive.

* * *

The district court abused its discretion by refusing to allow Heyne to
introduce testimony of Caruso's other female employees who claimed to

have been sexually harassed by him. Such testimony would have affected the jury's determination of whether Heyne's dismissal was motivated by a nondiscriminatory reason, her tardiness, or for a forbidden reason, her rejection of Caruso's sexual advances. The exclusion of such evidence tainted the verdict in light of the apparent closeness of the decision.

*   *   *

Heyne does not challenge the exclusion of the NERC investigative report but limits her appeal to the districts court's exclusion of the NERC probable cause finding. Heyne notified the district court, prior to trial, of her intent to introduce the NERC probable cause finding in evidence. The district court's awareness of Heyne's intent is evidenced by the court's pre-trial discussion with Heyne's counsel regarding the admissibility of the probable cause finding. Therefore, we conclude that Heyne made an offer of proof for the probable cause finding.

Id. at 1479–82 (footnote omitted).

*   *Cf.* Biggs v. Nicewonger Co., Inc., 897 F. Supp. 483 (D. Or. 1995). A former employee brought a Title VII action against former employer and supervisor alleging sexual harassment, retaliatory discharge, as well as an intentional infliction of emotional distress claim under Oregon law. The defendants moved the court for an order precluding Biggs from offering evidence of acts of sexual harassment or discrimination not witnessed by Biggs or related to her during her employment on the grounds that such evidence was irrelevant and prejudicial. The court held that evidence as to alleged incidents of sexual harassment to which Biggs had knowledge was admissible, but that evidence relating to alleged incidents of sexual harassment not witnessed by Biggs or not related to her while she was on the job was not relevant to prove a hostile work environment in this case.

Page 268, add to footnote 244:

See also Longmire v. Alabama State Univ., 151 F.R.D. 414 (M.D. Ala. 1992).

Page 268, add to footnote 246:

See also Webb v. Hyman, 861 F. Supp. 1094 (D.D.C. 1994). The court's admission of evidence of prior bad acts did not warrant a new trial.

Consonant with exceptions for notice, motive, and intent, three women were allowed to testify regarding events that took place within the past few years of the misconduct alleged in this case. Despite the District's contentions, the testimony each of them gave at trial was highly probative and relevant. Rather than being admitted for the purpose of propensity, Ms. Johnson's testimony provided direct evidence of a contemporaneous hostile environment regarding preferential treatment toward attractive women. Similarly, Ms. Washington's testimony concerned substantially similar behavior when compared with those acts alleged by Ms. Webb as well as contemporaneous harassment, thus pertaining both to intent as well as to a hostile working environment. Likewise, Ms. Bonds testified that Paylor recently treated her in a substantially similar way to that of Ms. Webb.

*   *   *

[P]erhaps most importantly, the Court anticipated and addressed the 404(b) and 403 issues through a limiting instruction, minimizing any prejudice by informing the Jury that the testimony of Officer Sharon Bonds and Ms. Teresa Washington "is offered only to show Mr. Paylor's motive or intent, and that the District of Columbia *may* have had prior notice of sexual harassment in the Department of Corrections. . . . This instruction was given both during the trial, *and* during the jury charge. . . .

In addition, several of the defense witnesses testified to the effect that Paylor did not commit the tortious and discriminatory acts charged. The testimony regarding Paylor's prior conduct allowed the Plaintiff the opportunity to present evidence of prior inconsistent behavior with the testimony of the defense witnesses.

Id. at 1111, 1112.

Page 269, add to footnote 249:

Fore v. Health Dimensions, Inc., 509 N.W.2d 557 (Minn. Ct. App. 1993). In a sexual harassment action by a female employee, who introduced evidence that three other women had experienced incidents with the supervisor, the district court properly declined to impute knowledge of the acts to the employer, who would thus have had an obligation to act before the plaintiff was harassed, when the district court found that a supervisor's conduct with the three other women did not amount to sexual harassment. The statutory scheme is remedial, not preventative; an employer has no duty to maintain a pristine work environment.

§ 6.34   EVIDENCE OF OTHER EMPLOYEES

Page 270, add to footnote 251:

Janopoulos v. Harvey L. Walner & Assocs., 866 F. Supp. 1086 (N.D. Ill. 1994). Testimony about coworkers' prior complaints against the employer and the employer's prior behavior toward coworkers was not considered necessary background for the coworkers' testimony about the employer's conduct toward the plaintiff so as to warrant circumventing the rule prohibiting inadmissible character evidence. Coworkers had complained about the alleged harasser to the plaintiff and thus was hearsay. Plaintiff also failed to lay a proper foundation for the evidence by establishing that the testimony about the alleged harassment of other employees would implicate the plaintiff's work environment. Unlike other cases in which testimony about a superior's previous behavior has been admitted to establish that an environment was hostile, the plaintiff here did not allege that a manager sexually harassed her and that the employer was aware of the harassment but failed to intervene; rather the plaintiff was suing the employer as the alter ego of his firm and alleged that the employer himself harassed here. "Thus, there is no issue here whether an employer was aware that one of its employees was engaging in ongoing harassment yet failed to intervene. Accordingly, Janopoulos fails to demonstrate how testimony about other women Walner allegedly harassed would be relevant to her claims." *Id.* at 1092 (footnote omitted).

Longmire v. Alabama State Univ., 151 F.R.D. 414 (M.D. Ala. 1992). A university employee who brought an action against the former president and the university could discover evidence of the president's other sexual activities with women at the university, but not with women at another university. The court noted that this ruling was based on the present state of the record; if the plaintiff had actual evidence, not argument, which would establish a good faith basis for the inquiry about the president's sexual activity at places other than this university and some relevance to this inquiry, the plaintiff could make an ex parte motion under seal requesting that the court allow such inquiry.

Page 270, add to footnote 252:

*   Hirase-Doi v. U.S. West Communications, Inc., 61 F.3d 777 (10th Cir. 1995). The court found that there was a genuine issue as to whether the defendant knew or should have known of a supervisor's harassing conduct based on the alleged overall pervasiveness of the conduct. A female employee brought an action against her employer and a male coworker

(Coleman) alleging hostile work environment sexual harassment in violation of Title VII and claims under Utah law against the employer for failure to adequately train, supervise, or control and for intentional infliction of emotional distress. The coworker's remarks included persistent requests for sex and inquiries of their sexual conduct. He also reportedly made open-ended invitations to all female employees to satisfy his sexual desires. The training supervisor informed Coleman that his conduct was inappropriate and could be construed as sexual harassment. Despite this warning, Coleman continued to make sexually offensive comments and overtures to female employees. Again, the training supervisor advised Coleman to refrain from such conduct, but his continued sexual overtures and innuendos caused the supervisor to conclude that Coleman had not taken her warnings seriously. Coleman continued to work as a directory assistance operator in an unsupervised area and engaged in sexually offensive behavior towards numerous other women in the area; he subjected one employee to comments, winking, and staring with possible sexual overtones, and the employee reported the behavior to her union representative, in accordance with a written U.S. West policy for reporting such conduct.

The court rejected the defendant's argument that the plaintiff could not solely rely on Coleman's harassment of other workers to establish a hostile work environment for herself. The court had resolved that issue to the contrary in *Hicks v. Gates Rubber Co.*, 833 F.2d 1406 (10th Cir. 1987). The plaintiff had provided evidence that she herself was subject to harassment by Coleman, and thus she could rely on Coleman's harassment of others to the extent that it affected her general work atmosphere, but she could only rely on evidence relating to harassment of which she was aware during the time that she was allegedly subject to a hostile work environment. Because it was undisputed that Coleman was neither acting within the scope of his employment nor acting or purporting to act as U.S. West's agent in committing the alleged acts of sexual harassment, in order to prove her claim against U.S. West, the plaintiff had to prove that U.S. West was negligent or reckless. The court concluded that U.S. West could be put on notice if it knew that the perpetrator had practiced widespread sexual harassment in the office place, even though U.S. West may not have known that this particular plaintiff was one of the perpetrator's victims. Thus the plaintiff could rely on U.S. West's notice of any evidence of sexual harassment by Coleman that was similar in nature and near in time to his sexual harassment of the plaintiff in order to raise a genuine issue of material fact as to whether U.S. West knew or should have known of Coleman's conduct. The court found that there was a genuine issue as to whether U.S. West knew or should have known of Coleman's conduct based on the alleged overall pervasiveness of that conduct, involving perhaps as many as 8–10 employees. Statements to a union vice president also could constitute notice to U.S. West under U.S. West's published employee policy manual. U.S. West's designation of union representatives to receive complaints was described as part of the company's internal review procedure, and the manual explicitly differentiated that from external entities to whom complaints could also be directed.

Cf. Schweitzer-Reschke v. Avnet, Inc., 881 F. Supp. 530 (D. Kan. 1995). The district court properly granted summary judgment for the defendants in an action by a former employee against her employer and supervisor for sexual harassment, constructive discharge, and negligent infliction of emotional distress. Evidence that the supervisor had a reputation of being a male chauvinist was inadmissible to prove intent to discriminate; the plaintiff did not cite any case authorizing the use of character evidence in the form of testimony concerning reputation to prove intent or motive to discriminate, and absent controlling authority to the contrary, the court would not read into Rule 404(b) a "narrow and specifically considered exception allowing for the use of evidence of specific acts, a channel for the admissibility of reputation evidence," as to do so would "so narrow the gap with the prohibition of character evidence to show conformity contained in Rule 404(a), that it would virtually disappear." *Id.* at 533.

§ 6.35   Testimony

Page 271, add to footnote 255 following "EEOC Policy" citation:

Fifth Circuit: Cuesta v. Texas Dep't of Criminal Justice, 805 F. Supp. 451 (W.D. Tex. 1991). The court found sexual harassment in an action by a female parole case worker against the parole officer and parole board. Although the defendant presented many credible witnesses who asserted that there was not a hostile environment toward all the female coworkers at this office, these witnesses could not testify as to what happened in private to the plaintiff or other targets of abuse. There was evidence that the parole officer "chose his victims carefully, seeking those women who were vulnerable and not likely to fight back." *Id.* at 456.

Page 271, add at end of footnote 255:

Kelly-Zurian v. Wohl Shoe Co., 22 Cal. App. 4th 397, 27 Cal. Rptr. 2d 457, 64 Fair Empl. Prac. Cas. (BNA) 603 (1994) (sexual harassment, constructive wrongful discharge, intentional infliction of emotional distress). The plaintiff's testimony was corroborated by other employees.

§ 6.36   Credibility of Witnesses

Page 272, add to footnote 259:

Hostility on the part of the alleged harasser may be implicating as well. Cuesta v. Texas Dep't of Criminal Justice, 805 F. Supp. 451 (W.D. Tex. 1991). The court found sexual harassment in an action by a female parole case worker against the parole officer and parole board. The court could not grant credibility to much of the parole officer's testimony when his demeanor was defensive and evasive, he made blanket denials of any harassment or improper interview questions, and he contradicted his own witnesses when he denied that, as a result of complaints about his interview techniques, the personnel office instructed him to have a third party present when he conducted interviews, or that he was insulted by this requirement. The court also noted that when confronted with discrepancies between his testimony and that of the plaintiff, he launched into an "improbable" conspiracy theory, "charging that a host of people—including some hitherto unrelated to the case—were plotting his downfall." *Id.* at 455.

§ 6.38   Expert Witnesses

Page 273, add to footnote 265:

Martin v. Cavalier Hotel Corp., 48 F.3d 1343 (4th Cir. 1995). Testimony regarding the plaintiff's psychological symptoms and personality traits were properly admitted when the district court specifically prohibited the plaintiff's experts from offering their opinions as to the plaintiff's truthfulness or the alleged harasser's guilt; the experts testified only that the plaintiff's personality was such that she might be an "easy victim" and that her symptoms were consistent with those of someone who had been sexually assaulted.

*

§ 6.39   Agency Records

Page 276, add to footnote 271:

E.E.O.C. v. Regency Architectural Metals Corp., 896 F. Supp. 260 (D. Conn. 1995). The Equal Employment Opportunity Commission (EEOC) and a female union member, Hodge, filed an action alleging sex discrimination and Title VII violations against her former employer, successor employer, union local, and international union, alleging that Hodge's employer, defendant Regency Architectural Metals Corp; knowingly assigned a male employee who was awaiting trial for allegedly raping Hodge to work beside her on two occasions, leading her to quit her employment. The plaintiffs also alleged that Hodge's union failed to represent Hodge in her efforts to challenge Regency's acts of alleged sexual harassment. Finally, the plaintiffs alleged that the union denied Hodge representation in her efforts to bring union charges against three members of the Local chapter, including the alleged rapist. The EEOC's determinations were given no weight, when they consisted largely of brief factual assertions which were the subject of testimony at the trial, and legal reasoning, which was the province of the court. There also was no foundation from the plaintiffs as to how the information in the determination was complied.

§ 6.40   Administrative Decisions

Page 277, add to footnote 277:

Cf. Heyne v. Caruso, 69 F.3d 1475 (9th Cir. 1995). The district court improperly excluded from evidence a probable cause finding of the Nevada Equal Rights Commission, and the error was not cured by mentioning the finding in jury instructions. The defendant's attempt to distinguish the reports of the NERC from the EEOC was not persuasive because whether information gathered for purposes of a probable cause determination was kept confidential did not affect the probative or prejudicial effect of introducing a finding of probable cause itself at trial. In the alternative, the defendant argued that section 233.190 of the state's law prohibited the plaintiff from receiving the investigative report in the first place, and thus, the report must be excluded from evidence. However, section 233.190 states that the report must be kept confidential until the NERC has determined to conduct a hearing on the matter. Once the NERC has determined to conduct a hearing on the matter, the report is no longer confidential, and section 233.190 does not state that the evidence collected for the hearing regains its confidentiality if the hearing is ultimately canceled.

Garrison v. State of Maryland, Great Oaks Ctr., 850 F. Supp. 366 (D. Md. 1994). A pro se plaintiff who brought a Title VII action claiming that she suffered discrimination because she was charged with sexual harassment and not given an opportunity to defend herself did not present a genuine issue for trial so as to preclude summary judgment for the employer. The EEOC had found no facts that even remotely suggested discrimination. Late filings by the defendants were excusable when at the time the complaint was filed and served, the plaintiff was still an employee and actively pursuing separate grievance proceedings involving the underlying incidents and the defendants reasonably could have believed that the complaint was related to the personnel action.

* *Page 277, add to footnote 281:*

Hartsell v. Duplex Products, Inc., 895 F. Supp. 100 (W.D.N.C. 1995). On the employer's motion to strike references in the plaintiff's answer to the employer's motion for summary judgment to testimony from an Employment Security Commission (ESC) hearing as absolutely privileged, the court held that North Carolina's statutory privilege protecting testimony from disclosure in any civil or criminal proceeding applied to the employee's Title VII sexual harassment claim against her employer. The ESC privilege encouraged full disclosure from unemployment benefits claimants and employers at hearings and prevented parties from conducting free discovery before litigation. The testimony offered little to justify its admission and expecting the jury to ignore the challenged testimony in considering state claims while considering the same testimony in assessing the Title VII claim was unrealistic. North Carolina distinguished ESC hearings and civil trials as distinct proceedings such that ESC hearings did not investigate Title VII allegations and ESC participants did not expect their testimony to appear later in subsequent federal Title VII proceedings. State law determines evidentiary privileges that apply to state law claims litigated in federal court, and thus state claims of intentional infliction of emotional distress and of negligent retention would be striken.

§ 6.43   Prima Facie *Quid Pro Quo* Case

Page 279, add to footnote 293 following "First Circuit":

EEOC v. Horizons Hotel Corp., 831 F. Supp. 10 (D.P.R. 1993). In an action by the EEOC on behalf of a former hotel restaurant cashier, the court found that the hotel's night auditor sexually harassed the cashier by subjecting her to a steady stream of comments about her body, almost on a daily basis, and invitations to his hotel room on at least two occasions. The plaintiff had complained on several occasions and was ultimately discharged by the director of personnel (the daughter of the alleged harasser). The plaintiff established that the rejection of harassment resulted in a tangible job detriment when the alleged harasser wrote a report alleging that the plaintiff was not performing her cashier duties adequately; at trial the defendant was unable to pinpoint a single instance of the plaintiff's committing any error in the restaurant logs prior to the day when the defendant asked her to approach him to discuss a mistake in her log. "This evidence, or better stated—lack thereof, thus, makes it more likely than not that [the defendant's] allegation that he wanted to discuss an error with plaintiff was merely a subterfuge to further harass her." *Id.* at 14. The employer was strictly liable for this quid pro quo harassment, despite the alleged harasser's contention that he lacked a supervisory role at the defendant's restaurant, when the auditor's influence in the plaintiff's discharge de facto led to the opposite conclusion. In addition, the defendant was also liable for failing to address complaints by the plaintiff concerning the auditor's conduct.

Page 279, add to footnote 293 following "Second Circuit":

Saulpaugh v. Monroe Community Hosp., 4 F.3d 134 (2d Cir. 1993), *cert. denied*, 114 S. Ct. 1189 (1994). The district court properly found that a public hospital employee who was subjected to sexual advances by her supervisor, and then was threatened and berated by him when she complained, was subjected to quid pro quo sexual harassment under Title VII. The court properly dismissed her First Amendment claim because the plaintiff's complaints were personal in nature and generally related to her own situation rather than matters of public concern, but the plaintiff's assertions that the defendant deprived her of both a property and a liberty interest without due process were sufficient to survive defendants' motion to dismiss.

Bridges v. Eastman Kodak Co., 885 F. Supp. 495 (S.D.N.Y. 1995). Quid pro quo sexual harassment does not require explicit sexual overtures; the crucial point is the exchange of job benefits for the toleration of the sexual harassment.

Cf. Donato v. Rockefeller Fin. Servs., 65 Fair Empl. Prac. Cas. (BNA) 1722 (S.D.N.Y. 1994). A female employee alleged that a coworker made a motion with his mouth, tongue, and lips simulating oral sex, on several occasions left notes on her desk commenting on her appearance, gave her a neck massage, once told her on the phone that he had heard she was a pro, and another time told her that he was at the airport with his pants down. She could not, however, make out a claim for quid pro quo sexual harassment, because the coworker had no supervisory authority over her and she did not claim that her job conditions were altered or that an economic benefit was conditioned on or withheld because she refused to submit to sexual demands. The plaintiff's retaliation claim, however, would not be dismissed as a matter of law because the defendant did not demonstrate legitimate, nondiscriminatory reasons for allegedly taking accounts away from the plaintiff, changing her hours, and giving her a poor performance review and distasteful job assignment.

Zvelter v. Brazilian Nat'l Superintendency of Merchant Marine, 833 F. Supp. 1089 (S.D.N.Y. 1993). Evidence supporting allegations of discriminatory retaliation in the form of a warning, after the plaintiff was propositioned, physically groped, and verbally harassed, that her failure to "play the game" would jeopardize her employment created a genuine issue of material fact regarding quid pro quo sexual harassment.

Cf. Johnson v. Tower Air, Inc., 149 F.R.D. 461 (E.D.N.Y. 1993). A former flight attendant trainee did not proffer evidence sufficient to support quid pro quo or hostile environment sexual harassment claims in an action charging that the plaintiff's supervisor made sexual advances and brushed up against plaintiff, on another occasion grabbed his crotch and shouted derogatory comments to the plaintiff, and during a two-week period made several other offensive gestures or comments. With respect to the claim of quid pro quo harassment, she did not submit proof that her rejection of sexual advances resulted in a supervisor's report that she was not seated in her "jump seat" as required by the FAA and Tower safety requirements and she admitted that she was not so seated. Nor did the plaintiff show that improper reasons caused her employer to deny her any condition of employment to which she was entitled.

Page 279, add to footnote 293 following Second Circuit case:

Fifth Circuit: Walker v. MacFrugals Bargains, 66 Fair Empl. Prac. Cas. (BNA) 1085 (E.D. La. 1994). An employer was not entitled to summary judgment on a quid pro quo claim of sexual harassment by an employee with whom a supervisor [Ybarra] had had a consensual relationship. When Ybarra repeatedly tried to resume the relationship and was rejected, his question provoked an angry, negative response from the plaintiff, to which Ybarra responded, "Bitch if that is the way you want it, you can have it your way." *Id.* at 1087. Over the course of the following week, Ybarra repeatedly criticized the plaintiff about her performance at work, and upset, the plaintiff told Ybarra that she was quitting and left work. Ybarra called the plaintiff that evening and apologized for his behavior earlier in the day. He also suggested that she make an appointment with the general manager and ask to be reinstated. The plaintiff met with the general manager, and during the meeting she complained that she and Ybarra had personality conflicts and disagreed over how best to complete their work duties. The plaintiff, however, did not inform the general manager about her personal relationship with Ybarra or about the incidents occurring after their relationship had been terminated. At the plaintiff's suggestion, the general manager agreed to hire additional personnel to assist the plaintiff and Ybarra and reassign some of the plaintiff's duties to Ybarra. After the plaintiff returned to work, Ybarra's sexual advances toward her temporarily ceased, and over the next several months, the plaintiff learned through gossip and her own observations that Ybarra was harassing two other women. The plaintiff also overheard Ybarra and other male supervisors gossiping about and criticizing the two women. Ybarra renewed his efforts to resume a sexual relationship with the plaintiff and numerous, unsolicited advances took the following forms:

(1) lewd comments about Walker's appearance and clothing; (2) benign oral requests to renew the relationship; (3) sexually explicit oral requests

to resume the relationship; (4) oral threats that "life could be made difficult" at work for Walker if his requests were not honored; (5) sexually explicit descriptions of how Walker could honor his requests to resume the relationship; (6) beginning work-place rumors that Walker was intimately involved with another supervisor; (7) unsolicited touching; and (8) harassing phone calls to Walker's home.

Id. at 1088. The plaintiff rejected Ybarra's advances and complained to the assistant general manager about rumors Ybarra had started. She did not disclose Ybarra's other conduct. After he was confronted by the assistant general manager, Ybarra threatened to reveal their affair, and shortly thereafter, the assistant general manager made some comments to the plaintiff that she interpreted as meaning that he would transfer her from under the supervision of Ybarra if she started seeing the general manager. The plaintiff resigned the following day. The court rejected the defendant's contention that it was entitled to summary judgment because the undisputed facts demonstrated that the plaintiff was never denied a tangible job benefit and never suffered a tangible job detriment as a result of the supervisor's alleged harassment:

> While it is true that plaintiff's refusal to resume a consensual relationship with Ybarra did not lead to poor performance reviews, lost pay raises, or formal discipline, . . . it is undisputed that plaintiff's resistance led Ybarra to criticize her performance, verbally reprimand her, threaten to "make her life at work difficult," and threaten to expose her extra-marital relationship to her husband. . . . By threatening to make plaintiff's life at work "more difficult" if she did not capitulate to his demands, Ybarra was explicitly stating that he intended to change plaintiff's working conditions for the worse in the event she continued to refuse his requests to resume their relationship. In those instances when Ybarra was not explicit in his demands and was merely hostile, it was implicit that plaintiff's capitulation would have evoked an altogether more pleasant work environment. . . . As such, Ybarra clearly linked the acceptance or rejection of his harassment to Walker's working conditions.

Id. at 1089. The plaintiff could use the assistant general manager's conduct as proof of a hostile environment. Although taken alone his conduct might well be insufficient to serve as the basis of a hostile environment claim under Title VII, the focus of plaintiff's claim was on whether she was subjected to recurring acts of discrimination, not whether a given individual harassed her recurrently. The absence of formal or informal notice did not automatically insulate the defendant from liability. That Ybarra was subjected to some mild form of discipline after the women employees either formally or informally complained did not alter the fact that Ybarra continued his conduct unabated.

Sixth Circuit: Wilson v. Wayne County, 856 F. Supp. 1254 (M.D. Tenn. 1994). This Title VII sexual harassment and retaliatory discharge action was brought by a former dispatcher, the alleged victim of discrimination, and a male coworker deputy sheriff who alleged that he was fired for opposing the harassment. The court found that the female plaintiff was subjected to quid pro quo and hostile environment harassment when her supervisor lured the plaintiff into his office in the dead of night, locking off her only route of escape, fondled her, placed her hand on his crotch, and pulled her to the floor and penetrated her. The fact that the 18-year-old plaintiff wore shorts during the summer months, wore a bathing suit on a canoe trip, and engaged in nonsexual horseplay with a coworker her own age should not be perceived by a 53-year-old man as a willingness to have sex with him. The supervisor also called the plaintiff into his office for sex right after she asked if she could stay on as a dispatcher in the fall. The condition of sex for continued employment need not be explicit:

> Ms. Wilson admits that the sheriff never explicitly offered her continued employment in exchange for sexual favors. In fact, her lawyer disclaims that Ms. Wilson even understood that the sheriff might be conditioning her continued employment on what would happen on the floor of his office. The Court, however, concludes that these points are irrelevant. According to the United States Court of Appeals for the Sixth Circuit, a plaintiff may prove quid pro quo harassment by showing that submission to unwelcome sexual advances was "an express *or implied* condition for receiving job benefits." [Highlander v. K.F.C. Nat'l Management Co., 805 F.2d 644, 648 (6th Cir. 1986)] . . . Ms. Wilson may have not realized what the conditions were for her to stay on as a dispatcher, but this Court is not so naive.

Id. at 1260. The male plaintiff proved retaliation for his opposing the sheriff's harassment of the female plaintiff. Among the actions he took in opposition to the harassment were the following: he notified an assistant district attorney of the female plaintiff's allegations, obtained a rape detection kit, contacted a sheriff's department sergeant, took the female plaintiff to the hospital for examination, and testified before the county grand jury. The court rejected as pure pretext the sheriff's explanation that he laid off the plaintiff because of budget restrictions, when the plaintiff was the only employee laid off that summer and another employee was hired within a month. The case was dismissed, however, because Title VII does not allow actions against individual defendants in their individual capacities.

Page 279, add to footnote 293 following "Seventh Circuit":

Bristow v. Drake St. Inc., 41 F.3d 345 (7th Cir. 1994). A female associate producer of a play alleged that when she terminated a sexual relationship with the producer, and until he ultimately fired her, he subjected her to a protracted series of outrages that included firing her between 12 and 40 times and promptly rehiring her, yelling at her, following her around work, stalking her during nonworking hours, banging on the door of her apartment late at night, calling her 10 to 30 times a night and leaving messages on her answering machine that he hated her and wished her dead. She did not demonstrate, though, that the producer closed the show for the purpose of discharging her. The district court concluded that the producer had such strong financial reasons for closing the show that he would have done so even absent his hostility toward the plaintiff. Although the district court did not place the burden of persuasion on the employer to show that he would have fired the employee even if there had been no discriminatory motive, and thus did not apply the test of *Price Waterhouse*, reversal was not warranted:

> Burdens of persuasion affect the outcomes only of cases in which the trier of fact thinks the plaintiff's and the defendant's positions equiprobable. Burdens of persuasion are, in other words, tie-breakers. If the trier of fact, having heard all the evidence, comes to a definite conclusion, [she or] he has no occasion to invoke a burden of persuasion. Judge Zagel thought that Powers would not have closed the show for nonfinancial reasons. For Powers was not only the producer; he was the playwright. Vanity alone would have made it unlikely that he would close his own show merely to get back at Bristow. He would be cutting off his nose to spite his face, as Judge Zagel put it. If this is what the judge believed, he would have believed it whether or not he had ever heard of *Price Waterhouse*. The doctrine of that case, we repeat, is designed for the situation in which the trier of fact cannot figure out what would have happened had the unlawful motive been absent.

*   *   *

"[C]lose the show and fire Bristow." But these are distinct acts. One can imagine Power's closing the show only because it was losing, but breaking his contract with Bristow because of her refusal to have sex with him. (After all, she recorded a phone conversation, six months before her last firing, in which he told her, "I'm firing you for not fucking me, period.") But she has not tried to separate these issues, save as regards the post-closing employment. She seems to concede that if Powers closed the show purely for financial reasons, he fired her for the same reasons. Which makes sense. If he was unwilling to pay to keep the show open, he was unlikely to be willing to pay her $1,300 a week for another twenty months, which would come to more than $100,000, especially if he believed that the contract entitled him to terminate her in these circumstances without liability. He might well have fired her even if he had not closed the show; but under *Price Waterhouse*, a plaintiff cannot obtain damages if the trier of fact is convinced that even if sex had played no role in the decision to fire her (however large a role it played in fact), she would have been fired; for she has suffered no harm by reason of sex that she would have not have suffered anyway.

*   *   *

Bristow had the burden of persuading the judge that sex was a, not necessarily the, motive for closing the show (had "*any* role in the decision to close the show"). Because she had the burden of persuasion on the question whether sex was a motive, the determination that the evidence was in equipoise doomed her case. Only if she had shown that sex was a motive would the burden have shifted to the defendant to show that, even so, she was not harmed, because she would have been fired even if the unlawful motive had been absent. If the evidence on *that* issue had been in equipoise, she would have been entitled to a judgment; but that issue could not even arise unless and until she showed that sex was one motive; the judge held that it was no motive. So this is not even a mixed-motives case, and the issue of causality does not arise.

Id. at 353, 354–55.

Johnson v. Indopco, Inc., 846 F. Supp. 670 (N.D. Ill. 1994). A former employee stated a cause of action against her employer for quid pro quo sexual harassment when she alleged that, prior to her termination and on two separate occasions, her supervisor asked her to convince him that she should be hired, and one of those requests came after taking the plaintiff to his apartment under false pretense. While at the apartment, the supervisor suggested that if the plaintiff opened up to him he was sure she would advance at the company and that he could do a lot for her. These actions were construed in light of his other sexually suggestive inquiries and braggadocio. Damages, available under the Civil Rights Act of 1991, were not barred by the state workers' compensation.

Page 279, in footnote 293, add to "Saxton" citation:

The Seventh Circuit affirmed, Saxton v. American Tel. & Tel. Co., 10 F.3d 526 (7th Cir. 1993), noting that under *Harris*, a court must consider not only the effect the discriminatory conduct actually had on the plaintiff, but also the impact it likely would have had on a reasonable employee in her position. Here the alleged harasser's offensive behavior was relatively limited, presumably because the plaintiff "was forthright and persistent in making clear that the advances were unwelcome." *Id.* at 534.

Page 280, add to footnote 293 following Seventh Circuit cases:

Tenth Circuit: Noland v. McAdoo, 39 F.3d 269 (10th Cir. 1994). A female employee alleged that a coworker made sexual advances during the time he was a fellow employee in the county office and that later, after he was appointed county assessor (and therefore the plaintiff's supervisor), he eventually terminated her as a result of her rejection of his sexual advances. These claims created a genuine issue of material fact concerning whether the defendant subjected her to sexual harassment, as did testimony that, during the years she worked with the defendant, he would invite her out, buy her gifts, touch her, tell her he loved her, and block her way so that she would have to rub up against him to get by. The district court properly dismissed a § 1983 claim against the assistant district attorney defendant, which alleged that he had deprived her of a liberty interest in her reputation without benefit of due process when he told a reporter, who later published the remarks in a local newspaper, that the plaintiff was a whore and a barfly. Although the attorney admitted making these statements 20 days after the plaintiff's termination, in response to questions about sexual harassment charges against the county assessor by the plaintiff, the plaintiff failed to establish a sufficient nexus between the assistant district attorney's remarks and her termination.

§ 6.43   PRIMA FACIE QUID PRO QUO

Cf. Sauers v. Salt Lake County, 1 F.3d 1122 (10th Cir. 1993). A former secretary with the county attorney's office failed to establish a prima facie case of quid pro quo sexual harassment when the plaintiff offered no evidence that her supervisor made a sexual advance that the plaintiff rejected, other than a comment about swapping spit.

Page 280, add to footnote 293 following "Eleventh Circuit":

Virgo v. Riviera Beach Assocs., 30 F.3d 1350 (11th Cir. 1994). The district court did not err in finding constructive discharge and quid pro quo sexual harassment in an action by a female general manager of a hotel. She alleged that, over the course of her employment, she had been subjected to a sexually harassing course of conduct by a supervisor, who touched her without her permission and told her she would have to have sex with him or he would write disparaging job performance reviews; she eventually succumbed and then subsequently resigned because of the harassment. Even though the plaintiff resigned without filing a formal sexual harassment complaint, there was no showing of a formal grievance procedure, and the plaintiff attempted to notify several people about the harassment.

Splunge v. Shoney's, Inc., 874 F. Supp. 1258 (M.D. Ala. 1994). See § 6.44.

Hodges v. Gellerstedt, 833 F. Supp. 898 (M.D. Fla. 1993). A female employee stated claims for hostile environment and quid pro quo sexual harassment when she alleged that her supervisor offered her money and material goods for a sexual relationship and that, after she refused the harassment, continued through the display of sexual literature and sexual devices in the office in her presence and attempts to touch her.

Page 280, footnote 293, add to District of Columbia Circuits cases :

Cf. Ryczek v. Guest Servs., Inc., 877 F. Supp. 754 (D.D.C. 1995). A female former employee who brought a Title VII suit against her employer, alleging sexual harassment by her female supervisor, did not establish quid pro quo sexual harassment when the only relevant allegation involved a *belief* by the plaintiff that her evaluation would suffer if she did not submit to her supervisor's advances. She did not contend that she submitted to the sexual demands or that she received an unfavorable evaluation from her supervisor.

TRYING THE CASE

* *Page 280, add to footnote 296:*

Cf. Talada v. Int'l Serv. Sys., Inc., 899 F. Supp. 936 (N.D.N.Y. 1995). An employee and a former employee proved that they were subjected to quid pro quo and hostile environment sexual harassment. One plaintiff alleged that her supervisor on one occasion approached her directly, walked right up close to her, and immediately attempted to put his arms around her. He began touching her, placing one hand on her buttock. He made several comments to one plaintiff, claiming "I've been waiting a long time for this," telling her she had a "nice ass," and attempting to kiss her. She immediately pushed him away, stating, "Get the hell away from me." She finished the day's work at the side of a male coworker, and only after leaving for the day did she confide in him exactly what had transpired. About a month later, her supervisor approached her and stated, "I have something hard and nice for you," and reached for her, told her he could make her job easier with more days off. He attempted to kiss her and she told him to get away from her. She pushed the elevator button and fled to the ladies restroom on the first floor where she remained for some time. The other plaintiff alleged that the supervisor took her to an isolated telephone room, approached her and pressed her between the columns of wires, stating, "I have waited 13 years for this." He took her hand and put it against his penis, stating he had something "nice and hard" for her and that if she cooperated, he could arrange a deception allowing her shorter work hours while still receiving full wages. He attempted to unfasten her pants and continually handled her, putting his hands on her breasts and buttocks for approximately 15–20 minutes. He forced his tongue into her mouth and she bit his tongue, and forced her knee into his groin which enabled her to break free from her flanked and cornered position. The alleged harasser's conduct was resisted and reported by the plaintiffs. Talada even found it necessary to use physical force to manage escape from the treatment.

The court concluded that the "use of this supervisory power to effectually blackmail an employee into acting in a manner in which she otherwise would not, has been loathed from long before the enactment of these two Civil Rights Acts." *Id.* at 949. The court noted that the

> continued attempts of sexual conduct by Rice against both women, seemingly sanctioned through management's relative inaction and fellow supervisors' active support, undermined any sense of security held by these women. Management removed Rice from their work area and began an investigation which did not include interviews of the victims or their

associates. No disciplinary action was taken, and no recognition was granted of the incidents even occurring.

Id. at 951.

Page 281, add to footnote 300:

*   Hartleip v. McNeilab, Inc., 83 F.3d 767 (6th Cir. 1996). In an action by an employee against her former employer for sexual harassment in violation of Michigan civil rights law, for intentional infliction of emotional distress, and for breach of contract, the district court properly concluded that the plaintiff did not present evidence raising a genuine issue of fact regarding whether her rejection of Barnes's, a sales trainer, advances was used as a factor in decisions affecting her employment. Barnes started calling the plaintiff and sending her cards and messages after they met at a training session at company headquarters. The court found that apart from Barnes's cards, phone calls and/or messages, and a visit, Barnes did not personally engage in any other activities that Hartleip found to be of a harassing nature. The plaintiff did testify that she had been told that Barnes had sexual fantasies about her and another female employee. Hartleip also testified that she had been warned to be careful because Barnes might show up on her doorstep and that she was afraid of Barnes because she was told by another sales representative that Barnes had also harassed her. The other woman feared that Barnes would attempt to "blackmail" her by threatening to divulge information to the company about a romantic liaison she had allegedly had with a married man whom she met on a business trip. Hartleip's complaint expressly stated that Barnes's alleged harassment ceased "when the Anita Hill/Clarence Thomas hearings began" in 1991. The court found that because Hartleip conceded that Barnes never had supervisory authority over her, she could not argue that he was directly responsible for any employment decisions affecting her. But she did argue that because Barnes told her he was "close friends" with Gerald Bruce, who did have an impact on these decisions, an inference could be made that Barnes influenced Bruce and, presumably, that Barnes was therefore somehow responsible for the decisions.

> Hartleip did not notify her supervisor of Barnes' alleged harassment until after she had already resigned from McNeilab. Hartleip's failure to avail herself of the company policy for reporting the harassment weighs strongly against imposing liability on McNeilab.

* * *

> Hartleip argues that she told other employees—though not her supervisors—about the harassment. She apparently believes that this was sufficient to place the company on constructive notice and to require it to take remedial action. However, Hartleip's deposition testimony merely indicates that she told "some people"—presumably unidentified coworkers—about the harassment, and the testimony does not even indicate when she did so.

Id. at 776–77.

Johnson v. Plastic Packaging, Inc., 892 F.Supp. 25 (D. Mass. 1995). A genuine issue of material fact existed as to whether an employer could be liable for sexual harassment by a supervisory employee. The offensive conduct included the unwanted touching of Johnson's thighs and buttocks in the office of the head of the maintenance department, Caputo, when she delivered production reports to Caputo as required by her job duties. Caputo also made unwanted sexual advances while in a car with Johnson after they gave a sick employee a ride home, and repeatedly propositioned her, offering to Johnson a number of incentives, including opportunities to become friendlier with top management and to receive pay raises if Johnson were to become Caputo's lover. He also offered her cash and a car in exchange for sexual favors. Johnson alleged that these unwanted overtures were pervasive enough to alter the conditions of her job and establish a hostile work environment. The court rejected the defendant's argument that summary judgment was warranted because the plaintiff had not established a critical element of her claim: a basis for employer liability. The defendant blurred a distinction courts have made between the standards for determining employer liability in a coworker sexual harassment case and one involving a supervisor and an employee on a lower rung in the job hierarchy. Agency principles typically guide courts in drawing this distinction on a case-by-case basis. Caputo had let the plaintiff know that he had close ties to the company president and would be able to provide her with tangible job benefits if Johnson would provide him with sexual favors. She was required routinely to come into contact with Caputo and to provide him with information she collected in the course of her duties. Based upon Caputo's initiative and actual position of authority, management asked him to investigate allegations of Johnson's drug dealing that Caputo himself had raised. Caputo also exercised his authority by threatening to fire Johnson after she refused his sexual advances.

Menchaca v. Rose Records, 67 Fair Empl. Prac. Cas. (BNA) 1334 (N.D. Ill. 1995). A nonemployee who allegedly sexually harassed a cashier in a store by making sexual comments and attempting to grab her could not be held liable for quid pro quo sexual harassment when he could not grant or deny tangible benefits to her. A material factual issue existed as to whether the customer's harassment was sufficiently severe and pervasive to affect her employment when the jury could conclude that she occasionally was the only cashier on the floor and that she was a captive recipient of the customer's conduct. There was a dispute as to whether the customer's actions were not as abusive as the plaintiff characterized and that there was only one incident of harassment before an incident in which he picked up the plaintiff and dangled her by the ankles.

Thompson v. Berta Enter., Inc., 72 Wash. App. 531, 864 P.2d 983 (1994). An employer is strictly liable for quid pro quo sexual harassment perpetuated by supervisory personnel.

> Adopting this standard is sound public policy because it requires employers, who themselves have the power to hire and fire supervisory personnel to be responsible for insuring that those they cloak with apparent authority to affect terms and conditions of their employee's jobs do not abuse that authority. Therefore, it places the burden for preventing quid pro quo sexual harassment on those best situated to prevent it. We also believe this holding is consistent with the legislative mandate that RCW 49.60 be construed liberally to accomplish the purposes of the statute.

Id. at 987.

Page 282, add to footnote 301:

See also Gardinella v. General Elec. Co., 833 F. Supp. 617 (W.D. Ky. 1993). In a sexual harassment action brought by a male employee, alleging that his female direct supervisor discriminated against him because he refused to continue a sexual relationship with her, the court rejected the defendant's contention that because the plaintiff was male, the court should apply a modified version of the *McDonnell Douglas* test used by the circuit in reverse race discrimination cases brought under Title VII, *Murray v. Thistledown Racing Club, Inc.,* 770 F.2d 63 (6th Cir. 1985), under which a white plaintiff may establish a prima facie case of race discrimination by showing that background circumstances support the suspicion that the defendant is an unusual employer who discriminates against the majority, rather than the test of *Kauffman v. Allied Signal, Inc.*, 970 F.2d 178 (6th Cir.), *cert. denied*, 113 S. Ct. 831 (1992).

> *Murray* and *McDonnell Douglas* do not apply in quid pro quo sexual harassment cases. The *McDonnell Douglas* test was developed to allow a minority plaintiff to establish a *prima facie* case of discrimination without direct evidence of discriminatory intent by showing that [she or] he was treated differently than similarly situated nonminority employees, from which discrimination can be inferred. . . . The test must be altered in reverse discrimination cases because absent unusual circumstances, disparate treatment does not warrant an inference of discrimination against majority employees . . . .
>
> In a quid pro quo sexual harassment case a plaintiff does not seek to prove discrimination by inference, but by direct evidence of a supervisor's unwelcome sexual advances. Gardinella's sole burden in opposing summary judgment is to raise a genuine issue of material fact as to each [of] the *Kauffman* elements, which together constitute a statutory violation.
>
> *Kauffman's* requirement of membership in a "protected class" does not alter this analysis. "Any individual," male or female, is protected against sex discrimination in employment under the plain language of the Kentucky Civil Rights Act. . . . Requiring a male plaintiff who produces direct evidence of sex discrimination to jump through an additional hoop would derogate the clear intent of the statute.

833 F. Supp. at 620. The court also rejected the defendant's contention that the plaintiff could not show that the defendant took any adverse employment action against him because the defendant reduced his workload when he complained that he was overburdened, assigned him to a different supervisor when he first complained of harassment, gave him "light duty" work when he became physically unable to perform his normal duties, placed him on extended medical leave when suitable work was no longer available, held his position open through the date required by a contract with the union, and even now kept his name on a recall list so that he would be eligible for reemployment when physically able. This argument failed because the defendant relied on actions it took to remedy adverse employment conditions or job detriments already imposed upon the plaintiff by his supervisor, allegedly because he rebuffed her sexual advances. An employer's response after learning of

an employee's harassment may negate liability in a hostile environment case, but is not relevant under the quid pro quo theory.

Page 282, add to footnote 302:

Alphonse v. Omni Hotels Management Corp., 643 So. 2d 836 (La. Ct. App. 1994). The trial court properly found sexual harassment in an action by a former hotel employee who alleged that her supervisor ordered her to take meals with him at the hotel, take walks with him at lunch in the French Quarter, accompany him to hotel functions as his date, ride to and from work with him, and generally hold herself out as his "showpiece" until a point in time when his attitude changed and he began to berate her and assign her additional duties without additional pay or proper training. "Courts have consistently held that sexual harassment need not take the form of sexual advances or of other instances with sexual overtones." *Id.* at 839. The court rejected the defendant's argument that the supervisor managed by intimidation and screamed at all his employees, both male and female, when although no one witnessed the supervisor call the plaintiff a weak woman and make a comment about her menstrual cycle, the plaintiff testified that the incidents occurred, that she sought medical help because of her emotional distress and was ultimately forced to resign because of the harassment. The defendant did not offer any evidence to refute the allegations, and the court found the plaintiff's testimony to be credible and sufficient to establish her claims. The employer knew or should have known about the harassment because of the plaintiff's repeated attempts to report the offensive behavior. General damages of $85,000 and attorneys' fees of $16,500 were also proper.

Page 283, add to footnote 303:

Kopp v. Samaritan Health Sys., Inc., 13 F.3d 264 (8th Cir. 1993). See **§ 3.19.**

Bartlett v. United States, 835 F. Supp. 1246 (E.D. Wash. 1993). See **§ 3.19.**

Page 283, add to footnote 305:

Cf. Bedford v. Southeastern Pa. Transp. Auth., 867 F. Supp. 288 (E.D. Pa. 1994). A police officer who brought an action for sexual harassment, retaliatory discharge, and intentional infliction of emotional distress against the transit authority and a number of individuals stemming from an incident in which a SEPTA physician during a routine medical examination allegedly and unnecessarily placed a stethoscope under the plaintiff's brassiere and pressed his pelvic area against her buttocks while examining her back, did not state a claim for hostile environment harassment when although a single act of harassment may be sufficient to sustain a hostile environment claim if it is of such a nature and occurs in such circumstances that it may reasonably be said to characterize the atmosphere in which a plaintiff must work, the plaintiff here could not reasonably have perceived the encounter with the doctor and an exchange with an employee in the civil rights department, during which the plaintiff was told that nothing was going to happen to the doctor and that his reputation was at stake, as creating a hostile environment.

Page 283, add after "Nichols" citation in footnote 306:

aff'd, Nichols v. Frank, 42 F.3d 503 (9th Cir. 1994). The Ninth Circuit affirmed a finding of liability against the Postmaster General and the U.S. Postal Service and an award of back pay. The court agreed with the defendant that the district court applied the wrong test in holding the defendant liable for the supervisor's conduct with respect to the hostile environment claim, because the proper analysis is what management-level employees knew or should have known, not whether an employee was acting within the scope of employment; had the proper test been applied, the Postal Service could not have been held liable on a hostile environment theory. Nevertheless, the court still held the Postal Service liable for the supervisor's acts because the conduct constituted quid pro quo harassment in addition to the hostile environment harassment, and the Postal Service was liable for the supervisor's acts under the doctrine of respondeat superior. The plaintiff presented evidence that she was required to perform oral sex in order to obtain a two-week leave of absence, that her evaluations were sometimes conditioned on her willingness to perform the acts, that the supervisor conditioned her continued employment on such willingness, and that he asked her to perform oral sex after they had just discussed her sick leave and her attendance record.

The question of what constitutes sexual harassment is a complicated and increasingly important one in our society. There is no agreed upon definition of the newly popular term. In some versions, it appears to cover the widest possible range of sins, from physical assault to reading a magazine in a public facility. Whether particular conduct is appropriate or whether it crosses the line is the subject of disagreement and controversy, always heated and often legitimate. Public opinion can change rapidly. It is quite possible for conduct that is acceptable today to become unacceptable tomorrow. One's views are influenced by one's age, sex, national origin, religion, philosophy, education, and experience. There is no uniform attitude towards the role of sex nor any agreement on what is appropriate for inclusion in a code governing sexual conduct. Nevertheless, the right to be free from unwanted sexual attention is of fundamental importance, and answers to the relevant questions must be found. Nothing is more destructive of human dignity than being forced to perform sexual acts against one's will. Rape is still the ultimate violation. At the same time, unfounded charges, or charges based on misconceptions or misunderstanding, can wrongfully destroy careers, if not lives.

Workplace sexual harassment is a particularly complex and sensitive form of the genus. There are two competing concerns. On the one hand, courts are understandable reluctant to chill the incidence of legitimate romance. People who work closely together and share common interests often find that sexual attraction ensues. It is not surprising that those feelings arise when one of the persons is a superior and the other is a subordinate. As our workforce grows, and more and more of us find it necessary, or desirable, to earn our own living, we spend an increasing amount of our time at work. Sexual barriers to employment have lessened. We tend these days, far more than in earlier times, to find our friends, lovers, and even mates in the workplace. We spend longer hours at the office or traveling for job-related purposes, and often discover that our interests and values are closer to those of our colleagues than to those of people we meet in connection with other activities. In short, increased proximity breeds increased volitional sexual activity.

On the other hand, the opportunity to take unfair advantage of a co worker or subordinate has increased commensurately. Title VII embodies a most essential principle. It entitles individuals to a workplace that is free from the evil of sexual intimidation or repression. It is frequently difficult to reconcile the two competing values. In some cases, the difficulty arises shortly after an individual decides that he or she would like to explore the possibility of a romantic relationship with a co-worker. When does a healthy constructive interest in romance become sexual harassment? To what extent is pursuit of a co-worker proper but of a subordinate forbidden? Is wooing or courting a thing of the past? Must a suitor cease his attentions at the firm sign of disinterest or resistance? Must there be an express agreement before the person seeking romance may even hold the hand of the subject of his affection? Is it now verboten to steal a kiss? In the workplace? Everywhere? Under all circumstances or only some? Has the art of romantic persuasion lost its charm? Questions relating to love and sex are among the most difficult for society to answer—in or out of the workplace—and courts are hardly experts in that realm. Still, we must find ways to define sexual harassment, to protect potential victims against such conduct, and to enforce the rights of those who suffer injury; and we must do so with clarity, and understanding, and with wisdom.

Id. at 509–10. The court went on to define quid pro quo sexual harassment: "[W]e hold that quid pro quo sexual harassment occurs whenever an individual explicitly or implicitly conditions a job, a job benefit, or the absence of a job detriment, upon an employee's acceptance of sexual conduct." *Id.* at 511. The conclusion may be reached in two ways: one is the application of an objective standard, under which the court determines what would be the view of a reasonable person (using a hypothetical woman if the accuser is a woman, and a hypothetical man if the accuser is a man). The court noted that a reasonable person is not defined only by her or his sex. "Other immutable traits possessed by the person bringing the charge, including but not limited to race, age, physical or mental disability, and sexual orientation, may in particular cases be relevant to the inquiry as well." *Id.* at 512. In the alternative, the court can apply a subjective standard, under which the factfinder may inquire into whether the alleged harasser actually intended to subject the accuser to quid pro quo sexual harassment.

> Under this approach also, it is proper for the fact-finder to consider the fundamental or immutable characteristics of the individual bringing the charge. But here, in addition, the fact-finder may consider other individual traits or characteristics known to the accused that may make the victim especially or uniquely susceptible to quid pro quo sexual harassment. A defendant may be liable under the subjective test if he intentionally takes advantage of some particular fear or weakness that afflicts the accuser. By the same token, characteristics of and information about the accused which are known to the accuser may become part of the mix. A showing that either the subjective or objective standard is met is sufficient to support the imposition of liability.

Id. The court noted that difficult factual and legal questions arise whenever either the conditioning of benefits (or absence of detriment) or the request for sexual favors is not explicit, but rather implicit in the alleged harasser's communications or dealings with the employee.

For example, quid pro quo harassment is clear if a manager explicitly tells his subordinate "I will fire you unless you sleep with me." However, it is much less clear whether a violation has occurred if a manager simply asks the subordinate whether she would like to have a drink after work to talk about a possible promotion and then sometime after she refuses, awards the position to another employee. It is even less clear if the manager merely invites the employee out for a drink on one or more occasions but does not suggest that he wishes to discuss work-related matters; if the manager is spurned and subsequently withholds anticipated benefits, it may set off alarm bells, but further evidence would be required before a charge of sexual harassment could be sustained.

Harassment in cases of implicit conditioning can be inferred only from the particular facts and circumstances of the case. We must examine each such charge with the utmost care, for an error either way can result in a gross injustice and will often have a disastrous impact on the life of whichever person is truly the injured party.

The ability to identify implicit quid pro quo harassment accurately is important for two very different reasons. We have already mentioned the first: the possibility that the charge is erroneous or the result of a misunderstanding, and the disastrous consequences that may befall an innocent person. The second involves precisely the opposite concern. Implicit quid pro quo harassment is a most serious matter. It is far more likely to take place than is the explicit variety. As time goes by and harassers learn that they can no longer victimize their prey at will, their actions become less overt. . . .

In attempting to determine whether implicit quid pro quo harassment has occurred, the key is often the verbal nexus. That is one way of establishing a violation. The tighter the nexus between a discussion about job benefits and a request for sexual favors, the more likely that there has been an "implicit" conditioning by the harasser. However, each case differs, and no rule or set of rules will provide an answer in all circumstances. Five-part, seven-part or even ten-part tests frequently serve only to obfuscate the real inquiry. In truth, there is no substitute for a rigorous examination in each instance of all of the relevant facts and circumstances, as well as the application of common sense, sound general principles, and a true understanding of human nature.

Id. at 12–13. The court had no difficulty finding that the plaintiff here was subjected to quid pro quo sexual harassment. The nexus between the supervisor's discussion of work-related matters and his requests for oral sex were so close that there could be no doubt that a reasonable person in the plaintiff's position would have understood that the supervisor was conditioning the granting of job benefits on the performance of sexual acts.

Page 284, add before first full paragraph:

Nor is the plaintiff required to present evidence of actual, rather than threatened, economic loss in order to state a valid claim of quid pro quo sexual harassment. In *Karibian v. Columbia University*, 14 F.3d 773 (2d Cir.), *cert. denied*, 114 S. Ct. 2693 (1994), an action by a former university employee charging the university and supervisors with sexual harassment, the court stated that in the typical quid pro quo case,

> the employee who refuses to submit to her supervisor's advances can expect to suffer some job-related reprisal. . . . Accordingly, in such "refusal" cases, evidence of some job-related penalty will often be available to prove *quid-pro-quo* harassment. But that is not to say that such evidence is always essential to the claim. In the nature of things, evidence of economic *harm* will not be available to support the claim of the employee who *submits* to the supervisor's demands. . . . The supervisor's conduct is equally unlawful under Title VII whether the employee submits or not. Under the district court's rationale, only the employee who successfully resisted the threat of sexual blackmail could state a *quid pro quo* claim. We do not read Title VII to punish the victims of sexual harassment who surrender to unwelcome sexual encounters. Such a rule would only encourage harassers to increase their persistence.
>
> The relevant inquiry in a *quid pro quo* case is whether the supervisor has linked tangible job benefits to the acceptance or rejection of sexual advances. It is enough to show that the supervisor used the employee's acceptance or rejection of his advances as the basis for a decision affecting the compensation, terms, conditions or privileges of the employee's job. . . . In this case, Karibian stated that her work assignments, raises and promotions depended on her continued responsiveness to Urban's sexual demands. In addition, Karibian claimed that Urban implicitly threatened to fire her and to damage her career if she did not comply. If true, Urban's conduct would constitute *quid pro quo* harassment because he made and threatened to make decisions affecting the terms and conditions of Karibian's employment based upon her submission to his sexual advances.

*   *   *

Finally, we believe imposing an "actual economic loss" requirement in a *quid pro quo* case where the employee submits to the unwelcome sexual

158

overtures of her supervisor places undue emphasis on the victim's response to the sexual harassment. The focus should be on the prohibited conduct, not the victim's reaction. While the employee's submission to the supervisor's advances is certainly relevant, it bears only on the issue whether the sexual advances were unwelcome, not whether unwelcome sexual advances were unlawful. . . . Ultimately, the question whether Karibian submitted to Urban's advances out of a reasonable fear of some job-related reprisal is properly one for the finder of fact.

Id. at 778–79.

Page 284, add to footnote 309:

The threat of adverse employment action may be insufficient. Cram v. Lamson & Sessions Co., 49 F.3d 466 (8th Cir. 1995). A former employee could not recover for quid pro quo or hostile environment sexual harassment when according to the plaintiff's own testimony, her supervisor did not make any sexual comments, advances, or requests after their consensual relationship ended. The only evidence the plaintiff proffered to show that her supervisor was enforcing a quid pro quo against her was that as he left a restaurant following a nonwork-related quarrel a week before she left work early (which ultimately led to her termination), he said, "I'll get you for this." With respect to the hostile environment claim, the supervisor's workplace interactions with the plaintiff during the period following the breakup of their relationship were "brief, sporadic, nonsexual, nonthreatening, and polite." *Id.* at 474. The court rejected the plaintiff's contention that the district court should have applied a mixed-motives analysis under *Price Waterhouse* to her claims of discriminatory and retaliatory discharge. There was no evidence that her discharge was based on a discriminatory attitude toward women.

§ 6.44   Prima Facie Hostile Environment Case

Page 285, add to footnote 312:

Cross v. Alabama, 65 Fair Empl. Prac. Cas. (BNA) 1290 (11th Cir. 1994). Female former and present state employees established that the commissioner of the state department of mental health and mental retardation and the associate director of the mental illness division knew or should have known that the facility director harassed women and that they failed to take prompt remedial action to remedy the hostile environment. The plaintiffs thus demonstrated liability under Title VII and § 1983.

Page 286, add to footnote 314:

See also Bouton v. BMW of N. Am., 29 F.3d 103 (3d Cir. 1994). Under both Title VII and the state antidiscrimination law, a hostile environment claim requires proof of pervasive or severe intentional discrimination that affected the plaintiff and would also affect a reasonable person. Under agency law, employers are responsible for torts committed by their employees within the scope of their employment; masters are liable for their own negligence or recklessness, such as when they fail to take remedial action upon notice of harassment, and the master is required to answer if the servant relied upon the apparent authority or was aided by the agency relationship. Here, the plaintiff did not report any incidents that the Human Resources Department considered to be sexual harassment and, when queried, she indicated that she did not believe she had been sexually harassed and did not want an investigation. "If she had reported any event involving unwelcome touching or that the personnel department viewed as sexual harassment, personnel managers testified—and she agreed—that the company would have investigated regardless of her wishes." *Id.* at 107.

Page 286, add to footnote 315:

Cf. Donato v. Rockefeller Fin. Servs., 65 Fair Empl. Prac. Cas. (BNA) 1722 (S.D.N.Y. 1994). A female employee alleged that a coworker made a motion with his mouth, tongue, and lips simulating oral sex, on several occasions left notes on her desk commenting on her appearance, gave her a neck massage, once told her on the phone that he had heard she was a pro, and another time told her that he was at the airport with his pants down. She could not, however, make out a claim for hostile environment sexual harassment. Even if the coworker's actions sufficed to create a hostile environment, the plaintiff did not contend that the employer provided no reasonable avenue for complaint. She conceded that she was aware of the employer's sexual harassment policy and that it directed employees to report such conduct, but she discussed only one of the incidents with anyone with supervisory authority, and the head of personnel followed up on her complaint. Thus, the plaintiff did not show that the coworker's actions could be imputed to the employer. The plaintiff's retaliation claim, however, would not be dismissed as a matter of law when the defendant did not demonstrate legitimate, nondiscriminatory reasons for allegedly taking accounts away from the plaintiff, changing her hours, and giving her a poor performance review and distasteful job assignment.

Page 288, add to footnote 319:

Zvelter v. Brazilian Nat'l Superintendency of Merchant Marine, 833 F. Supp. 1089 (S.D.N.Y. 1993). See § **3.20.**

Page 288, add to footnote 320 after Second Circuit paragraph:

Currie v. Kowalewski, 842 F. Supp. 57 (N.D.N.Y. 1994). A female employee demonstrated that her employer created a hostile environment when he gave her full frontal body hugs, even after being told to stop, over a period of 11 months, and made sexual innuendoes, sexual advances, and sexual talk and admitted unwelcome touching. The plaintiff's subordinates started resenting her and created difficult working conditions. This resulted in a deterioration of her work performance and ability to delegate work to other employees, and the employees made complaints about her to the defendant. After she quit, the employer did not challenge the plaintiff's unemployment application, in order to avoid a pubic hearing, which was further proof that the alleged acts of sexual harassment had occurred. Although the plaintiff went into great detail about most incidents, she testified vaguely about acts of touching of her breasts and buttocks and reaching for her crotch. But even discounting that testimony, the totality of the circumstances demonstrated that the defendant had created a hostile work environment.

Page 289, add to footnote 320 after Seventh Circuit paragraph:

Johnson v. Indopco, Inc., 834 F. Supp. 1039 (N.D. Ill. 1993). A receptionist/secretary did not state a claim for sexual harassment when she alleged that the company personnel manager asked why she had married so young when she could have had fun with him, whether her husband satisfied her, and why she settled for second best, when the alleged questions, standing alone, could not be described as sexual advances sufficiently severe or pervasive as to alter the plaintiff's employment or create an abusive working environment.

TRYING THE CASE

Page 289, add to footnote 320 following Eighth Circuit paragraph:

Tenth Circuit: Ziegler v. K Mart, 65 Fair Empl. Prac. Cas. (BNA) 1694 (D. Kan. 1994). A hostile environment was not created by two incidents during the course of an eight-year employment period, in which the plaintiff received gag gifts of a calendar of male nudes and a bucket of candy suckers resembling black and white penises.

Geoffert v. Beech Aircraft Corp., 64 Fair Empl. Prac. Cas. (BNA) 1387 (D. Kan. 1994). Four incidents of sexual comments toward a female homosexual employee did not constitute conduct so pervasive as to affect a term or condition of her employment. There was no evidence that management tolerated sexual comments or that the comments affected her ability to perform her job.

Page 290, add to footnote 320 after Eleventh Circuit carryover paragraph:

Young v. Mariner Corp., 65 Fair Empl. Prac. Cas. (BNA) 555 (N.D. Ala. 1991)(one isolated incident, in which a supervisor made a few "mild" advances for a few minutes to a hotel's director of catering, after which he stopped and purportedly apologized with apparent embarrassment, was not sufficiently severe or pervasive to create a hostile environment).

Page 290, add to footnote 321:

Griffith v. State of Colo., Div. of Youth Servs., 17 F.3d 1323 (10th Cir. 1994). The district court properly granted summary judgment in favor of the employer in a sexual and racial harassment action by a female Caucasian employee against an African-American supervisor. The plaintiff had alleged that the supervisor had criticized her approach to children who were having behavior problems and told her to cuff and shackle them, in contradiction to DYS procedure, threatened to write her up for hugging the children, yelled at her in the presence of the children, made statements about her physical appearance as ugly and overweight, called her a stupid white woman, and cursed and used words such as fucking, Goddamn, and shit while professing to be a wonderful Christian. The plaintiff also alleged that when she told the supervisor that he was intimidating and overbearing, he remarked that the plaintiff would not say that if he were white. She also allegedly saw him put his arm around a female coworker's waist and kiss her on the neck, which she considered obscene, and heard rumors that the supervisor had affairs with others. The district court found from undisputed facts that the alleged harasser was immediately investigated and terminated, that the plaintiff was given four months of administrative leave, that she suffered no loss of wages, benefits, or tenure, and that the Division paid all of her therapy bills and provided her with workers' compensation to cover her job-related stress. The court further found that the plaintiff was not entitled to nominal damages because Title VII provided for equitable, not legal relief. The plaintiff had been made whole and had not demonstrated any actual damages.

Klessens v. United States Postal Serv., 66 Fair Empl. Prac. Cas. (BNA) 1630 (1st Cir. 1994). A female employee who alleged that her coworkers made explicit remarks about her body, made comments like, "If I don't get laid I'm going to take hostages," she was "a nice piece of ass," she had "small tits," and she should "go fuck herself," and spoke of their sexual exploits, did not prove a hostile environment. After she complained and management investigated, it offered the plaintiff a transfer that would take her away from one of the coworkers. She declined at first but later in the summer accepted the transfer; ultimately, the alleged harasser was also transferred to another post office. Before the transfers, however, the plaintiff and her alleged harasser regularly sat together in the plaintiff's car during breaks. The court noted that the sexual harassment issue was close, but that the lower court's finding that the post office responded appropriately to the plaintiff's complaints was insurmountable. With respect to a retaliation claim, the court properly found that the plaintiff was discharged because she had given false answers on her employment application, not because she had complained of sexual harassment.

Nelson-Cole v. Borg-Warner Sec. Corp., 881 F. Supp. 71 (D.D.C. 1995). A female former security officer stated a claim for sexual harassment against her employer when there was evidence that the defendants may not have had in place prior to the alleged harassment of the plaintiff a clear sexual harassment policy that was properly disseminated to supervisory personnel. At least one person stated in deposition that the company's sexual harassment policy was distributed after the plaintiff complained of harassment and that the policy was new. It also was far from clear that the defendants took prompt remedial action to alleviate the situation when, although the plaintiff was transferred to another supervisor after she complained, she allegedly received retaliatory comments. Moreover, investigators may have inadequately investigated the plaintiff's complaints. There was also evidence that the supervisor may have used his position to create the alleged abusive environment and that he allegedly touched the plaintiff in a sexually offensive manner while she was on duty.

Marquart v. McDonnell Douglas Corp., 859 F. Supp. 366 (E.D. Mo. 1994), *aff'd without op.*, 56 F.3d 69 (8th Cir. 1995). A female custodian alleged that she had been called a whore by coworkers, that a bag of horehound candy had been placed near her locker, that photographs of coworkers' wives and girlfriends in swimsuits were displayed in the workplace and that other pictures of other women in swimsuits were in the work area, that she had seen a male employee simulate sexual intercourse using a tool, that there was howling and whistling in the workplace, that on a single occasion a man's name had been placed over hers on a union campaign-for-office poster, that an American Cancer Society brochure on testicular cancer had been placed in her locker, and that some *Playboy* pictures and cartoons were in trash containers she was required to empty. These allegations did not make out a claim of hostile environment harassment when a supervisor responded to each complaint with immediate remedial action: photos were removed from display; it was determined that the employee was unaware that the plaintiff was watching him as he performed the act with the tool, but he was chastised nonetheless; coworkers were counseled and lectured on an individual and group basis that any form of harassment would not be tolerated. Neither female nor male coworkers liked the plaintiff, and the animus directed against her was brought about by her own actions. The plaintiff struck her fellow employees with her broom, swept over their feet, deliberately placed trash containers where her coworkers would stumble over them, allowed trash to accumulate around certain workers' benches, and took copious notes of all coworkers' activities.

Page 291, add to footnote 325:

Sudtelgte v. Reno, 63 Fair Empl. Prac. Cas. (BNA) 1257 (W.D. Mo. 1994). A female former employee who claimed that her mental illness was due to sexual harassment did not establish a hostile environment when, although she subjectively perceived the environment to be sexually abusive, much of the plaintiff's case was based on her feeling that she was being persistently picked on.

When the Court [in *Harris*] ruled that "Title VII bars conduct that would seriously affect a reasonable person's psychological well-being" (114

S.Ct. 371), I believe it effectively disposed of claims based on abnormal sensitivity, whether or not the sensitivity was simply unusual or produced by mental illness. This might be a different test than would be applied in standard tort law, where a tort-feasor takes the injured party as it finds him or her, but it likely comports with Congressional intent. Employers must police the environment for the benefit of the average person or "reasonable person" under the Civil Rights Act; particular disabilities may be subject to other legislative protection.

Id. at 1267.

Page 291, add to footnote 326:

King v. Hillen, 21 F.3d 1572 (Fed. Cir. 1994). The Merit Systems Protection Board improperly determined that the conduct of a senior civilian manager at the Army's Military Traffic Management Command toward five women, which included touching of the buttocks, thigh, and breast, suggestive comments and looks, and the telling of vulgar jokes, did not constitute sexual harassment. The Board stated that to establish sexual harassment under the EEOC Guidelines, a serious effect on the employee's psychological well-being must be shown and that it must be determined for each incident, standing alone, whether it met the criteria of sexual harassment, rather than considering the effect on the workplace of the totality of the conduct. This reasoning misapplied the fact that one victim did not complain until she learned that the alleged harasser would be placed in her chain of command, and erroneously required that the factfinder establish that the conduct was of a sexual nature.

Kulp v. Dick Horrigan VW Inc., 63 Fair Empl. Prac. Cas. (BNA) 1185 (E.D. Pa. 1994). An allegation that a female employee was called a "slut" by a coworker in the presence of management, which did not respond, was not sufficient by itself to support a claim of hostile environment sexual harassment. However, the plaintiff alleged facts to survive a motion to dismiss on her hostile environment claim when she also alleged that she was fired for occasional lateness, whereas male coworkers committed more egregious offenses without consequence; that special burdens were placed upon her and not on male coworkers; and that she was denied the perquisites and privileges routinely afforded male car salespersons.

Page 292, add to footnote 328:

See also Norman v. Gannett Co., Inc., 852 F. Supp. 46 (D.D.C. 1994). The plaintiff made a prima facie showing that her employer tolerated a sexually hostile and abusive environment in violation of the district's human rights act. Plaintiff alleged that:

1. In 1988 a reporter stood behind her and dropped his pants to the floor.
2. A year later, a production manager kissed her on the head twice within a couple of months, and then kissed her once again a year later.
3. Several employees made individual sexually and nonsexually oriented comments over the course of three years.
4. She observed several employees watching a pornographic video.

The sexual harassment claim was time-barred however, when none of the incidents relied on by the plaintiff occurring within the limitations period could be held to constitute unwelcome conduct of a sexual nature resulting in a hostile environment, and there was no basis for a finding of continuing violation.

Page 292, add to footnote 332:

Webb v. Hyman, 861 F. Supp. 1094 (D.D.C. 1994). Evidence supported a female former correctional officer's claims of hostile environment and quid pro quo sexual harassment and a jury verdict on her emotional distress claim:

> Ms. Webb's testimony on its own is sufficient to show this outrageousness, as she testified to repeated sexual assaults and retaliatory tactics by Paylor, her supervisor, which was known or should have been known by the Defendant District of Columbia. For example, she told the Jury that on June 20, 1992, Paylor locked her into a strip search room, forcibly kissing her and sticking his tongue into her mouth. In addition, she testified that Paylor fondled her, made a series of harassing phone calls, and, when she refused his advances, changed her work schedule and falsely accused her of stealing inmate property.

Id. at 1102. The court rejected the supervisor's assertion that his acts in 1992 could not have caused her to leave work in May 1993 when the plaintiff had alleged a course of conduct that lasted throughout that period; merely because the most offensive conduct subsided somewhat after the latter portion of 1992 did not prevent the jury from finding a continuing course of conduct. There was also sufficient evidence regarding her supervisor's efforts to silence her complaints and get back at her for refusing his solicitations.

Page 293, add to footnote 333 before Fifth Circuit paragraph:

First Circuit: EEOC v. Horizons Hotel Corp., 831 F. Supp. 10 (D.P.R. 1993). In an action by the EEOC on behalf of a former hotel restaurant cashier, the court found that the hotel's night auditor sexually harassed the cashier by subjecting her to a steady stream of comments about her body almost on a daily basis and invitations to his hotel room on at least two occasions. The plaintiff had complained on several occasions and was ultimately discharged by the director of personnel (the daughter of the alleged harasser). The auditor's conduct was severe and pervasive and management admitted at trial that they were aware of the auditor's conduct.

Third Circuit: Lazarz v. Brush Wellman, Inc., 857 F. Supp. 417 (E.D. Pa. 1994). A former employee failed to establish a hostile environment when she alleged that while walking past a coworker, he made a comment along the lines of "fucking up against the wall" with the plaintiff and the same alleged harasser two years later, as a manager, asked the plaintiff to have sex with him, a corporate counsel for the employer put his hand on her leg while she was driving him to the airport and kissed her goodbye when he got out of the car and on several later occasions lured the plaintiff to his hotel room to discuss business but instead grabbed her and told her he wanted to sleep with her.

Fourth Circuit: Hammill v. Albemarle County Sch. Bd., 65 Empl. Prac. Dec. (CCH) ¶ 80,883 (W.D. Va. 1994). While sexually explicit remarks may be sufficiently severe to establish a prima facie case of sexual harassment, offensive comments on the job are generally not alone sufficient to impose liability under Title VII. Here a female employee alleged that a coworker subjected her to such comments and displayed nude pictures for her. During her deposition, the plaintiff testified that the coworker began to harass her in 1979 by talking about sex, although there is evidence to indicate that she did not report such conduct until 1985. The plaintiff insisted, however, that the harassment occurred every day during her 13 years as a custodian in the school system and that the coworker continually asked her to have sex with him. The coworker also allegedly commented to the plaintiff that he needed a girlfriend and that she needed a boyfriend because the plaintiff's husband maintained a girlfriend, and the coworker allegedly asked her whether she knew about oral sex. As a result of these incidences, the plaintiff claimed and established that she suffered clinical depression for which she sought psychiatric treatment.

Troutt v. Charcoal Steak House, Inc., 835 F. Supp. 899 (W.D. Va. 1993). The plaintiff former waitress presented evidence that after her first month at work as a waitress, her supervisor began to make sexually suggestive remarks which escalated into physical contact, including putting his hands on her waist and breast, grabbing her buttocks, kissing her on the neck, reaching under her skirt and grabbing her crotch. This was more than sufficient to prove a hostile environment. The supervisor's conduct caused the plaintiff to suffer extreme emotional distress, sleeplessness, and depression, and she quit her job.

Sixth Circuit: Redman v. Lima City Sch. Dist. Bd. of Educ., 889 F. Supp. 288 (N.D. Ohio 1995). A female substitute school custodian stated a claim for hostile environment sexual harassment when she alleged that the principal sexually assaulted her, made numerous sexual comments to her, followed her around the school, and watched her work while he ate his lunch, despite the fact that the alleged incidents occurred over a short period of time. The court noted that although a number of the incidents in themselves may not have risen to an actionable level when they occurred over a period of short duration, "a rational fact-finder could conclude that plaintiff was subjected to sex-based conduct that was so severe and pervasive that she could prevail on her hostile environment claim." Id. at 293. The board of education was not liable for the sexual harassment, despite the plaintiff's allegations that the district's sexual harassment policy was inadequate, when the custodian complained on the day of the alleged assault, and the superintendent of custodians met her at school the following two mornings to prevent her from being alone with the principal, the superintendent notified a school district official the following weekend, the board immediately conducted an investigation that was completed within one month and that led to the alleged harasser's discharge, no harassment occurred after the official became aware of the allegations, and there was no evidence that the board was aware of the principal's alleged prior sexual comments to other employees.

§ 6.44   HOSTILE ENVIRONMENT

* *Page 293, add to footnote 333 following "Seventh Circuit":*

Sanfelice v. Dominick's Finer Foods, Inc., 899 F. Supp. 372 (N.D.Ill. 1995). Two female employees of a store stated an actionable claim for sexual harassment against the store owner under Title VII. Both plaintiffs complained of "continuous and constant" sexually harassing conduct including

> (1) on a number of occasions, he kissed her on the neck and mouth; (2) at least ten times he grabbed her buttocks, at times in the presence of others and other times while alone; (3) on multiple occasions, he grabbed her sides and tickled her; (4) he often whispered in her ear that she "had a nice ass," "smelled good," or "looked good"; and (5) on a number of occasions, he asked her to go out socially with him (including to dinner, a summer boat cruise, and after-work employee gatherings), all of which she refused.

Id. at 374.

Both plaintiffs complained to their immediate supervisors, and nothing was done to correct their situations. They never welcomed his conduct and often told him to stop it. Their doctors diagnosed them both with posttraumatic stress disorder caused by the sexual harassment. Common law claims were barred by the state workers' compensation act. Under state law, intentional torts committed by coemployees are accidental from both employee and employer's point of view, and thus the employer has the right to consider that the injured employee's sole remedy against the employer will be under the Illinois Workers' Compensation Act.

Page 293, add to footnote 333 following "Eighth Circuit":

Evans v. Ford Motor Co., 768 F. Supp. 1318 (D. Minn. 1991). A female former employer proved sexual harassment when she was subjected to repeated unwelcome harassment by management and employees in the form of comments about her body, sexual advances, and discussions about "blowjobs" and other sexual practices in her presence. The employer knew of the harassment because of the plaintiff's repeated complaints and because a lot of it was carried out by supervisory or management personnel. The plaintiff was entitled to past economic damages for discriminatory discharge and sexual harassment in the amount of $146,491, as well as to prejudgment interest. She was also awarded $10,000 under state law for mental anguish and suffering. Because the plaintiff was adequately compensated by the award of back pay, mental anguish and suffering, prejudgment interest, and an order reinstating her at Ford, the court determined that the compensatory damages should not be multiplied. The statutory maximum of $6,000 in punitive damages and attorney fees was also awarded.

Page 294, add to footnote 333:

Eleventh Circuit: Dibernardo v. Waste Management, Inc., 838 F. Supp. 567 (M.D. Fla. 1993). A female employee stated a claim for quid pro quo and hostile environment sexual harassment when she alleged that the general manager grabbed her from behind and pressed his body against hers, pinning her to a desk; repeatedly went out of his way to brush up against her; made sexually suggestive comments about her body; repeatedly propositioned her and asked her in a sexually suggestive fashion what she would do to get a favorable letter of reference; the operations supervisor followed her into a file room, closed the door, confined her to a corner, and said that he would like to "give it to her," touched her body on a daily basis, including breasts and buttocks, hugged her, put his arm around her and pushed his body against hers, and made sexually suggestive statements; and the controller told the plaintiff on several occasions to put the day's money deposits in his pants, implied to others that she had paid for sex with the defendants, repeatedly asked her to go out on dates, and when she refused, told the plaintiff he would make her life miserable and gave her extra work assignments, and made sexually suggestive remarks. The plaintiff alleged that she repeatedly made her alleged harassers and management aware of the conduct.

Page 295, add at beginning of footnote 338:

First Circuit: Dellert v. Total Vision, Inc., 875 F. Supp. 506 (N.D. Ill. 1995). A female employee did not state a claim for hostile environment sexual harassment; the company president commented once that glass frames would look better on her without a skirt, stated that he could not have her model eyeglasses like a barebacked model in an ad because he would have to "jump her," and asked the employee if she had any photographs of herself in lingerie or swimwear in her portfolio. The comments were made once during a one or two-day period early in the employee's employment and were never repeated, and when the president was told that the employee was not happy with his statements, he never said anything offensive again. The court diminished the effect of 5 to 10 telephone conversations, during which the president asked the plaintiff about whether she was still engaged:

> Unless . . . there was some reason to believe that underlying the question was an unstated intent that if she were not, Mr. Macklin intended to pursue her in a sexual manner, there was nothing wrong with the question. Ms. Dellert has not claimed that she had any belief, or any reason to believe, that such was the intent. She does complain that an additional instance of sexual harassment occurred in November, 1992, when she telephoned Mr. Mackin about her raise and he said he would call her back at her home, since she was not scheduled to be at work. In that conversation, Mr. Macklin asked her with whom she lived and she said female roommates. At that, Mr. Macklin stated he would be right over. Defendants have not suggested any proper reason for Mr. Macklin to have asked her who she lived with but it is also clear that Mr. Macklin was not about to come right over and that Ms. Dellert knew that: She called Mr. Macklin in California, where he lived. As it turned out, that was the last instance in which Mr. Macklin ever said anything offensive to Ms. Dellert, because she complained after that remark and the remarks stopped. After that, Mr. Macklin did not even ask if she were engaged.

Id. at 512.

Page 295, add to footnote 338 following "Seventh Circuit":

Rennie v. Dalton, 3 F.3d 1100 (7th Cir. 1993), *cert. denied.* 114 S. Ct. 1054 (1994). In an action by a former temporary employee at a civilian facility operated by the Navy against the Navy, the plaintiff did not prove a hostile environment or retaliation when she failed to establish that an instructor's conduct (an off-color joke and a conversation about a strip bar) unreasonably interfered with her work performance. Such conduct might be considered offensive and in poor taste, but was not persistent and did not poison the work environment.

*   Sink v. Knox County Hosp., 900 F.Supp. 1065 (S.D. Ind. 1995). Three incidents of conduct of a sexual nature by the hospital worker plaintiff's coworker—a joke and personal questions during the ride home from a conference—did not rise to the necessary level of severity of pervasiveness on which to base a Title VII claim. Nonsexual conduct alleged was not connected to the sexual conduct and thus did not make up part of a sexually hostile environment. Courts consider not only the actual effect of the conduct, but also the effect such conduct would have on a reasonable person in the plaintiff's position. The claimant's perception, however, was only part of the inquiry, and the evidence supported a finding that the environment was "merely unpleasant rather than hostile and deeply repugnant. . . . Sink fails to point to sufficient evidence to support a reasonable conclusion that Warthan, as a spurned suitor, proceeded on a campaign of criticism, tattling and bickering against her because of her sex." *Id.* at 1076. The alleged harasser was reprimanded, his office was moved, he was instructed on the topic of sexual harassment, and Sink's future contact with him was minimized. By Sink's own testimony, the resolution of the problem was satisfactory to her. However, a genuine issue of material fact existed as to whether Bailey, "a supervisor with considerable input into the decision to discharge Sink, harbored a retaliatory motive that substantially influenced that action." *Id.* at 1077.

Page 295, in footnote 338, add to "Saxton" citation:

The Seventh Circuit affirmed, Saxton v. American Tel. & Tel. Co., 10 F.3d 526 (7th Cir. 1993), noting that under *Harris*, a court must consider not only the effect the discriminatory conduct actually had on the plaintiff, but also the impact it likely would have had on a reasonable employee in her position. Here the alleged harasser's offensive behavior was relatively limited, presumably because the plaintiff "was forthright and persistent in making clear that the advances were unwelcome." *Id.* at 534. Management began an investigation the day after it was advised of the plaintiff's complaint; a detailed report was completed two weeks later and the alleged harasser was transferred to another department within five weeks after it learned that the plaintiff was not interested in a transfer herself. In light of the fact that nearly a year had passed since the principal events underlying the sexual harassment claim had occurred, the employer "acted with considerable alacrity." *Id.* at 535 (footnote omitted).

Page 295, add at end of footnote 338:

Ninth Circuit: Bradshaw v. Golden Road Motor Inn, 885 F. Supp. 1370 (D. Nev. 1995). A female former employee of a hotel casino failed to establish sexual harassment when there was no evidence that the plaintiff's supervisor called her a "cunt" or a "fucking bitch" to her face or within her earshot or that he used these references around the workplace or to other employees generally, but only to other supervisors. Nor did a customer who said "you motherfucker" three times while playing at her "21" table create a hostile environment when although the first supervisor she approached, but whom she did not ask to relieve her of her table, decided not to approach the customer at the time, a second supervisor relieved her about five minutes later and other supervisory personnel dealt with the customer.

Tenth Circuit: Griffith v. State of Colo. Div. of Youth Servs., 17 F.3d 1323 (10th Cir. 1994). A state agency was not liable for the sexually harassing conduct of one of its supervisors when the plaintiff's affidavit disclosed only possible isolated occurrences, "entirely speculative," that the employer might have been aware of, such as a meeting during which the supervisor used the word "fucking" once, and rumors of possible affairs with staff members.

Page 295, add to footnote 339:

* Ascolese v. Southeastern Pa. Transp. Auth., 902 F. Supp. 533 (E.D. Pa. 1995). An employee of the public transportation authority did not demonstrate a hostile environment when the alleged conduct was better characterized as episodic indifference than a pattern of hostility. SEPTA had held a luncheon to explain a fitness program to female officers, who it anticipated might have more difficulty meeting fitness standards than would males. Under this program, the officers were to undergo a physical examination, including both a medical exam and fitness testing. Officers expressed reservations about the fact that the medical tests required for the program would be administered by SEPTA's medical staff, whom the plaintiff felt were "not professionals" and were motivated by the desire "to keep you from reporting an injury if you are injured." *Id.* at 537. Because the women at the meeting had not had bad experiences with a particular doctor, he offered to conduct the examinations himself. With respect to the plaintiff, the doctor opened the examination by requesting that she call him "Louie," and asking that she wear her gown open in the front; she chose instead to wear her gown open at the back, and under it she wore her bra and a pair of boxer shorts. The doctor also told Ascolese that she would be tested for pregnancy, and Ascolese objected to such a test as an invasion of her privacy. In fact, a technician had already obtained a urine sample from Ascolese before the examination for use in this pregnancy test. It was not clear whether a pregnancy test was actually conducted.

In the course of the examination, the doctor examined Ascolese's hips and spinal column by having her bend over an examination table and move her hips from left to right. The plaintiff alleged that during this process, he stood behind her, with his body in contact with her from his waist to his knees, and touched her hips and spine with his hands. He also allegedly complimented her on a tattoo on her shoulder during this process. Later in the examination, he told her that he was going to examine her liver and spleen, then tore her paper gown in the front to do so, placing his hand under her boxer shorts; during this examination, his hand allegedly touched her pubic hairline.

Ascolese did not immediately bring the alleged events at this examination to SEPTA's attention, but she submitted a memorandum to SEPTA stating that she was pregnant and requesting that SEPTA provide her with a light-duty assignment. During a meeting with the Deputy Chief of Police, he made a number of remarks that expressed a lack of sympathy for her situation, including that she "would look humorous eight months pregnant in uniform," that she should not ask for special treatment, that he did not know why she had to eat every three hours, and that she was a "troublemaker." The court found that with the exception of Ascolese's encounter with the Deputy Chief of Police, her other difficulties were entirely of a bureaucratic character.

> While perhaps Kafkaesque, these difficulties did not involve the element of immediate personal threat that ordinarily contributes the most to the "hostility" or "abusiveness" of a work environment, and that was, for instance, at issue in *Harris*. This is not to say that misfeasances of a bureaucratic nature can never establish the existence of work difficulties sufficiently pointed, and gender-defined, so as to satisfy the *Harris v. Forklift Systems Inc.*, 114 S. Ct. 367 (1993) standard, but rather that such difficulties must be intense, comprehensive and sustained. The conduct alleged by Ascolese, while certainly unacceptable, seems better characterized as episodic indifference than as a pattern of "abusiveness" and "hostility." Therefore, it is not actionable under *Harris*.

Id. at 544.

Battaglio v. General Elec. Co., 66 Fair Empl. Prac. Cas. (BNA) 1513 (E.D. Pa. 1995). A plaintiff was not subjected to a hostile environment when she alleged that the following six incidents, which took place over one year, created an actionable hostile work environment: (1) a comment by the plaintiff's supervisor in September 1991 that cleaning up the shop was "women's work"; (2) a remark about the plaintiff's chest size made by a nonsupervising employee, who worked in another organization, to a group of shop employees, not in her presence, in March 1992; (3) the display of a picture of an unidentified male coworker with an unidentified naked woman in March 1992; (4) a poster depicting cartoon figures of nude skiers hung up for approximately two weeks in the office that she shared with two others; (5) a comment by her supervisor to her in July 1992 about the chest size of a woman depicted in a "biker" magazine brought in by the plaintiff's friend; and (6) defacement of pictures of the Philadelphia Eagles on the plaintiff's desk in August 1992 on which male genitalia were drawn. *Id.* at 1513. The court did not disagree that the plaintiff's sensibilities may have been offended by the incidents but concluded that it was not likely that a reasonable woman in the plaintiff's position would have been so detrimentally affected so as to compel her to transfer out of the department. The six alleged incidents were far from severe and were infrequent, spanning a 12-month period.

Page 296, add to footnote 342:

Johnson v. Tower Air, Inc., 149 F.R.D. 461 (E.D.N.Y. 1993). A former flight attendant trainee did not proffer evidence sufficient to support quid pro quo or hostile environment sexual harassment claims in an action charging that plaintiff's supervisor made sexual advances and brushed up against the plaintiff, on another occasion grabbed his crotch and shouted derogatory comments to the plaintiff, and during a two-week period made several other offensive gestures or comments. A hostile environment was not established when, although the plaintiff's supervisor was not a pleasant person for whom to work, it was clear that he was unpleasant to each member of the crew, irrespective of their sex, and his comments, while offensive, appeared to be far more hostile and angry than sexual. "Behavior that is immature, nasty, or annoying, without more, is not actionable sexual harassment." *Id.* at 469. *Accord* Porras v. Montefiore Medical Center, 742 F. Supp. 120, 127 (S.D.N.Y. 1990).

Page 296, add to footnote 343:

Stahl v. Sun Microsystems, Inc., 19 F.3d 533 (10th Cir. 1994). The district court properly found that the plaintiff did not present a viable claim of hostile environment harassment with evidence that a supervisor used vulgar language when referring to female employees, and that at least one other employee had filed an internal complaint against the supervisor.

Page 297, add to footnote 345:

The Ninth Circuit affirmed a finding of liability against the Postmaster General and the U.S. Postal Service and an award of back pay. Nichols v. Frank, 42 F.3d 503 (9th Cir. 1994). The court agreed with the defendant that the district court applied the wrong test in holding the defendant liable for the supervisor's conduct with respect to the hostile environment claim, because the proper analysis is what management-level employees knew or should have known, not whether an employee was acting within the scope of employment; had the proper test been applied, the Postal Service could not have been held liable on a hostile environment theory. The court still held the Postal Service liable for the supervisor's acts because the conduct constituted quid pro quo harassment in addition to the hostile environment harassment and the Postal Service was liable for the supervisor's acts under the doctrine of respondeat superior. The plaintiff presented evidence that she was required to perform oral sex in order to obtain a two-week leave of absence, that her evaluations were sometimes conditioned on her willingness to perform the acts, that the supervisor conditioned her continued employment on such willingness, and that he asked her to perform oral sex after they had just discussed her sick leave and her attendance record. See **§ 6.44**.

Eleventh Circuit: Splunge v. Shoney's, Inc., 874 F. Supp. 1258 (M.D. Ala. 1994). Four female restaurant employees made out a prima facie case of hostile environment sexual harassment. Allegations included that the store and area managers made sexual comments about one or more of their breasts and buttocks, rubbed up against them with their bodies or hands, stared at their breasts, showed them pictures with sexual content, trapped one in the walk-in freezer and threatened to keep her there until she kissed him, and asked them out for drinks. One plaintiff made out a claim of quid pro quo sexual harassment when she alleged that another employee with less seniority than her was allowed to take a test upon which pay raises were conditioned. The employee who was allowed to take the test was having an affair with one of the assistant managers, and thus the "inference which logically may be extracted is that management allowed Splunge's co-employee to take the test because she provided sexual favors to one of the assistant managers." *Id.* at 1270. Although the plaintiffs did not complain to higher management about the harassment, there was clearly a genuine issue of material fact as to whether the openness and pervasiveness of the harassment inferred knowledge on the part of the defendant.

Page 299, add to footnote 347 following "Eighth Circuit":

Hatley v. Store Kraft Mfg. Co., 859 F. Supp. 1257 (D. Neb. 1994). A female employee established a hostile environment claim with persuasive evidence that the employer never took proper remedial measures against alleged sexual harassment despite four well-documented complaints. That the plaintiff engaged in pranks, some of which had sexual overtones, with other coworkers did not prove that the alleged harasser's overtures were welcome when it was obvious to everyone that the plaintiff was being singled out as a woman and that she found the conduct offensive. It was not surprising that the plaintiff did not complain to her union since she was the only female on the final assembly line, and the plaintiff testified that after union meetings stag films were often shown. For conduct that occurred after the effective date of the Civil Rights Act of 1991, a jury awarded $125,000 in lost wages and fringe benefit damages and $100,000 for emotional pain, suffering, inconvenience, mental anguish, loss of enjoyment of life, and other nonmonetary damages. For conduct occurring before the effective date of the Act, the plaintiff was awarded nominal damages of $1.00.

Page 299, add to footnote 347:

Eleventh Circuit: Dibernardo v. Waste Management, Inc., 838 F. Supp. 567 (M.D. Fla. 1993).

Minnesota: *Cf.* Giuliani v. Stuart Corp., 512 N.W.2d 589 (Minn. Ct. App. 1994). The trial court properly found that a property manager had been sexually harassed, in violation of the state human rights act, by her supervisor, who was vice president of the defendant real estate management firm. Knowledge of the sexual harassment was imputed to the employer, which did not respond to allegations of sexual harassment until almost two years after the original incident and had no sexual harassment policy. Although the court was not willing to state that strict liability applied, it noted that companies that fail to institute sexual harassment policies will naturally find themselves vulnerable to the likelihood that knowledge will be imputed to them. The fact that the plaintiff asked a supervisor to keep her confidences about the harassment a secret did not waive her claim; the persons in whom she confided recognized their legal obligation to report her allegations to company officials, but chose not to.

* *Page 299, add to footnote 349 following "Second Circuit":*

Talada v. Int'l Serv. Sys., Inc., 899 F. Supp. 936 (N.D.N.Y. 1995). An employee and a former employee proved that they were subjected to quid pro quo and hostile environment sexual harassment. One plaintiff alleged that her supervisor on one occasion approached her directly, walked right up close to her, and immediately attempted to put his arms around her. He began touching her, placing one hand on her buttock. He made several comments to one plaintiff, claiming "I've been waiting a long time for this," and telling her she had a "nice ass," attempting at one point to kiss her. She immediately pushed him away, stating, "Get the hell away from me." She finished the day's work at the side of a male coworker, and only after leaving for the day, did she confide in him exactly what had transpired. About a month later, her supervisor approached her and stated, "I have something hard and nice for you," and reached for her, telling her he could make her job easier with more days off. He attempted to kiss her and she told him to get away from her. She pushed the elevator button and fled to the ladies restroom on the first floor where she remained for some time. The other plaintiff alleged that the supervisor took her to an isolated telephone room, approached her and pressed her between the columns of wires, stating, "I have waited 13 years for this." He took her hand and put it against his penis, stating he had something "nice and hard" for her and that if she cooperated, he could arrange a deception allowing her shorter work hours while still receiving full wages. He attempted to unfasten her pants and continually handled her, putting his hands on her breasts and buttocks for approximately 15–20 minutes. He forced his tongue into her mouth and she bit his tongue, and forced her knee into his groin which enabled her to break free from her flanked and cornered position. The alleged harasser's conduct was resisted and reported by the plaintiffs. Talada even found it necessary to use physical force to manage escape from the treatment.

The court concluded that the "use of this supervisory power to effectually blackmail an employee into acting in a manner in which she otherwise would not, has been loathed from long before the enactment of these two Civil Rights Acts." *Id.* at 949. The court noted that the

> continued attempts of sexual conduct by Rice against both women, seemingly sanctioned through management's relative inaction and fellow supervisors' active support, undermined any sense of security held by these women. Management removed Rice from their work area and began an investigation which did not include interviews of the victims or their associates. No disciplinary action was taken, and no recognition was granted of the incidents even occurring.

Id. at 951.

* *Page 300, add to footnote 349 following "First Circuit":*

E.E.O.C. v. Regency Architectural Metals Corp., 896 F. Supp. 260 (D. Conn. 1995). The Equal Employment Opportunity Commission (EEOC) and a female union member, Hodge, filed an action alleging sex discrimination and Title VII violations against her former employer, successor employer, union local, and international union, alleging that Hodge's employer, defendant Regency Architectural Metals Corp. knowingly assigned a male employee who was awaiting trial for allegedly raping Hodge to work beside her on two occasions, leading her to quit her employment. The plaintiffs also alleged that Hodge's union failed to represent Hodge in her efforts to challenge Regency's acts of alleged sexual harassment. Finally, the plaintiffs alleged that the union denied Hodge representation in her efforts to bring union charges against three members of the Local chapter, including the alleged rapist.

While Hodge worked at Regency, there were less than five female workers out of the total of about thirty-five to forty workers. The atmosphere in the shop was coarse, with much sexually explicit talk among the male workers; occasionally sexually explicit behavior was directed at the female workers, and at other times it was done with no attempt to hide it from the female workers. For example, coworkers created imitation penises out of styrofoam, stuck them in their groin area, and paraded around the shop. At other times, these three also performed the same act with extendible tape measures. Some would stick out their tongues at female workers "like they wanted oral sex," drop their pants and moon their coworkers. *Id.* at 264. The plaintiff attended a party where she allegedly was taken away and raped by three men, including one coworker and union brother. Hodge stayed away from work for 11 weeks following this incident, receiving total disability payments from her union health plan. Management reassured her and told her she could press charges and get her job back, but the union business agent told her that there was some sentiment among her coworkers that she had been drunk at the time of the alleged rape, and that her sexual habits were generally loose.

The court concluded that Regency officials displayed an "egregious lack of insight into the psychology of a putative rape victim, especially given that they had ample warning of Hodge's precarious emotional state." Their insensitivity created a hostile working environment for Hodge, and thus gave rise to a colorable claim of discrimination on the basis of sex. The court also found that the local chapter intentionally avoided asserting her claim.

> When Hodge grieved orally to Seravalli about Vaughn having been assigned to work near her . . . , he did not make an earnest effort to settle her grievance, as required by the International's constitution. The fact that he has offered contradictory explanations for failing to help her (he investigated and concluded Regency had done no wrong; she refused to put her claim in writing; he was the wrong person to initiate the first step of the grievance process) requires us to look deeper for his actual motivation.
>
> Seravalli's position as business agent was an elected one, and accordingly he had a strong reason to cater to the prejudices of his overwhelmingly male constituency. . . . We thus conclude that Seravalli's desire to cater to the prejudices of the members of Local 832 was a motivating factor in his failure to adequately assert Hodge's claim against Regency.

Id. at 269. However, the court concluded that the Local's failure to hold a union trial on Hodge's charge against Seravalli was not a violation of Title VII. There was little or no useful evidence concerning this omission, but the court decided that the union's motivation in failing to hold the trial was deference to Seravalli's clout, rather than any improper discriminatory motivation. The court also held that the international union was not vicariously liable for the local's conduct:

> When a union selectively withholds its internal union disciplinary procedures from women, this has the direct effect of strongly discouraging them from using the union in regard to employment. The end result is that women may receive fewer employment opportunities. We conclude, following Title VII and *Goodman [v. Lukens Steel Co.,* 580 F. Supp. 1114 (E.D. Pa. 1984)] that unions may not restrict female union members' access to internal disciplinary procedures, either out of prejudice on the

part of union decisionmakers, or in deference to the prejudices of the rank and file.

However, the plaintiffs have failed to meet their burden showing by a preponderance of the evidence that a motivating factor for the International's actions was sexual prejudice, or desire to cater to the prejudices of the rank and file. The International did not have the same motivation to cater to the demonstrated prejudices of the rank and file that Seravalli did, as an elected official of Local 832. Instead, the best explanation for the International's obstructionism is that the International simply did not want to give a forum to a person they saw as mentally unstable and somewhat of a troublemaker.

Moreover, we note that the International's interference with internal union action against certain members of the Local was not a proximate cause of Hodge's damages in this case. She had been constructively discharged by her employer many months earlier. The conducting of union charges against union members would not have recaptured her position with Regency.

Id. at 270.

Page 300, add to footnote 349 following "Third Circuit":

*   Stewart v. Weis Markets, Inc., 890 F. Supp. 382 (M.D. Pa. 1995). A female former employee brought a successful action against her former employer for violating Title VII and the Pennsylvania Human Relations Act by subjecting her to a sexually hostile working environment. Her manager, Botsford, addressed comments to her with the epithets: "sleazebag," "douchebag," and "bitch." He would also frequently ask her if she "got any last night," would tell her to "bend over, Helen Baby," and would state "while you're down there," to Stewart while flipping up his work apron. He also suggested that Stewart must like young men, and told a coworker to take her into the cooler and "take care of her." After an elderly woman customer complimented Stewart on her work by stating, "You are very good," Botsford stated to the customer, "How do you know, have you ever had her?" He addressed similar comments to other female employees under his supervision. Other employees overheard Botsford's sexual harassment of female employees under his supervision. The evidence amply demonstrated that Stewart suffered intentional discrimination because of her gender. Sexually related epithets and insults were directed at her that were not and would not have been directed at a man. Botsford's sexually explicit derogatory language and mannerisms toward Stewart were unwelcome, uninvited, and offensive, subjecting her to a discriminatorily hostile and abusive work environment; the harassment was pervasive and regular, and had a detrimental effect on Stewart and would have had the same effect on any reasonable person in her position. Sufficient evidence also existed to support a finding of respondeat superior liability. The harassment was sufficiently frequent and done with such disregard for who was in a position to overhear or observe it, that the on-site store management, specifically, the on-site store manager, knew or must have known that it was occurring. The manager did nothing to halt the harassment or bring Botsford's conduct to the attention of other supervisory personnel. The court rejected the defendant's assertion that the remarks were made in jest and were part of a general joking atmosphere in the produce department at the store. Although the defendant asserted that Botsford addressed sexually related comments to the males in his department as well, that was not borne out by convincing testimony.

Weis Markets conducted a prompt investigation by questioning plaintiff about her concerns, and by immediately interviewing other employees in the produce department; although as soon as the situation was brought to the attention of the district supervisor it was put to an end, this prompt action did not nullify liability for the months that the situation was tolerated by on-site management level employees who knew or should have known that it was occurring. "Management level employees cannot turn a deaf ear or a blind eye to situations of obvious harassment." *Id.* at 391.

The court did find that the plaintiff was not constructively discharged by harassment of a more general nature after she reported her supervisor's misconduct to management. The plaintiff admitted that Botsford's sexually related conduct ceased immediately after she complained to Botsford's supervisor. The court finds, even assuming the plaintiff was "closely supervised," that she did not leave her employment because of the alleged sexual harassment. Although Stewart charged that Botsford then became abusive toward her in a more general manner, attacking her job performance, the conduct that she described at trial did not rise to the level of intolerable conduct necessary to sustain her claim of constructive discharge. A jury awarded the plaintiff $139,125 as compensatory damages against Weis Markets for the harassment.

Pittman v. Correctional Healthcare Solutions, Inc., 868 F. Supp. 105 (E.D. Pa. 1994). A former employee stated a claim of hostile environment sexual harassment when she alleged that her supervisor made sexist remarks frequently, referring to his penis and to the plaintiff's large breasts. The tendency of such remarks to cross into harassment was magnified by the plaintiff's allegations that in connection with the statements, she was denied benefits and raises, suffered mental anguish, and was ultimately terminated. The court rejected the company's argument that none of the plaintiff's allegations tied it to the alleged conduct of the supervisor when the alleged harasser was a supervisor, and thus the requirement of respondeat superior is a fortiori alleged and moreover, the alleged decisions to deny the plaintiff raises and benefits and to terminate her were alleged to be part of the pattern of harassment and these decisions may have been made at the corporate level or at least known to corporate-level employees.

Page 300, add to footnote 349 following "Fourth Circuit":

Cf. Spicer v. Commonwealth of Va. Dep't of Corrections, 44 F.3d 218 (4th Cir. 1995). A female rehabilitation counselor at an all-male prison was granted injunctive relief on her hostile environment claim, based on a barrage of sexual comments, usually about her breasts, and a memorandum in which the "revealing" clothing of the plaintiff and other women staff was discussed. There was sufficient evidence to support the district court's finding that the Department's remedial response was inadequate: one employee was "begrudgingly" counseled for 5 to 10 minutes, and the person responsible for investigating complaints of sexual harassment and conducting the training sessions conceded that he had not conducted any training on sexual harassment in quite a while, thought his training was mandatory but did not require anyone to attend, did not know who attended, did not remember much of what was taught, and resisted the notion that jokes of a sexual nature could create a hostile
* environment. The court, en banc, vacated the panel decision, Spicer v. Commonwealth of Va., Dept. of Corrections, 66 F.3d 705 (4th Cir. 1995), reversing its conclusion that the Department of Corrections failed to take effective remedial action and its award of attorneys' fees. A review of the record revealed that the district court's conclusion that the employer failed to take effective remedial action either was an error of law, or, if interpreted as a finding of fact, was clearly erroneous. Undisputed facts in the record show that on the very day Spicer complained to her employer about the memorandum and the sexually offensive remarks, action was taken (1) to assure that the memorandum was not publicly posted, (2) to counsel those involved in writing and

distributing the memorandum about treating such matters more sensitively, and (3) to admonish those making inappropriate sexual remarks that such conduct would not be tolerated. In addition, two training sessions were conducted to educate employees and to prevent the recurrence of such remarks. The court found no evidence in the record to suggest that the incident was other than "the brief, isolated result of an inartfully drafted memorandum addressing a legitimate and important concern." *Id.* at 710.

> While we have never suggested that an employer must make the most effective response possible and we have consistently held that an employer is only liable for sexual harassment committed by its employees if no adequate remedial action is taken, the record in this case does not even colorably support a conclusion that the Virginia Department of Corrections' response was accurate. This is especially true in light of Spicer's concession that no further offensive remarks were made after the Department's equal employment officer intervened. . . .
>
> To hold the Virginia Department of Corrections liable under these circumstances would be tantamount to imposing strict liability on an employer for all workplace conversations that are inappropriate, regardless of the employer's knowledge of them or response. Such a holding would dramatically change the law regarding employer liability for sexual harassment in the workplace.
>
> The workplace is a complex and diversified community in which employees work closely and continuously in each other's presence over long hours, during which, experience has shown, inappropriate conduct occurs from time to time. While employers can and should be required to adopt reasonable policies aimed at preventing illegal conduct and to take responsible measures to enforce these policies, they cannot be held to a standard under which they are liable for any and all inappropriate conduct of their employees. When presented with the existence of illegal conduct, employers can be required to respond promptly and effectively, but when an employer's remedial response results in the cessation of the complained of conduct, liability must cease as well. Employers cannot be saddled with the insurmountable task of conforming all employee conduct at all times to the dictates of Title VII, irrespective of their knowledge of such conduct or the remedial measures taken in response to such conduct.

Id. at 711. Here the record, considered in the light most favorable to the Department of Corrections, indicated that the warden removed Spicer from the work committee because of their philosophical differences about the committee, because of inmate and staff complaints, and because she chaired work committee meetings when she was not authorized to do so. That evidence rationally supports the verdict returned by the jury.

The dissent noted that it was undisputed that the Department never officially or unofficially retracted or apologized for the public dissemination of the August 1 memorandum, even though the Department itself admitted that public dissemination of the memorandum was improper. It was similarly undisputed that, other than counseling, the Department undertook no disciplinary action against any employee for that employee's part in making or disseminating the harassing statements; indeed, shortly after these incidents, the Department promoted the author of the memorandum.

> There was abundant evidence that the counseling and training that were undertaken by the Department were ineffective. For example, both the author of the memorandum and the warden, although they had assertedly been "counseled" and "trained, " testified at trial that in their respective views the memorandum was neither "too explicit" nor "inappropriate." Further, the Department's EEO manager, who conducted the Department's remedial training sessions, had, in his own words, "not conducted any training on sexual harassment in quite awhile," did not require anyone to attend the training sessions and did not remember much of what was taught.

Id. at 712-13 (Motz, J., dissenting).

Page 300, add to footnote 349 following "Fifth Circuit":

DeAngelis v. El Paso Mun. Police Officers Ass'n, 51 F.3d 591 (5th Cir. 1995);

Page 300, add to footnote 349 following "Seventh Circuit":

Howard v. Board of Educ. Sycamore Dist., 876 F. Supp. 959 (N.D. Ill. 1995). A female former director of music and band director stated claims for hostile environment sexual harassment and retaliation when she alleged that during her employment, notes referring to the plaintiff in a sexually offensive manner were posted, a male teacher made offensive comments about a female teacher, and male students made offensive comments. The plaintiff complained about such conduct but was told not to further complain or "heads would roll." Although throughout her employment the plaintiff's performance evaluations reflected her satisfactory job performance, she was forced to submit a letter of resignation in lieu of termination proceedings, and she was replaced by a less qualified male who did not even meet the minimum requirements for the position.

Ficek v. Griffith Lab. Inc., 67 Fair Empl. Prac. Cas. (BNA) 1396 (N.D. Ill. 1995). Thirty-six incidents of sexual harassment amounted to a hostile environment; acts of coworker harassment included comments about the plaintiff's "big booty," a sexual assault during which a coworker tried to remove her panty hose in the parking lot of a bar, comments about her underwear showing through her white uniform, calling her a "lazy bitch," making masturbation gestures, telling her to bend over to show her a "real man," running into her with a forklift, and graffiti in the men's room. The plaintiff sometimes broke into tears when she heard the remarks, and she felt humiliated.

Sassaman v. Heart City Toyota, 879 F. Supp. 901 (N.D. Ind. 1994). Evidence of sexually charged comments and actions and differential treatment supported a jury verdict finding sexual harassment of a female salesperson by four male supervisory employees of a car dealership. According to the plaintiff:

> Roger Ellis had a way of humiliating her every day: he would stand in the show room and flick his tongue at her; Mr. Ellis told her about his sexual exploits with his wife and asked her to join them; he bragged to her about sliding under a female sales-person in the showroom and seeing a "juicy pussy"; when she would pick up the clean up man Louis, Mr. Ellis would ask her if they had fun and if she liked black dicks better than white ones.
>
> Mr. McDonald had a way of getting too close to her—putting his arm around her and rubbing against her elbow. Once, Mr. McDonald brushed across her breasts. Mr. McDonald asked her many questions about being single and about her male companionship. Mr. Cunningham would laugh when Mr. Ellis flicked his tongue at Ms. Sassaman. Charles Barett, a former salesman at Heart City, testified that he worked with Ms. Sassaman and observed her with used car management. Mr. Barrett testified that Mr. McDonald treated her with disrespect and did not treat her like he treated the males. Mr. Barrett testified that on numerous occasions the management failed to assist Ms. Sassaman.
>
> Ms. Sassaman testified that Mr. Cunningham treated her differently than he treated the salesmen. She testified that: she had to clean the popcorn machine when the male salespersons did not; Mr. Cunningham would not allow her to let customers go alone on demonstration rides

when male salespersons were so allowed; Mr. Cunningham would not let her smoke although smoking was allowed on the premises and men were allowed to smoke; everything Mr. Cunningham gave her he either threw at her or mixed up; Mr. Cunningham insisted that she tell him when she was taking her lunch break, but that other salesmen would come and go as they pleased; Mr. Cunningham would not permit her to use the computer locator system, but permitted other salespersons to use it; and Mr. Cunningham made it difficult for her to work deals with customers.

According to Ms. Sassaman's testimony, Mr. Cunningham told Ms. Sassaman to tell one customer to "fuck [her]" because he did not want to deal with him. When Ms. Sassaman switched days off with another salesperson to have her birthday off and to spend the weekend in Chicago, Mr. Cunningham ordered her to take a test at Lochmandy Motors on the day she was to have off. He would not show her how to run the computerized test; rather, he told her, "You're a woman, you can figure it out." She later learned that she could have taken the test at any time and did not have to take the entire test at once. Mr. Cunningham sent Ms. Sassaman to a seminar in Indianapolis on less than a day's notice and insisted that she ride with a new salesman, Craig. After the trip, Mr. Ellis and Cunningham asked Craig if he "got any pussy" while in Indianapolis.

On the day that Ms. Sassaman was terminated, Heart City was participating in a dealer show. Mr. Cunningham told Ms. Sassaman to stay at the store, even though she was the first on the "up" list. Although Mr. Cunningham said he would soon send a salesman to relieve her, he did not do so until noon. Mr. Cunningham brought sandwiches for all the male sales representatives, but not for Ms. Sassaman. When Mr. Cunningham told Ms. Sassaman that she was fired, he offered as an explanation that women are not cut out to be car sales people and that they should be home with their kids.

Ms. Sassaman testified that Gerald Suszko, Heart City's general manager, would inquire of her as to her love life; he persisted in questioning her although she told him it was not his concern. Ms. Sassaman testified that Mr. Susko was aware of the sexual treatment from Mr. Ellis and Mr. Cunningham since Mr. Susko was present on many occasions.

Id. at 908–09 (footnotes omitted). Although the company had a sexual harassment policy, the plaintiff testified that she did not receive a copy of the policy until two weeks before she was terminated. Although she did not complain about the sexual harassment to any other management employees, the jury could reasonably find that management employees knew or had reason to know of the sexual harassment, based on the employee's testimony that the dealership's general manager was present on many occasions when the plaintiff was being harassed by male sales managers, and the company president testified that he was at the dealership for several hours a day.

Al-Dabbagh v. Greenpeace Inc., 873 F. Supp. 1105 (N.D. Ill. 1994). A female former employee stated a cause of action for sexual discrimination under Title VII against Greenpeace when she alleged that a coworker suddenly attempted to kiss her as she was preparing to leave the office at the end of the day, and then responded to her rejection of his actions by slapping her, tearing off her shirt, beating her, hitting her on the head with a radio, shocking her with a phone cord, and ultimately raping her. The plaintiff escaped in the early morning hours, phoned the police, and was treated for her injuries at a local hospital. She was allowed to return to work over a week later, but resigned by telephone two weeks after returning to work, citing an atmosphere of distrust and tension and constant encouragement by Greenpeace to seek other employment. Although the alleged harasser had a history of "womanizing" and substance abuse, the only action the defendant took against him was an oral reprimand for having reported to work in an intoxicated state. The court concluded that a reasonable person would have found the environment hostile or abusive (the objective prong) and that the victim did in fact perceive it as such (the subjective prong):

> Al-Dabbagh alleges that Greenpeace had turned a blind eye to Mitchell's sexual abuse of female employees in its Chicago office before she fell victim to it and subsequently suffered grave bodily and psychological injury. As already stated, Greenpeace's single response to Mitchell's earlier conduct—an oral reprimand for his drinking—fell far short of addressing the more serious problems posed by his conduct. There is no question that those allegations, credited as they must be on the present motion, amply support the first (objective) element of a hostile-environment claim—the evaluation of Mitchell's conduct by a reasonable person.
>
> As for the second (subjective) factor, Greenpeace advances the frankly outrageous argument that because newly-hired Al-Dabbagh was unaware of Mitchell's depredations before she fell prey to his sexual advance and rape, she lacked the required perceptions of the work environment as hostile. If accepted, that proposition would insulate Greenpeace against liability for a known miscreant's first attack on each recently hired nubile young woman. This Court rejects that offensive notion, holding instead that Al-Dabbagh's reaction to the actual experience—her natural reaction to being personally exposed to the offending employee's violent sexual

misconduct—establishes the requisite subjective prong even though she had not previously known of Mitchell's proclivities.

Id. at 1111 (footnote omitted). The court noted that the plaintiff's claim of constructive discharge was unnecessary to prove her Title VII claim, but provided her with the potential for additional recovery—compensatory or punitive damages or both, and perhaps reinstatement or back pay "for a Title VII violation that was already complete when she suffered the rape itself." *Id.* at 1112.

Page 301, add to footnote 349 following "Eighth Circuit":

Olmer v. Iowa Beef Processors, 66 Fair Empl. Prac. Cas. (BNA) 843 (D. Neb. 1994). The defendant employer intentionally discriminated against a female employee plaintiff under Title VII when she was terminated ostensibly for fighting with a coworker, who was only suspended for one day in an altercation that the plaintiff alleged was started by the coworker. During her employment, the plaintiff was subjected to harassment by a coworker, Bateman, and her immediate supervisor, Wunderlich. Two of the plaintiff's former coworkers testified regarding the nature of the harassment, alleging that Bateman would continually call the plaintiff names such as "the bitch," "worthless bitch," or "fucking bitch" in front of coworkers and supervisors, that Wunderlich would always refer to plaintiff as the "fucking bitch" and wondered aloud "how she got her fat ass into her coveralls." *Id.* at 844. Wunderlich himself admitted to calling the plaintiff a "bitch." The plaintiff complained to Wunderlich about Bateman's name calling; Wunderlich admitted that he knew that Bateman hated women and the plaintiff in particular, and testified that Bateman picked on plaintiff and called her "bitch" and other derogatory names. Wunderlich warned Bateman that further harassment would result in his termination. Bateman's harassment exceeded name calling. Bateman would often direct his hostility specifically toward the plaintiff. On one occasion, Bateman blew his nose in a napkin and placed it on the plaintiff's breakfast that she was about to eat during the maintenance crew's morning break. This incident was reported to supervisors who warned Bateman. The plaintiff also alleged that on one occasion, a coworker spilled coffee onto a floor the plaintiff had just cleaned, stating, "I wanted to show you what a woman's period looks like." The plaintiff reported this incident to her supervisors. She also testified that she was often told by employees of IBP that "this is a man's world." The court concluded that the defendant's proffered reason for terminating the plaintiff was pretextual. Although this case was not pleaded as a sexual harassment case, the history of harassment in this case revealed an animus of discrimination toward the plaintiff on the basis of her gender. While there was some testimony that perhaps some of the hostility directed toward the plaintiff was due to her personality, there, was ample evidence to support a finding that the plaintiff was singled out because she was a female. The court found compelling the fact that the plaintiff's immediate supervisor, Wunderlich, was present during the investigation but offered no input, explanation, or recommendations. Although he knew of Bateman's hostility toward women, frequent temper tantrums, and use of vulgar and derogatory language toward the plaintiff, and had even warned Bateman that further harassment could result in his termination, he chose to remain silent throughout the investigation. In addition, Wunderlich's supervisor, Mel Olmer, openly discussed with Wunderlich his hatred for the plaintiff because of strained family relations and because she was a woman. Olmer also discussed his desire to see the plaintiff terminated. In addition, Wunderlich himself had made remarks about the lack of need for women in the work force at IBP and admitted to calling the plaintiff a "bitch." The court found that it was incumbent upon Wunderlich to inform the investigatory team of all that he knew, and thus his deliberate failure to do so directly resulted in the plaintiff's termination and constituted unlawful intentional discrimination.

Page 301, add to footnote 349 following "Ninth Circuit":

Fuller v. City of Oakland, Cal., 47 F.3d 1522 (9th Cir. 1995). The district court improperly ruled for the defendant city in a Title VII sexual harassment action by a female former police officer when the city failed to take any appropriate remedial steps once it learned of the sexual harassment. After ending a relationship with a fellow police officer, the coworker allegedly started harassing the plaintiff and was eventually transferred into a supervisory position with authority over the plaintiff. Among the acts of harassment were calling and hanging up, sometimes 25 times a day, threatening to kill himself, attempting to run the plaintiff and her new boyfriend off the road, and forcibly extracting her new unlisted phone number from her.

Steiner v. Showboat Operating Co., 25 F.3d 1459 (9th Cir. 1994), *cert. denied*, 115 S. Ct. 733 (1995). A former casino employee, the first female "floorperson," established a prima facie case of hostile environment sexual harassment in an action alleging sexual harassment, retaliation, constructive discharge, and intentional infliction of emotional distress. She proved without contradiction that her supervisor habitually referred to her and to other female employees in a derogatory fashion, using sexual explicit and offensive terms such as "dumb fucking broad," "cunt," and "fucking cunt." The evidence suggested that the defendant was consistently slow to react to the plaintiff's claims, and did not seriously investigate them or strongly reprimand the supervisor until after the plaintiff had filed a formal complaint. Moreover, the defendant twice changed the plaintiff's shift to get her away from the supervisor, rather than changing his shift or work area within the casino "or indeed, firing him outright and early on." *Id.* at 1464.

Page 301, add to footnote 349 following "Tenth Circuit":

Henry v. Gehl Corp., 867 F. Supp. 960 (D. Kan. 1994). A genuine issue of fact existed on hostile environment, retaliatory discharge and disparate treatment claims as well as whether the employer was liable for a hostile work environment claim when the plaintiff alleged that her office manager daily engaged in sexual banter, made sexual innuendoes about her, told crude sexual jokes, embarrassed her with comments about her body and clothes, and stood so the plaintiff was forced to brush against him. Following an incident at a bar with coworkers where the office manager put his hand on her thigh twice, plaintiff called in sick. When she eventually complained to the office manager about his conduct, she was fired immediately. The court rejected the defendants' claim that the plaintiff was terminated for poor attendance and production and not in retaliation when there was evidence that only after the office manager fired the plaintiff did he prepare and insert into the plaintiff's personnel file most of the negative comments about her performance and attendance and his secretary testified that the office manager even forged the plaintiff's signature on an employee reprimand prepared after her termination. There was a factual and legal basis for imposing liability on the employer based on agency principles when the office manager had the ultimate authority to hire and fire the plaintiff and thus exercised significant control over her conditions of employment. There were also issues of material fact regarding liability based on conduct outside the scope of delegated authority when the office manager allegedly capitalized on his authority over the plaintiff to create an intimidating and sexually charged atmosphere in which the plaintiff realized the almost certain termination facing if she challenged the offensive conduct. The company handbook contained no alternative to taking complaints to the supervisor.

Page 302, add to footnote 349 following "Eleventh Circuit":

Splunge v. Shoney's, inc., 874 F. Supp. 1258 (M.D. Ala. 1994).

Page 302, add following "District of Columbia Circuit":

Webb v. Hyman, 861 F. Supp. 1094 (D.D.C. 1994).

Page 302, add to footnote 349 following "First Circuit":

Third Circuit: Cook v. Applied Data, 66 Fair Empl. Prac. Cas. (BNA) 395 (D.N.J. 1989). The plaintiff failed to prove that a second supervisor created a hostile environment. The court concluded that although the supervisor's staring and leering for prolonged periods of time at the plaintiff could be characterized as offensive and unbefitting an officer of a corporation, it was not pervasive or severe enough to be sex discrimination. The court noted that in holding that this party's conduct did not constitute sexual harassment, it was not ruling on whether the cumulative effect of the behavior of all parties rose to the level of sexual harassment under Title VII.

* Fourth Circuit: Hopkins v. Baltimore Gas and Elec. Co., 77 F.3d 745 (4th Cir. 1996). A former employee did not prove that conduct by his supervisor, including bumping into the plaintiff, placing a magnifying glass over the plaintiff's crotch, staring at the plaintiff in the bathroom, and making inappropriate sexual comments, was sufficiently severe or pervasive to create a hostile environment in an action against his former employer under Title VII alleging that his supervisor's conduct created a sexually hostile work environment and that he was retaliated against for making a complaint about the harassment. The plaintiff alleged conduct that was

> temporally diffuse, ambiguous, and often not directed specifically at him. First, the incidents that Hopkins recounts occurred intermittently over a seven-year period, with gaps between incidents as great as a year. That alone suggests the absence of a condition sufficiently pervasive to establish Title VII liability. . . .

Second, Swadow's alleged conduct toward Hopkins was sexually neutral or, at most, ambiguous. According to Hopkins, Swadow bumped into him, positioned a magnifying glass over his crotch, flipped his tie over to see its label, gave him a congratulatory kiss in the receiving line at Hopkins' wedding, and stared at him in the bathroom. Notably, Hopkins has not asserted that Swadow ever made an overt sexual proposition or touched Hopkins in a sexual manner. While Swadow's conduct was undoubtedly tasteless and inappropriately forward, we cannot conclude that it was "of the type that would interfere with a reasonable person's work performance . . . to the extent required by Title VII." . . .

Third, several of the incidents upon which Hopkins relies occurred in group settings, and only Hopkins subjectively perceives them to have been directed solely at him. On one occasion, Hopkins was offended by Swadow's comment during a group discussion concerning how to use a sexual organ to survive a plane crash. On another occasion, he was offended by Swadow's comment—"Was it as good for you as it was for me?"—made after Swadow forced himself into a revolving door with a third party.

While we do not approve of Swadow's apparent willingness to offend and provoke employees with his ambiguously sexual innuendos, Title VII was not designed to create a federal remedy for all offensive language and conduct in the workplace.

Id. at 753-54 (citing *Harris v. Clyburn,* 1995 WL 56634, at *3 (4th Cir. 1995) (unpublished) (per curiam) (affirming summary judgment for employer where "only specific factual allegation of sexual harassment [was] occasional tickling [by her male superior] in the hallway"); *Cobbins v. School Bd. of Lynchburg, Va.,* No. 90-1754, slip op. at 7-10, 1991 WL 1828 (4th Cir. Jan. 14, 1991) (unpublished) (per curiam) (holding that where male teacher asked female teacher out for a drink, asked her to perform tasks she perceived as secretarial, and struck her in a fight, purported harassment was not gender-based and was not sufficiently severe or pervasive).

Page 303, add to footnote 349 following "Seventh Circuit":

Although "reluctant to upset a jury verdict challenged only for resting on insufficient facts," the Seventh Circuit did so when it concluded that the plaintiff did not establish a case of actionable sexual harassment when during the incidents spread over seven months, the supervisor never touched the plaintiff or invited her to have sex or go out on a date with him. Baskerville v. Culligan Int'l Co., 50 F.3d 428, 430 (7th Cir. 1995). The plaintiff alleged that during this time period, her supervisor called her "pretty girl" and made suggestive comments, such as his office was not hot until she stepped foot into it:

> We do not think that these incidents, spread out over seven months, could reasonably be thought to add up to sexual harassment. The concept of sexual harassment is designed to protect working women from the kind of male attentions that can make the workplace hellish for women. (Sexual harassment of women by men is the most common kind, but we do not mean to exclude the possibility that sexual harassment of men by women, of men by other men, or women by other women would not also be actionable in appropriate cases.) It is not designed to purge the workplace of vulgarity. Drawing the line is not always easy. On one side lie sexual assaults; other physical contact, whether amorous or hostile, for which there is no consent express or implied; uninvited sexual solicitations; intimidating words or acts; obscene language or gestures; pornographic pictures. . . . On the other side lies the occasional vulgar banter, tinged with sexual innuendo, or coarse or boorish workers. . . . It is not a bright line, obviously, this line between a merely unpleasant working environment on the one hand and a hostile or deeply repugnant one on the other; and when it is uncertain on which side the defendant's conduct lies, the jury's verdict, whether for or against the defendant, cannot be set aside in the absence of trial error. Our case is not within the area of uncertainty. Mr. Hall, whatever his qualities as a sales manager, is not a man of refinement; but neither is he a sexual harasser.
>
> He never touched the plaintiff. He did not invite her, explicitly or by implication, to have sex with him, or to go out on a date with him. He made no threats. He did not expose himself, or show her dirty pictures. He never said anything to her that could not be repeated on primetime television. The comment about Anita Hill was the opposite of solicitation, the implication being that he would get into trouble if he didn't keep his distance. The use of the word "tilly" (an Irish word for something added for good measure, and a World War II British slang term for a truck) to refer to a woman is apparently an innovation of Hall's, and its point remains entirely obscure. Some of his repartee, such as, "Not until you stepped your foot in here," or "Were we dancing, like in a nightclub?," has the sexual charge of an Abbott and Costello movie. The reference to masturbation completes the impression of a man whose sense of humor took final shape in adolescence. It is no doubt distasteful to a sensitive woman to have such a silly man as one's boss, but only a woman of Victorian delicacy—a woman mysteriously aloof from contemporary American pop

culture in all its sex-saturated vulgarity—would find Hall's patter substantially more distressing than the heat and cigarette smoke of which the plaintiff does not complain. The infrequency of the offensive comments is relevant to an assessment of their impact. A handful of comments spread over months is unlikely to have so great an emotional impact as a concentrated or incessant barrage. . . .

We are mindful of the dangers that lurk in trying to assess the impact of words without taking account of gesture, inflection, the physical propinquity of speaker and hearer, the presence or absence of other persons, and other aspects of context. Remarks innocuous or merely mildly offensive when delivered in a public setting might acquire a sinister cast when delivered in the suggestive isolation of a hotel room. So too remarks accompanied by threatening gestures or contorted facial features, or delivered from so short a distance from the listener's face as to invade the listener's private space. . . . Even a gross disparity in size between speaker and listener, favoring the former, might ominously magnify the impact of the speaker's words.

But even if we are wrong, and Hall's remarks could reasonably be thought to cross the line that separates vulgarity (not actionable) from harassment (potentially actionable), the plaintiff must lose because the company took all reasonable steps to protect her from Hall.

Id. at 430–31.

* Sanfelice v. Dominick's Finer Foods, Inc., 899 F. Supp. 372 (N.D. Ill. 1995). Judgment as a matter of law was not appropriate in an action by female employees of store who brought an action against the store owner for sexual harassment under Title VII and for intentional torts under Ilinois state law. One plaintiff alleged that a manager committed the following acts: (1) on a number of occasions, he kissed her on the neck and mouth; (2) at least 10 times he grabbed her buttocks, at times in the presence of others and at other times while alone; (3) on multiple occasions, he grabbed her sides and tickled her; (4) he often whispered in her ear that she "had a nice ass," "smelled good," or "looked good"; and (5) on a number of occasions, he asked her to go out socially with him (including to dinner, a summer boat cruise, and after-work employee gatherings), all of which she refused. She never welcomed his conduct and often told him to stop it. On one occasion in 1993, after telling Whetter that she was tired of being touched, he smiled, said that he thought she liked it, and walked out of the room in laughter. Sanfelice alleged that the conduct affected her job performance; there were times when she could not concentrate on the customers, and the manager of the deli department in which she worked noted this. She also experienced migraine headaches when she went to work and had nightmares while at home. Her intimate relationship with her boyfriend (currently, her husband) also suffered and her doctor diagnosed her with posttraumatic stress disorder, caused by Whetter's sexual harassment. The other plaintiff made similar allegations. Both women complained to their immediate supervisors, and nothing was done to correct their situations. Sanfelice's supervisor did attempt to contact both the store's human resources representative and the district manager but they did not respond. Sanfelice herself even tried to contact human resources but to no avail.

Page 303, add at end of footnote 349 :

Tenth Circuit: Ballou v. University of Kan. Medical Ctr., 871 F. Supp. 1384 (D. Kan. 1994). Although a female manager of collections in a hospital accounting office alleged that her supervisor pestered her constantly for dates, walked by her desk 30 to 40 times a day, sat on her desk and leaned toward her, stared, invited himself to have lunch with her, interrupted her when she was speaking to other men, and then warned her not to push him when he found out that she had complained about him to management, she did not state a claim for hostile environment when although these actions may have caused the plaintiff to be uncomfortable, there was no indication that this conduct would cause a reasonable person to find such a work environment hostile and abusive. The court found that the plaintiff never alleged any inappropriate physical contact and that there was no evidence that the behavior was related to her sex or that it rendered her environment hostile.

*   Eleventh Circuit: Faragher v. City of Boca Raton, 76 F.3d 1155 (11th Cir. 1996). In an action by former city lifeguards against the city and supervisors for sexual harassment under § 1983, with one plaintiff, Faragher, claiming sexual harassment under Title VII and alleging pendent state law claims against supervisors for battery, and against city for negligent retention and supervision of one supervisor, the district court properly entered judgment for the plaintiff on her § 1983 claim against supervisors, for supervisors on the second plaintiff's, Ewanchew's, § 1983 claim, for the plaintiffs on their battery claims, and for the city on their negligent retention claims, but improperly ruled against the city on Faragher's Title VII claim.

"The tight quarters and high male-female ratio apparently led to a rambunctious atmosphere among the lifeguards." *Id.* at 1157. Alleged supervisor conduct included one pressing himself against a plaintiff's buttocks and simulating sexual movement while the two were at the water fountain and another engaging in a pantomime depicting cunnilingus. Other female lifeguards similarly were subjected to the supervisors' uninvited and offensive touching and to their demeaning and offensive comments. Offensive comments included saying to Faragher, after tackling her, "If you had tits I would do you in a minute," and to Ewanchew, "There are a lot of tits on the beach today." Neither plaintiff complained to Parks and Recreation Department management about the conduct while they were employed with the city or when they resigned, but they did speak about it with one of their supervisors. The trial court found that Ewanchew's request for reemployment after resigning "makes it illogical to find a perception of hostility in the work environment on her part." *Id.* at 1159. With respect to Faragher, parts of the opinion made it at least arguable that the district court relied on conduct of which the plaintiff was unaware in determining that the supervisors' conduct was so pervasive and severe as to alter her conditions of employment. Thus the district court erred to the extent that it relied on such conduct.

District of Columbia: Stoeckel v. Environmental Management Sys., Inc., 882 F. Supp. 1106 (D.D.C. 1995). Conduct by a vice president, including comments about the plaintiff's dress, the rubbing of plaintiff's neck and shoulders on at least one occasion, winking at and following the plaintiff around the office, holding her head in his hands in an elevator, and comments about his dating life, all over a four-month period, did not constitute a hostile environment. The court had no doubt that the conduct was objectionable and unwelcome, though it noted that the plaintiff never verbally ordered him to stop, and that the conduct caused her discomfort, but noted that the plaintiff never testified that she found any of the incidents, except the one in the elevator, physically threatening in any way. Corrective action was taken immediately by her supervisor when she complained, an apology ensued, and the unwanted behavior ceased. "While Miller's conduct comes close to the line, the Court cannot find it was sufficiently egregious to rise to the level of a violation of Title VII." *Id.* at 1115 (footnote omitted).

Ryczek v. Guest Servs., Inc., 877 F. Supp. 754 (D.D.C. 1995). A female former employee, a student who worked for the defendants as part of a school program and who alleged that over the course of a month, her female supervisor told her about her sexual preference for women, inquired about the plaintiff's sexual practices, made other inappropriate comments, stuck the plaintiff's finger into a pot of sauce and licked the finger, looked at the plaintiff suggestively, leaned against her, and removed the supervisor's own shirt while she was riding in the elevator with the plaintiff, did not state a claim for hostile environment sexual harassment. At the end of the month, the plaintiff requested a transfer to another location and got it, and a month later, when she was told that she would be reassigned to work at her original workplace again, she told human resources representatives about her supervisor's conduct and they immediately began conducting an investigation. After she was interviewed but before the investigation had ended, the plaintiff left the defendant's employment and returned to school. The defendant completed its investigation, uncovered no evidence of harassment by the supervisor except for the use of vulgar language, ordered a counseling session for the supervisor, and placed a memo about the incident in her file. At best, the record reflected that the defendant should have been aware that the supervisor used foul language, but this was not a sufficient basis for Title VII liability. In response to the plaintiff's allegations that the investigation was not fair because management was accusatory, asked intrusive questions, and did not believe her, the court found that even viewing the facts in the light most favorable to the plaintiff, this did not demonstrate that the defendant failed to take prompt and appropriate remedial action. "Even if the investigation was not handled perfectly, the plaintiff has presented no evidence to suggest that the defendant did anything that would have allowed any harassment to continue." *Id.* at 759.

Some courts still seem to display judicial bias in focusing on the absence of physical injury or sexual advances. For example, in Gross v. Burggraf Constr. Co., 53 F.3d 1531 (10th Cir. 1995), a supervisor's alleged "crude" comments, such as referring to the plaintiff truck driver as a "cunt," saying to another truck driver in response to his inability to elicit a response from the plaintiff on his CB, "Mark, sometimes, don't you just want to smash a woman in the face?," referring to the plaintiff as "dumb" and using profanity in reference to her, and threatening to retaliate against her for contemplating filing an EEOC charge, did not constitute a hostile environment. The plaintiff failed to present percipient witnesses to testify regarding the statements she attributed to the supervisor; the record did not contain admissible evidence that the supervisor used the word "cunt" in referring to the plaintiff. There was no evidence in the record that the supervisor ever threatened the plaintiff with violence or ever attempted to harm her physically. The court asserted a questionable approach to the relationship between workplace and harassment:

§ 6.44   HOSTILE ENVIRONMENT

In the real world of construction work, profanity and vulgarity are not perceived as hostile or abusive. Indelicate forms of expression are accepted or endured as normal human behavior. . . .

Accordingly, we must evaluate Gross' claim of gender discrimination in the context of a blue collar environment where crude language is commonly used by male and female employees. Speech that might be offensive or unacceptable in a prep school faculty meeting, or on the floor of Congress, is tolerated in other work environments [citing *Rabidue*]. . . .

Id. at 1537–38. The court's that's-the-way-it's-always-been reasoning is circular. In Gearhart v. Eye Care Ctrs. of Am., Inc., 888 F. Supp. 814 (S.D. Tex. 1995), the court referred to a kick in the buttocks as "casual touching." A female former employee who had worked as an eyewear specialist at an eyewear store failed to establish that comments made by her supervisor constituted intentional infliction of emotional distress or a hostile work environment. Alleged offensive incidents included a comment that she could be promoted into management and gain a weekend off if she were to "sleep with the boss," comments that she should not wear dark pantyhose because they covered up her legs and others implying that the alleged harassers used *Cosmopolitans* for masturbation, touching her breast and hair, and kicking her in the buttocks. Although it did not condone the conduct, the court concluded that her allegations were nothing more than some flirting, casual touching, and sexual innuendos or jokes. Moreover, the employer responded immediately to the plaintiff's complaints, asking her if she would be comfortable remaining in the store pending an investigation if the alleged harasser were not present, and the plaintiff indicated that that would be fine. The employer subsequently relocated the alleged harasser.

Page 304, add to footnote 350:

See also Spain v. Gallegos, 26 F.3d 439 (3d Cir. 1994). An investigator in an EEOC office made a prima facie showing of hostile environment, despite atypical allegations that she was the subject of false rumors that she was having a sexual relationship with a supervisor and had gained influence over him as a result of their relationship, when in fact her private meeting with the supervisor allegedly resulted from the supervisor's improper solicitation of funds from the plaintiff, a practice that lasted for several years. The plaintiff alleged that her work environment was affected in several ways: she was subjected to the spreading of false rumors about her sexual affairs that impugned the integrity of her job performance, she was treated like an outcast, the rumors and resulting poor interpersonal relationships at work led supervisory personnel to evaluate the plaintiff negatively for advancement purposes, the supervisor exacerbated the situation by perpetuating the rumors and continuing to demand loans, and subsequently denied her a promotion.

The first element of a hostile work environment claim under *Andrews* is that the employee have suffered intentional discrimination because of her sex. . . . Spain's charge that she suffered such discrimination can withstand a motion for summary judgment as to this element. . . . We find that the first *Andrews* element is satisfied because the crux of the rumors and their impact upon Spain is that Spain, a female, subordinate employee, had a sexual relationship with her male superior. Unfortunately, traditional negative stereotypes regarding the relationship between the advancement of women in the workplace and their sexual behavior stubbornly persist in our society. Because we are cognizant that these stereotypes may cause superiors and co-workers to treat women in the workplace differently from men, we find that a reasonable jury could concluded that Spain suffered the effects she alleges because she was a woman. . . .

We note that there is no suggestion in the record that males who worked with Nelson [the supervisor] were harassed similarly. However, the district court erred in requiring Spain to produce evidence that males in a similar position were treated differently. A jury reasonably could conclude that if Spain had been a male, rumors would not have started that she had gained influence with Nelson through physically using her sex, particularly the ability to create problems for a fellow employee who "rubbed her the wrong way." Our discussion above leads us to believe that even if a male had a relationship bringing him into repeated close contact with Nelson, it would have been less likely for co-workers to have believed that the relationship had a sexual basis. Thus, the resulting poor interpersonal relationships, negative evaluations, and denial of advancement might not have occurred for a male as they allegedly did for Spain, inasmuch as the situation which caused them simply would not have been created. Furthermore, while it is true that the rumors also implicated Nelson, the rumors did not suggest that his involvement in the alleged relationship had brought him additional power in the workplace over his fellow employees, and the employees had no reason for resenting him in the way they did Spain. Accordingly, he did not have to endure a hostile working environment brought about due to his sex.

In addition, Spain's allegations that Nelson's improper conduct first created the conditions under which the rumors developed and then perpetuated them distinguishes Spain's claims from claims in other scenarios which might not support a sexually hostile work environment cause of action. . . . Thus, this is not a case in which rumors concerned the behavior of a co-worker outside of the workplace, or in which rumors developed as the result of other employees' misperception of a supervisor's and an employee's frequent but necessary job-related interaction. Rather, here there are factual questions for trial of whether the rumors developed and persisted as a result of Nelson's improper behavior. . . . Consequently, Spain properly has alleged, and supported with materials developed in discovery, that the rumors directed at her and her resulting ostracization and adverse evaluation for advancement purposes were both sex-based and intentional.

Id. at 448–49. The court noted that the plaintiff's claims were not predicated on sexually neutral conduct; she alleged that the harassment resulted from the rumors that she was having an affair with her supervisor.

Williams v. Marriott Corp., 864 F. Supp. 1168 (M.D. Fla. 1994). The repeated criticism and harassment of a female former security officer was properly found by a jury to constitute a hostile environment, even though the treatment of the employee was gender neutral, when there was ample evidence at trial from which the jury could reasonably have concluded both that the environment was hostile and that the hostility was due to the plaintiff's gender.

Page 304, add at end of section:

Some courts have found that the plaintiff's own conduct, not necessarily sexual, vitiates a claim of hostile environment. In *Munday v. Waste Management of North America, Inc.*, 858 F. Supp. 1364 (D. Md. 1994), an action by a female truck driver against her employer for breach of a settlement agreement for earlier charges of sexual discrimination, the court concluded that what happened to the plaintiff when she returned to work after the settlement agreement was not sexual harassment or sex discrimination but rather a pattern of retaliation designed to encourage the plaintiff to resign, as well as constructive discharge. With respect to the sexual harassment charge, the plaintiff "greatly contributed to the difficulties of which she complains by her own abrasive conduct and by her tendencies to blame her problems on others and to assume little responsibility for her own errors, as well as by her general dissatisfaction with her life." *Id.* at 1372. The court also noted that the type of employment was difficult and demanding and the entire work atmosphere could only be described "as a rather tough one." *Id.*

§ 6.45 Prima Facie Retaliation Case

Page 305, add to footnote 352:

Trent v. Valley Elec. Ass'n Inc., 41 F.3d 524 (9th Cir. 1994). The district court improperly granted summary judgment in favor of the employer utility company in an action by a meter reader alleging retaliatory discharge when the plaintiff had a reasonable belief that it was unlawful under Title VII to be subjected to a series of sexually offensive remarks at a mandatory safety meeting and thus she engaged in a protected activity, despite the fact that the plaintiff complained of conduct by an outside consultant. To establish the first element of a prima facie case, the plaintiff need only show that she had a reasonable belief that the employment practice she protested was prohibited under Title VII. "After all, Trent was obligated to attend the safety lecture to learn about an essential aspect of her job. She certainly would be justified in believing that Title VII would protect her from the offensive remarks she endured while attending the meeting." *Id.* at 527.

Redman v. Lima City Sch. Dist. Bd. of Educ., 889 F. Supp. 288 (N.D. Ohio 1995). An alleged harasser's refusal to allow a female plaintiff to work, because she had complained to management of sexual harassment, was not in response to the plaintiff's failure to submit to his advances but was instead in response to the plaintiff's complaints of sexual harassment; so this was not a quid pro quo claim but one of retaliation.

Page 306, add to footnote 354:

Hoeppner v. Crotched Mountain Center, 31 F.3d 9 (1st Cir. 1994). Summary judgment was properly granted in favor of the defendant employer in an action by a former teacher claiming that she was discharged for complaining about alleged sexual harassment by one teaching assistant. There was insufficient evidence that the employer had a practice of silencing employees by fabricating false negative evaluations against them, or of retaliating against teachers who made reports of teaching assistant misconduct and sexual harassment, and the plaintiff failed to establish the causal link between her report of sexual harassment and her discharge: that the defendant's alleged silencing practice was applied to the plaintiff in this case through the fabrication of the complaints against her and through her subsequent discharge when she continued to make waves by reporting incidents of sexual harassment. The plaintiff's evidence that she was a good teacher and that her teaching assistants were troublemakers did not by itself establish the necessary element of causality between the sexual harassment report and the discharge to support her Title VII action.

Ward v. Johns Hopkins University, 861 F. Supp. 367 (D. Md. 1994). Plaintiff's claim that an alleged harasser retaliated against her by not speaking to her and giving her less favorable assignments in the "dirtier" part of the basement for reporting his conduct did not amount to adverse employment action as a matter of law.

Johnson v. Tower Air, Inc., 149 F.R.D. 461 (E.D.N.Y. 1993). A former flight attendant trainee did not proffer evidence sufficient to support a claim of retaliatory discharge when a letter responding to a report indicating that the plaintiff did not follow FAA procedure did not mention allegations of sexual harassment.

Page 306, add to footnote 355:

Cf. Steiner v. Showboat Operating Co., 25 F.3d 1459 (9th Cir. 1994), *cert. denied,* 115 S. Ct. 733 (1995). The transfer to the day shift from swing shift of a former casino employee, the first female casino "floorperson," who alleged sexual harassment, retaliation, constructive discharge, and intentional infliction of emotional distress by a supervisor, was an instance of insufficient remediation but was not retaliatory in nature, as the employer was trying to avoid trouble between the supervisor and the plaintiff. The plaintiff also failed to show that her three low marks on the employer's employee evaluation were an act of retaliation, when her low marks were based on the employer's contention that she needed to learn to supervise games other than blackjack, there was no indication that the marks had been used as the basis for any adverse actions against the plaintiff, and at least two male dealers received worse marks than the plaintiff.

Page 307, add to footnote 356:

Ashkin v. Time Warner Cable Corp., 52 F.3d 140 (7th Cir. 1995). A female employee failed to establish that she was engaged in a protected activity so as to state a claim for retaliatory discharge when the magistrate judge properly found that she did not complain of any sexual harassment that she claimed invited retaliation but that her complaints arose solely out a nonsexual personality clash between two aggressive individuals. The court noted that this was not a case in which the plaintiff complained of sexual harassment, but did not use the "magic" phrase. The plaintiff and her attorney were ordered to each pay one-half of the defendant's attorneys' fees stemming from this appeal when it appeared that the plaintiff was aware of the insurmountable challenge she faced on appeal. Once the magistrate judge concluded that the plaintiff was not credible, and had therefore failed to prove the elements of her claim, the possibility of success on appeal was virtually nonexistent.

Sauers v. Salt Lake County, 1 F.3d 1122 (10th Cir. 1993). The district court's finding of no impermissible retaliation in violation of Title VII was not clearly erroneous. In an action by a former secretary with the county attorney's office, although the plaintiff demonstrated that she was reassigned after the supervisor indicated concern about someone filing sexual harassment charges against him, the defendants presented nondiscriminatory reasons behind the transfer, including an attempt by another supervisor to transfer her six weeks earlier because of dissatisfaction with her work, a backlog of work, and the need for assistance at the office to which she was transferred, thereby rebutting any case of retaliation raised by the plaintiff.

Marquart v. McDonnell Douglas Corp., 859 F. Supp. 366 (E.D. Mo. 1994), *aff'd without op.*, 56 F.3d 69 (8th Cir. 1995). A terminated female custodian alleged that she had been called a whore by coworkers, that a bag of horehound candy had been placed near her locker, that photographs of coworkers' wives and girlfriends in swimsuits were displayed in the workplace and that other pictures of other women in swimsuits were in the work area, that she had seen a male employee simulate sexual intercourse using a tool, that there was howling and whistling in the workplace, that on a single occasion a man's name had been placed over hers on a union campaign-for-office poster, that an American Cancer Society brochure on testicular cancer had been placed in her locker, and that some *Playboy* pictures and cartoons were in trash containers she was required to empty. These allegations did not make out a claim of retaliation when the plaintiff repeatedly displayed abnormal behavior at work and failed to comply with the employer's direct order that she obtain psychiatric diagnosis and treatment.

Page 307, add to footnote 360:

Dey v. Colt Constr. & Dev. Co., 28 F.3d 1446 (7th Cir. 1994). A plaintiff need not succeed on a charge of sexual harassment to make out a prima facie case of retaliatory discharge; the plaintiff need only have a reasonable belief that she or he is challenging conduct that violates Title VII. Here, allegations of sexual harassment were not baseless. The timing of the plaintiff's discharge, four weeks after she complained of sexual harassment to the alleged harasser and the vice president, and two weeks after she was given an unusually large raise by the president, supported the inference of a causal link between her complaints and her eventual discharge. The court rejected the defendant's contention that such an inference was unreasonable because the president allegedly did not know of the plaintiff's protected activity. Although the president denied knowing of her complaints, he admitted that he solicited the alleged harasser's opinion and that the latter agreed that the plaintiff should be fired. With respect to pretext, the plaintiff's detailed refutation of events which served as the basis for the employer's negative performance assessment demonstrated that the employer may not have honestly relied on the identified deficiencies, such as poor job performance and the plaintiff's uncooperative nature, in making its decision.

Page 307, add to footnote 362:

Cf. Van Zant v. KLM Royal Dutch Airlines, 870 F. Supp. 572 (S.D.N.Y. 1994). Sexual harassment claims were time-barred in an action by a former employee alleging that coworker bragged about his sexual skills, made lewd gestures behind the backs of women employees over a long period of time, and exposed himself to her in her office one day. The alleged harasser was reprimanded following an investigation and he was later terminated when the employer discovered that he had made a false statement on his application for employment about a prior conviction. A year and a half later, the plaintiff was greatly upset by the appearance of the alleged harasser, who had been allowed on the premises by a coworker. The employer offered the plaintiff a voluntary, paid leave of absence for several months, subject to periodic reviews in which the plaintiff refused to participate. Eight months later she was terminated for failing to report to a relevant evaluation. The plaintiff did not have the continuing violation theory available to her. Retaliation, itself, is a separate cause of action and not a part of any continuing discrimination claim.

Page 307, add at end of section:

Parties need have only a good faith, reasonable belief that matters about which they complain constitute sexual harassment in violation of Title VII. In *Hargens v. USDA*, 865 F. Supp. 1314 (N.D. Iowa 1994), a former U.S. Department of Agriculture employee made out a prima facie case of retaliation for complaining of alleged sexual harassment, despite the defendant's claim that the conduct about which he complained (not discussed in the opinion) was not sexual harassment. The plaintiff demonstrated temporal proximity between his challenges to conduct that he believed to be sexual harassment and an adverse employment action against him.

§ 6.46   Prima Facie Constructive Discharge Case

Page 308, add to footnote 364 after Sixth Circuit paragraph:

Seventh Circuit: Saxton v. American Tel. & Tel. Co., 10 F.3d 526 (7th Cir. 1993). Nothing in the record indicated that the employer treated the former employee plaintiff so badly that a reasonable employee in her position would have felt compelled to resign, and thus she was not constructively discharged.

Ninth Circuit: *Cf.* Steiner v. Showboat Operating Co., 25 F.3d 1459 (9th Cir. 1994), *cert. denied*, 115 S. Ct. 733 (1995). A former casino employee, the first female casino "floorperson," alleged sexual harassment, retaliation, constructive discharge, and intentional infliction of emotional distress by a supervisor. She thus raised triable issues of fact regarding her claim of intentional infliction of emotional distress. The court was unprepared to hold as a matter of law that public humiliation of an employee by her employer, "accomplished through rude, crude sexually explicit remarks and actions, cannot constitute intentional infliction of emotional distress." *Id.* at 1467.

§ 6.46   CONSTRUCTIVE DISCHARGE

Page 308, add to footnote 364 after Eleventh Circuit paragraph:

Virgo v. Riviera Beach Assocs., 30 F.3d 1350 (11th Cir. 1994). The district court did not err in finding constructive discharge and quid pro quo sexual harassment in an action by a female general manager of a hotel. She alleged that, over the course of her employment, she had been subjected to a sexually harassing course of conduct by a supervisor, who touched her without her permission and told her she would have to have sex with him or he would write disparaging job performance reviews. She eventually succumbed and then subsequently resigned because of the harassment. Even though the plaintiff resigned without filing a formal sexual harassment complaint, there was no showing of a formal grievance procedure, and the plaintiff attempted to notify several people about the harassment.

Cf. Young v. Mariner Corp., 65 Fair Empl. Prac. Cas. (BNA) 555 (N.D. Ala. 1991). One isolated incident, in which a supervisor made a few "mild" advances for a few minutes to a hotel's director of catering, after which he purportedly apologized with apparent embarrassment, was not sufficiently severe or pervasive to create a hostile environment. The plaintiff's claim of constructive discharge failed because, despite her claim that management was out to get her, there was no evidence that anything happened during the relevant period that could be considered retaliatory; she admitted that she was able to perform her job as competently as she had been able to before she raised her allegation, and that the conditions of her employment had not changed. The documentation of communications did not constitute "case building."

Page 308, add to footnote 365:

Martin v. Cavalier Hotel Corp., 48 F.3d 1343 (4th Cir. 1995). A female employee proved constructive discharge in an action charging that the general manager sexually harassed and assaulted her on a number of occasions by attempting to kiss her, telling her he wanted to take her to a hotel and "stick something between her legs" (*id.* at 1349), taking her into his office after placing a "Meeting in Progress" sign on his office door, locking it, putting his hand over her mouth to prevent her from screaming, and committing oral and anal sodomy on her, forcing her to commit oral sex in a hotel conference room, forcing her to lick his penis in the hotel's accounting office, and raping her. The plaintiff did not tell anyone about the abuse because the supervisor threatened to fire her if she did. After finally resigning, she was unable to work for several months and was diagnosed with depression and posttraumatic stress disorder and suffered from nightmares, insomnia, and severe weight loss. Before the effective date of her resignation, the plaintiff told her successor about the sexual harassment, and at trial the successor stated that he did nothing about it because he did not believe her. A jury found against the plaintiff on her sexual harassment, wrongful termination, and intentional infliction of emotional distress claims, but in favor of her and against the general manager on her common law assault and battery claims and against the employer on her constructive discharge claim. Because the general manager used his apparent authority to sexually assault the plaintiff, the hotel was liable for the constructive discharge. Hotel policy required that complaints be directed to the manager, and no other grievance process existed. To prove constructive discharge, an employer must necessarily be held to intend the reasonably foreseeable consequences of its actions. Here the plaintiff established that intent despite the employer's contention that the manager did not intend to make her quit, but wanted her to stay at the job so he could continue to assault her. Even if the evidence did not demonstrate the requisite employer intent, the plaintiff established the intent element by showing that when she protested, the manager told her to submit or be fired, and that when she resigned and tried to explain why, the manager snickered. In addition, there was no evidence that management took any remedial measures or that the manager treated other employees similarly.

§ 6.49   Settlements

Page 314, add to footnote 399:

Cf. Degerman v. S.C. Johnson & Son, Inc., 875 F. Supp. 560 (E.D. Wis. 1995). The canceling of a status conference by the plaintiff's attorney in a sexual harassment action did not necessarily indicate that a final agreement had been reached, and thus the court denied the defendant's motion to enforce a settlement agreement. The plaintiff agreed that a tentative agreement had been reached on most of the terms of the alleged settlement during a telephone conversation, but that a material term—the confidentiality clause—remained unsettled. The court rejected the defendant's assertion that the plaintiff's filing for unemployment benefits was evidence of the existence of a settlement agreement, because she did so after the parties agreed that the defendant would not contest her application for such benefits. However, the plaintiff filed for benefits, not immediately, but a month after the alleged settlement, and thus the court did not find the timing of the filing to be probative of the evidence of a settlement agreement.

See also Sheng v. Starkey Lab., 64 Fair Empl. Cas. (BNA) 1558 (D. Minn. 1994). A settlement agreement between an employer and a former employee who had alleged sexual harassment was enforceable despite the absence of agreement on the appropriate tax treatment of the cash settlement, and despite the fact that the court mistakenly issued an order granting summary judgment to the employer the day before the parties reached the agreement. The court's order was not filed and the court vacated the order before it had any effect and before the parties became aware of it. The court found that the parties entered a binding oral settlement agreement with two essential terms: that the plaintiff would release all claims and voluntarily dismiss the action and that the defendant would pay $73,500 to the plaintiff. The court denied an award of prejudgment interest when it determined that the settlement payment was adequate to make the plaintiff whole and effectuate the purposes of Title VII.

§ 6.50   Remedies

Page 314, add to footnote 401:

United States Equal Employment Opportunity Comm'n. v. Clayton Residential Home, Inc., 874 F. Supp. 212 (N.D. Ill. 1995). In an action by the EEOC, alleging that a class of female employees were subjected to a hostile environment, the EEOC could not recover injunctive relief when the last of the alleged unlawful employment practices was 3³/₄ years ago, the alleged harasser had not worked for the defendant since 1991, and the defendant now had an antidiscrimination policy.

A permanent injunction may require the continuing supervision of the court, which is costly. . . . Clayton has shown by the dearth of complaints against it in the last four years that there is little likelihood of recurrent violations. Thus, the purpose of Title VII will not be advanced further by enjoining Clayton from doing what it is already not doing, engaging in unlawful employment practices. Burdening the court, Clayton and the E.E.O.C. with the costs incumbent in a permanent injunction is not justified.

Id. at 216.

Page 314, update Landgraf citation in footnote 403:
aff'd on other grounds, 114 S. Ct. 1483 (1994).

Page 314, add to footnote 403:

Cuesta v. Texas Dep't of Criminal Justice, 805 F. Supp. 451 (W.D. Tex. 1991). The court found for the plaintiff in an action by a female parole case worker against the parole officer and parole board, and issued a declaratory judgment finding sexual harassment and a hostile environment; an injunction restraining the parole officer from engaging in sexual harassment against the plaintiff; an order that the defendant board remove the "no rehire" status on the plaintiff's file; and an award to the plaintiff of nominal damages and attorneys' fees.

Page 315, add to footnote 405:

Cf. Dombeck v. Milwaukee Valve Co., 40 F.3d 230 (7th Cir. 1994). A female employee's request for a permanent injunction prohibiting an alleged harasser from working in the same area as the plaintiff was not mooted by the fact that she and the alleged harasser were currently assigned to different work areas. Evidence indicated that the current assignments were not permanent and that, absent injunctive relief, the defendant could alter those assignments at any time.

EEOC v. Wilson Metal Casket Co., 64 Fair Empl. Prac. Cas. (BNA) 1402 (6th Cir. 1994). The district court properly issued an injunction that enjoined the alleged harasser from "asking any female employee to accompany him off the premises of the Company unless accompanied by at least one other employee, and kissing or placing his hands on any female employee in the work place." The court rejected the defendant's contention that none of this conduct was in and of itself unlawful and thus the injunction was overly broad:

> In the instant case, a distinct pattern of sexual harassment emerged. Wilson either waited until female employees were alone with him in isolated portions of the facilities or transferred them to isolated areas. Once they were isolated, he grabbed them and fondled their breasts and buttocks. With Barbara Ellis, in addition to unwanted fondling, Wilson forced her to engage in oral sex and sexual intercourse. Wilson also sexually propositioned female employees and asked them to accompany him

off the company's premises. Based on this pattern of behavior, the injunction approximately enjoins conduct which allowed sexual harassment to occur.

Id. at 1406.

Frederick v. Reed Smith Shaw & McClay, 63 Empl. Prac. Dec. (CCH) ¶ 42,864 (E.D. Pa. 1994). After a jury verdict finding on behalf of a defendant law firm on all and against the alleged harasser [Glanton] on some of plaintiff's claims, the court denied plaintiff's motion for injunctive relief by the law firm, rejecting the plaintiff's claim that such relief should be granted because it was the place of business where the conduct occurred and Glanton was a partner in the firm. The jury specifically found Glanton to be the only one in the firm who harassed the plaintiff and that the firm did not know nor should have known that he was engaging in sexually harassing conduct. Moreover, although the jury concluded that Glanton created a hostile environment, the injury to the plaintiff was so de minimis that an award of monetary damages was unnecessary to compensate her and thus injunctive relief would be unjustifiable. There was also no support for a request for a written apology, nor was it warranted when the law firm was exonerated of all charges.

Page 315, add to footnote 407:

Schmidt v. Maiorino, 619 N.Y.S.2d 139 (Sup. Ct. 1994). A former employee of a dentist did not establish her entitlement to a constructive trust over a pension account, and her claim that she was entitled to a constructive trust over future percentage bonuses allegedly orally promised by her employer was barred by the statute of frauds because it involved an oral agreement that could not be performed within one year. A constructive trust over the pension funds was not necessary, as the employer admitted that the plaintiff had a vested right to benefits of almost $50,000, but pursuant to the terms of the pension plan, such benefits would not be payable until the plaintiff was 65.

§ 6.51   —Front Pay

Page 316, update "Snider" citation in footnote 409:

cert. denied, 113 S. Ct. 981 (1993).

Page 316, add to footnote 409:

Hutchison v. Amateur Elec. Supply, Inc., 42 F.3d 1037 (7th Cir. 1994). An office manager who alleged that the owner and president of the defendant company regularly quizzed female employees about the frequency and nature of their sexual relations, engaged in numerous sexually explicit telephone conversations with his brother, leaving his office door open to ensure that the plaintiff and the other female office workers would overhear his comments, and refused to stop the conversations despite complaints from the plaintiff on behalf of the staff, failed to exercise reasonable diligence to mitigate her damages by failing to utilize temporary or full-time employment services specializing in the placement of persons with her skills. Moreover, the plaintiff had a duty to seek and accept employment paying less than what she earned at her previous employment; a reasonable jury could have concluded that absent the employer's unlawful discrimination, the plaintiff would have been in the market because the premium wages she received may have been tied to her continued tolerance of the employer's abuse and comparable nonabusive employment would then be compensated at the market rate.

Virgo v. Riviera Beach Assocs., 65 Fair Empl. Prac. Cas. (BNA) 1317 (11th Cir. 1994) (victim of quid pro quo sexual harassment was awarded $173,460 in back pay, $247,210 in front pay, and attorneys' fees and costs).

An award of front pay is discretionary. Saulpaugh v. Monroe Community Hosp., 4 F.3d 134 (2d Cir. 1993), *cert. denied*, 114 S. Ct. 1189 (1994).

§ 6.53 —Back Pay

Page 318, add to footnote 419:

Martin v. Cavalier Hotel Corp., 48 F.3d 1343 (4th Cir. 1995) (back pay award of $22,320).

Virgo v. Riviera Beach Assocs., 30 F.3d 1350 (11th Cir. 1994) (victim of quid pro quo sexual harassment was awarded $173,460 in back pay, $247,210 in front pay, and attorneys' fees and costs).

Olmer v. Iowa Beef Processors, 66 Fair Empl. Prac. Cas. (BNA) 843 (D. Neb. 1994) (plaintiff was awarded back pay in the amount of $36,299 and reinstatement).

Currie v. Kowalewski, 842 F. Supp. 57 (N.D.N.Y. 1994) ($13,419 in back pay and $3,011 interest awarded).

Page 319, add to footnote 431:

Saulpaugh v. Monroe Community Hosp., 4 F.3d 134 (2d Cir. 1993), *cert. denied*, 114 S. Ct. 1189 (1994). The district court improperly awarded the successful plaintiff in a sexual harassment action only simple interest in the amount of 7.22% a year, rather than a compound rate on her back pay award.

* *Page 320, add to footnote 440:*

Cf. Humpreys v. Medical Towers, Ltd., 893 F. Supp. 672 (S.D. Tex. 1995). A former building manager brought suit alleging claims for intentional infliction of emotional distress, violations of Title VII, and violations of the Texas Commission on Human Rights Act (TCHRA) including sexual harassment, sex discrimination, and retaliation. The court rejected the defendants' argument that the plaintiff failed to mitigate her damages by turning down a job offer and that any award of back pay should not extend beyond the time when she began taking teaching courses, when the plaintiff had turned down a job offer as a real estate sales person, not as a property manager. This position would not necessarily be the substantial equivalent of a position as a building manager, and if not, Humphreys was not required to accept it in order to mitigate her damages. However, she was not entitled to back pay for any time period in which she was not actively seeking employment as a property manager or in a substantially equivalent position, and she was not entitled to back pay during the time she was attending school full time.

Page 321, add to footnote 441:

Troutt v. Charcoal Steak House, Inc., 835 F. Supp. 899 (W.D. Va. 1993). The court rejected the employer's contention that a waitress, who quit her job after being subjected to ongoing sexual harassment, was not entitled to back pay because she could not prove that she was constructively discharged when she later returned to work at the restaurant and thus could not have found the environment to be intolerable. After the plaintiff's first month at work as a waitress, her supervisor began to make sexually suggestive remarks which escalated into physical contact, including putting his hands on her waist and breast, grabbing her buttocks, kissing her on the neck, reaching under her skirt, and grabbing her crotch. This was not the case of an overly sensitive employee reacting to inconsequential conduct. The fact that the plaintiff tolerated the conduct longer than someone else might have proved only that she needed the job badly, and she returned to the restaurant because she could not find another job that paid as well.

* *Page 321, add to footnote 443:*

Taylor v. Central Pa. Drug & Alcohol Serv. Corp., 890 F. Supp. 360 (M.D. Pa. 1995). A back pay award in a sexual harassment suit was not reduced by unemployment benefits collected by the plaintiffs, nor by the federal income tax which they would have paid on the wages earned. Back pay is normally computed at the rate the individual was paid at the time of discharge, and may include other benefits, if paid to other employees. The court rejected the defendants' contention that one plaintiff's right to back pay ceased when she started her own business ventures—that by opening a shop she voluntarily removed herself from the job market, legally terminating her right to continued back pay.

> Here, we find that that burden has not been met by defendants. Taylor testified convincingly that she remained available for work during the period she was operating the shops and would have closed the shops or found someone to operate them and immediately accepted other employment had a position been offered to her, because neither venture ever earned a profit.
>
> Further, Johnson's attempt to mitigate her back pay damages by starting her own business when no offers of employment were forthcoming was a laudable effort and should not be used against her to cut off her right to receive back pay. A ruling to the contrary would serve as a disincentive to Title VII plaintiffs unable to secure employment. Individuals in that position would have no incentive to use whatever talents or income-earning abilities they may have to earn money through self-employment as a stop-gap measure until full-time employment becomes available.

Id. at 372–73.

§ 6.54 —Compensatory and Punitive Damages

Page 323, add to footnote 451:

Cf. Hennessy v. Penril Datacomm Networks, Inc., 69 F.3d 1344 (7th Cir. 1995). Evidence supported a jury award of punitive damages in a sex and pregnancy discrimination case, alleging that a supervisor [Burns] took an employee to a "striptease" bar and behaved boorishly, propositioned the employee during an out-of-town trip, expressed surprise to find the employee pregnant, saying he had believed her to be a "career woman," and told the employee "not to worry" about her probationary status while he sent critical memoranda to his supervisor and others regarding her. However, the amount awarded, $300,000 against the employer and $50,000 against the alleged harasser, was excessive. In particular, two incidents involving Burns when he was not the plaintiff's supervisor were prominently mentioned in the evidence. Once when a number of Penril employees were in Portland, Oregon, on business, Burns took the plaintiff's supervisor, McFadden, the plaintiff, another female sales representative (Marshall), and two other men to a striptease bar where during a "performance," Burns and other male customers began yelling and cheering for the plaintiff and Marshall, the only women in the bar who were not entertainers, to get up on stage and perform with the bar's dancers. But they refused. As the group drove home, Burns mentioned how other women's breasts compared with the breasts of the dancers. The plaintiff stated she was uncomfortable during the evening and got the impression that Burns viewed her and other women as sex objects. At a later Christmas party, Burns confessed to the plaintiff that he was no longer sexually attracted to his wife, but that he had always found the plaintiff, who he said was intelligent, to be very sexually attractive. The plaintiff said her marriage was happy, and the topic was abandoned. The conversation, the plaintiff said, left her feeling "very uncomfortable."

It is, of course, beyond dispute that a punitive damage award is appropriate in certain cases to punish a wrongdoer for outrageous conduct and to deter others from engaging in similar conduct. An award of punitive damages, however, must be supported by the record and may not constitute a windfall to the prevailing party. . . .

Hennessy's case does not rest on a classic claim of sexual harassment; she claims she was terminated on account of her gender and because of her pregnancy. Yet a smidgen of what may be a claim of sexual harassment is lurking here because, as part of her argument for punitive damages, Hennessy points to the events in Portland and Seattle in 1990 concerning Mr. Burns. These events—the trip to the striptease bar and the poorly camouflaged proposition in the lounge after the Christmas party—and the legal significance that attaches to them bring to the fore the difficult question of what sort of sexual interaction between men and women is legally permissible in the workplace as we approach the end of the twentieth century. While this is not the time or place to delve into a lengthy discussion about the subject, a few general observations, we believe, are appropriate.

Studies tell us that many women, especially those who have spent substantial time in the work force, believe they have at one time or another been the subject of some sort of sexual harassment. The stories of harassment are as varied as the women who tell them. Judge Alex Kozinski of the United States Court of Appeals for the Ninth Circuit tells of the lawyer whom he knows well who put herself through school waiting tables at a Hungarian restaurant, where the owner's son often took the opportunity to grope her as she passed through the kitchen with her arms full of food. "You learn to wriggle past him without spilling the goulash," she explained.

Women deal with sexual harassment in the workplace in different ways. Some quit, while others, if the harasser is not the boss, appeal to a higher authority within the company. Others endure or learn, as Judge Kozinski notes, to "wriggle without spilling the goulash."

Sexual harassment in the workplace raises sensitive and complex concerns. For courts, these concerns are often competing. On one hand, we should not be in the business of throwing a wet blanket over activities that can lead to consensual amour. On the other hand, a major purpose of Title VII is to immunize the workplace from sexual intimidation and repression.

In 1994, Warner Bros. presented Demi Moore aggressively pursuing Michael Douglas in its movie, "Disclosure." The situation depicted in the movie, however, is atypical. The lion's share of sexual harassment situations features the man as the harasser and the woman as the harassee. But in the workplace, what is fair and what is foul? The extremes are easy; "Have sex with me or you're fired" lands deep in foul territory, but "I like your dress" is a fair ball. Deciding between the extremes is not an easy task today, and it won't get any easier to do in the future. As the work force grows and people spend more of their time at work, the workplace inevitably becomes fertile ground for the dating and mating game. It is certainly not unusual, and it may even be desirable, for love to bloom in the workplace. Contiguity can lead to sexual interest, which can lead to soft music, candlelight dinners, serious romance, and marriage, or any stops along the way. And more often than not, still at this moment in time, it is the man who usually makes the first move. Within this context, we look to what happened between Hennessy and Burns in Portland and Seattle in 1990.

Although Hennessy probably wishes she had stayed behind, it is undisputed that nobody dragged her kicking and screaming to the striptease bar in Portland. While Burns' actions in the bar, accepting Hennessy's view of them, were boorish, as were his comments on the way home, it was, from the evidence in this case, an isolated incident of bad taste. On the state of this record, even Hennessy does not argue that Burns was some sort of an overbearing sexist. The not-so-veiled proposition in the lounge in Seattle was a different sort of event. While Burns might have been a louse for saying unkind things about his wife and for being a married man trying to get something going with a married woman, that was really all he did, and Hennessy wasn't interested.

It is somewhat interesting to note that had Hennessy voluntarily become romantically involved with Burns and her fellow sales reps complained that she was receiving preferential treatment, they probably would have had no recourse under Title VII. . . .

Because there is no evidence that Burns ever followed up on his proposition—we are confident Hennessy would have told the jury about it if he had—we can only conclude that Burns accepted Hennessy's turn-off and that he never tried to work that field again. . . .

*   *   *

In our case, the jury, as we have seen, denied compensatory damages—pain and suffering, emotional distress, and that sort of thing—to Hennessy. The question then becomes whether 100 percent of the [$100,000] available damages to Hennessy in this case can be soaked up by a punitive damage award. We don't believe that it can. Although we believe, as we have noted, that the jury could have awarded punitive damages in this case, we do not think the case is so egregious that an award at 100 percent of what can legally be awarded against a company of Penril's size is appropriate. In fact, given the much more egregious nature of some sex discrimination cases—the legion of "quid pro quo" sexual harassment cases, like *Nichols v. Frank,* 42 F.3d 503 (9th Cir. 1994) for example—we think the punitive damages must be reduced to a smaller figure.

Id. at 1352–54.

Reese v. United States, 24 F.3d 228 (Fed. Cir. 1994) (punitive damages a taxpayer received as part of a sexual harassment suit were not excluded from gross income).

Prunty v. Arkansas Freightways Inc., 64 Fair Empl. Prac. Cas. (BNA) 451 (5th Cir. 1994). A former female employee who was found by the district court to have suffered severe emotional distress at the hands of her supervisor, who made daily vulgar, offensive, and degrading comments about the plaintiff both to her and to coworkers, could not recover compensatory damages under Title VII or the state antidiscrimination law when she did not present any evidence of damages whatsoever.

Faragher v. City of Boca Raton, 864 F. Supp. 1552 (S.D. Fla. 1994). A female former city lifeguard, alleging that among other things, the supervisors touched her on the waist, neck, breasts, and buttocks, made sexual comments such as "There are a lot of tits on the beach today," and referred to women as "cunts" and "bitches" proved sexual harassment. A second lifeguard, however, did not prove that she found the alleged conduct intolerable for purposes of her § 1983 claim when she tried to obtain a part time job again after she left city employment. The court awarded the first lifeguard nominal damages of $1.00 for the Title VII claim, and $10,000 in compensatory damages on the § 1983 claim. The second lifeguard, who prevailed on a battery claim against a supervisor, was awarded $35,000 in compensatory damages. Punitive damages against the supervisor were assessed at $500 for the first lifeguard and $2,000 for the second.

Hatley v. Store Kraft Mfg. Co., 859 F. Supp. 1257 (D. Neb. 1994). A female employee established a hostile environment claim with persuasive evidence that the employer never took proper remedial measures against alleged sexual harassment despite four well-documented complaints. That the plaintiff engaged in pranks, some of which had sexual overtones, with other coworkers did not prove that the alleged harasser's overtures were welcome when it was obvious to everyone that the plaintiff was being singled out as a woman and that she found the conduct offensive. It was not surprising that the plaintiff did not complain to her union since she was the only female on the final assembly line, and the plaintiff testified that after union meetings stag films were often shown. For conduct that occurred after the effective date of the Civil Rights Act of 1991, a jury awarded $125,000 in lost wages and fringe benefit damages and $100,000 for emotional pain, suffering, inconvenience, mental anguish, loss of enjoyment of life, and other nonmonetary damages. For conduct occurring before the effective date of the Act, the plaintiff was awarded nominal damages of $1.00.

Munday v. Waste Management of North Am., Inc., 858 F. Supp. 1364 (D. Md. 1994) (damage award of $50,000 proper when the treating physician's opinions regarding major mood disorder and posttraumatic stress syndrome were not accepted).

Johnson v. Board of County Comm'rs, 859 F. Supp. 438 (D. Colo. 1994). In a sexual harassment action by two female dispatchers and one deputy sheriff against the board of county commissioners and the former sheriff, a damages award would not intrude upon the state function of establishing an autonomous sheriff's department in violation of the Tenth Amendment doctrine of state immunity. In EEOC v. Wyoming, 460 U.S. 226 (1983), the Supreme Court held that the extension of the Age Discrimination in Employment Act to cover state and local governments was a valid exercise of Congress's power under the commerce clause and was not precluded by the constraints of the Tenth Amendment. The defendant failed to articulate how an award of damages would fall within requirements that must be satisfied to show congressional commerce-power legislation is invalid.

Page 323, add to footnote 452:

* McKinnon v. Kwong Wah Restaurant, 83 F.3d 498 (1st Cir. 1996). The court of appeals affirmed a $2,500 compensatory damage award to each waitress plaintiff in a sexual harassment case alleging that the owners and employees subjected the plaintiffs to repeated verbal and physical sexual harassment, but remanded the case to the district court for clarification and explanation as to what evidence the court relied upon in declining to award the plaintiffs punitive damages. The district court held a hearing without a jury to determine damages, and awarded $13,094.84 to McKinnon, and $13,189.45 to Poulin, plus attorneys' fees. The award included 135 weeks of back pay (adjusted for mitigation) and $2,500 per plaintiff in compensatory damages. The court declined to award front pay, punitive damages, or prejudgment interest. The court of appeals noted that in weighing the evidence the court found it difficult to distinguish between the emotional suffering caused by the defendants' behavior, and the suffering caused by prior independent sources. The district court reasoned that a $2,500 award was sufficient because the causal connection between the harassment and the plaintiffs' emotional trauma was complicated by other factors similarly causing such suffering. With respect to the denial of punitive damages, although compensatory damages are available to victims of intentional discrimination under Title VII, a plaintiff must demonstrate that the defendant acted with malice or reckless indifference before he or she can receive punitive damages. *Id.* The legislative history of the section notes that plaintiffs must first prove intentional discrimination, then must prove actual injury or loss arising therefrom to recover compensatory damages, and must meet an even higher standard (establishing that the employer acted with malice or reckless or callous indifference to their rights) to recover punitive damages. H.R. Rep. No. 40(I), 102d Cong., 1st Sess. at 72 (1991), 1991 U.S.C.C.A.N. 610.

> There is no question that Defendants' repeated sexual harassment was offensive. In fact, in many cases, this behavior might be strong evidence of malice or, at least, reckless indifference to Plaintiffs' rights. In this case, however, the Court believes that the behavior of at least some Defendants was influenced by language, cultural, and educational barriers. With this consideration and all of the other evidence in mind, the Court concludes that Defendants were not acting with either malice or reckless indifference to Plaintiffs' rights. No award of punitive damages is therefore appropriate.

Id. at 508. That the defendants' acts "were patently offensive" and repeated could provide cause for compensatory damages but did not necessarily mandate a finding of punitive damages. Heavy reliance on cultural and educational factors was inappropriate in this case.

> Ignorance of the law or of local custom is not a defense under Section 1981a to the alleged offensive conduct of the defendants.
> A defendant's cultural background is not irrelevant in evaluating the appropriateness of punitive damages. In certain circumstances, a defendant's background will likely have an impact on his consciousness of wrongdoing. In the instant case, however, the district court's only explicit reason for denying punitive damages was the cultural, ethnic, and educational background of the defendants, and this is not the dispositive factor.

Id. at 509.

Mills v. Amoco Performance Prods., Inc., 872 F. Supp. 975 (S.D. Ga. 1994). In an action by a female employee and her husband, a former employee, alleging that the female employee was sexually harassed, that the employer retaliated against both of them, and that the female employee was subjected to intentional infliction of emotional distress, the court held that the female plaintiff could recover compensatory and punitive damages for harassment that occurred after the enactment of the Civil Rights Act of 1991, but not for preenactment conduct. The female plaintiff alleged that on numerous occasions male coworkers referred to her as a "stupid bitch" and tried to look into the restroom at her and that one coworker gestured at her by grabbing his crotch. The plaintiffs stated a claim for hostile environment when the alleged conduct

> consisted of a continual pattern of offensive, sexually suggestive and explicit acts and comments by her male counterparts and supervisors. The alleged conduct was frequent and nondiscrete; it would not easily go unnoticed by shift supervisors or others in managerial positions who interacted with Mills and her coworkers on a regular basis.

Id. at 987. The defendant corporation could not be held liable for a claim of intentional infliction of emotional distress when the alleged sexual harassment was not committed in furtherance of the defendant's business, but outside the scope of the employees' jobs.

Preston v. Income Producing Management, Inc., 871 F. Supp. 411 (D. Kan. 1994). An employer was not immune from punitive damages for the acts of a comanager. The jury properly awarded $8,000 in compensatory damages and $25,000 in punitive damages. The evidence was clear that at pertinent times the alleged harasser had authority to hire and fire store employees and had the further responsibility of disciplining and/or counseling employees on areas of discriminatory practices.

> He, in the face of notice and complaint, did neither. To put the problem in perspective, we are dealing with a store co manager who, along with others, frequently teased plaintiff about her large breasts. He regularly addressed the young male employees as "hard dicks." This and other evidence relating to Poland's conduct convinces the court that the jury verdict is entirely understandable. To say now that IPM somehow is immune from punitive damages for the acts of Poland while co-manager is nonsense. Further discussion on the subject is unnecessary.
>
> It should be sufficient here to say that the price paid by a defendant for its conduct as an employer, through its store managers, is punitive damages. One lesson learned is that when and if a defendant, for whatever reason, imposes managerial responsibility on an untrained and undisciplined misfit such as Poland, it puts at risk the very result found by the jury in its

verdict. Another lesson which needs to be learned is that it is time for the president of the defendant company to see that such a circumstance does not reoccur.

Id. at 415.

Munday v. Waste Management of North Am., Inc., 858 F. Supp. 1364 (D. Md. 1994) (punitive damages of $40,000 in an action by a female truck driver against her employer for breach of a settlement agreement for earlier charges of sexual discrimination, in which the court concluded that what happened to the plaintiff when she returned to work after the settlement agreement was not sexual harassment or sex discrimination but rather a pattern of retaliation designed to encourage the plaintiff to resign, as well as constructive discharge).

A court may assess civil penalties as well. *See* Giuliani v. Stuart Corp., 512 N.W.2d 589 (Minn. Ct. App. 1994). The trial court properly found that a property manager had been sexually harassed, in violation of the state human rights act, by her supervisor, who was vice president of the defendant real estate management firm. It assessed a civil penalty of $500 to be awarded to the state.

Page 323, add at end of section:

In *In re Kininson*, 67 Fair Empl. Prac. Cas. (BNA) 381 (Bankr. E.D. Mo. 1995), the bankruptcy court held that any recovery that a debtor would receive for the personal injury aspect of a potential sexual harassment claim, such as medical expenses or recovery for emotional distress or other harms was exempt from the bankruptcy estate, but any recovery for injury to property, such as loss of wages and punitive damages, would become part of the bankruptcy estate for distribution to creditors.

§ 6.55   Awards of Attorneys' Fees

Page 323, add to footnote 454 after First Circuit paragraph:

Second Circuit: Saulpaugh v. Monroe Community Hosp., 4 F.3d 134 (2d Cir. 1993), *cert. denied*, 114 S. Ct. 1189 (1994) (attorneys' fees awarded in amount of $85,305).

Third Circuit: Stair v. Lehigh Valley Carpenters Local 600, 855 F. Supp. 90 (E.D. Pa. 1994) (attorneys' fees and expenses of $74,040 awarded to plaintiff).

§ 6.55   ATTORNEYS' FEES

Page 323, add to footnote 454 following "Fourth Circuit":

Martin v. Cavalier Hotel Corp., 48 F.3d 1343 (4th Cir. 1995) (attorneys' fee award of approximately $100,000).

Page 324, add to footnote 454:

Federal Circuit: Reese v. United States, 24 F.3d 228 (Fed. Cir. 1994) (victim of sexual harassment awarded $250,000 in damages and costs and attorneys' fees of $239,437).

Page 328, add to footnote 469:

Scheeler v. Crane Co., 21 F.3d 791 (8th Cir. 1994). An offer of $15,000 by the defendant in a sexual harassment suit was not more favorable than a judgment of $12,500 plus interest, for purposes of the offer of judgment rule, when attorneys' fees were costs to be subtracted from the awarded amount, and the plaintiff had already incurred fees in the sum of $3,500.

Page 328, add to footnote 470:

Marquat v. Lodge 837, 26 F.3d 842 (8th Cir. 1994), was an action by an employee alleging that her union retaliated against her because she asserted her Title VII rights, or, in the alternative, that the union acquiesced in or conspired with her employer to retaliate against her on the basis of her sexual harassment complaint by refusing to process her grievances. The plaintiff voluntarily dismissed her complaint without prejudice four days before trial and the trial court awarded fees to the defendant on the grounds that the union was a prevailing party and that the plaintiff's claims were without foundation. The court of appeals held that although the district court may award attorney fees to a defendant when the plaintiff voluntarily dismisses her or his Title VII complaint, the standards established in *Farrar* "cannot be transformed into a definition for prevailing party in general." *Id.* at 851.

> [T]he *Farrar* Court delineated the extreme contours of what constitutes a prevailing civil rights plaintiff for purposes of fee-shifting. These contours are meant to be extreme because, under the broad, policy-oriented, *Christiansburg* definition, a prevailing plaintiff is entitled to attorneys' fees except under very special circumstances. Justice Thomas, writing for

the *Farrar* majority, granted "prevailing party" status to even the " technical" civil rights plaintiff victor. . . .

This very definition of what constitutes a prevailing plaintiff falls within both the adversarial and the public policy conception of the role of the judiciary. By adopting a definition of prevailing plaintiff as one who achieves a material alteration of the legal relationship among the parties, the Court recognizes that the parties are adversarial and that a judicial determination of the issues will alter the legal relationship among these parties. On the other hand, by adopting such a broad definition of prevailing plaintiff, the courts have the power and latitude to award attorneys' fees to many more plaintiffs, especially in circumstances where the courts might feel that such plaintiffs have succeeded in their role as "private attorney general," but have not had a full-blown trial on the merits. . . .

While a wholesale importation of the *Farrar* "material alteration of the legal relationship between the parties" definition of prevailing plaintiff into a definition for prevailing defendant comports with the adversarial conception of the judicial role as fee-shifters, it does not comport with the dominant, public policy conception. Under such a test, the Union would technically be a prevailing party because [the plaintiff's] voluntary dismissal of her complaint *with prejudice* materially altered the legal relationship between her and the Union to the benefit of the Union. We believe, however, that the Supreme Court would expressly disapprove of such a test because it has had the opportunity to adopt a general definition of prevailing party several times and has chosen not to do so. Had it wished to adopt such a general definition it probably would have done so.

Id. at 850–51. In the Eighth Circuit, most recent decisions awarding attorney fees to prevailing defendants in civil rights cases indicate that a defendant must prove that the plaintiff's case is meritless in order to recover fees. When there are disputed issues of fact, it is necessarily impossible to prove that a plaintiff's case is meritless shy of a fullblown trial on the merits. Here there was no evidence that the plaintiff withdrew her complaint to escape a disfavorable judicial determination on the merits; the decision to withdraw a complaint with prejudice and to pursue state law claims is a legitimate litigation strategy.

Page 328, add to footnote 471:

Johnson v. Tower Air, Inc., 149 F.R.D. 461 (E.D.N.Y. 1993). A Rule 11 sanction in the amount of $1,000 was assessed against an attorney who failed to make a reasonable inquiry into the legal basis for a § 1983 claim of sexual harassment.

Sanctions may also be assessed under other federal and local rules and statutes, such as Fed. R. Civ. P. 16, 26 and 37, Appellate Rule of Civil Procedure 38, and 28 U.S.C. § 1927. *See, e.g.*, Carmon v. Lubrizol Corp., 17 F.3d 791 (5th Cir. 1994). Double costs as sanctions under Fed. R. App. P. 38 and 28 U.S.C. § 1927 were assessed jointly and severally against the plaintiff and her counsel for filing "nothing more than a five-page 'slap-dash' excuse for a brief—a brief that fails to raise even one colorable challenge to the district court's judgment." 17 F.3d at 795. The sexual harassment claim was disposed of on an entirely different ground than that asserted by the brief.

Page 328, add to footnote 472:

Sassaman v. Heart City Toyota, 879 F. Supp. 901 (N.D. Ind. 1994). Evidence of sexually charged comments and actions and differential treatment supported a jury verdict finding sexual harassment of a female salesperson by four male supervisory employees of a car dealership. Although the plaintiff did not win her claim for sex discrimination, both the sex discrimination and sexual harassment claims arose from the same underlying facts and sought relief from essentially the same course of conduct, and thus the claims were sufficiently related for purposes of attorneys' fees. Although it was a more difficult question, the court could not find that an unsuccessful retaliation claim was distinct in all respects from the sexual harassment claim. Had the plaintiff proved her retaliation claim at trial, the claim would have been premised in part upon the filing of a claim for underlying sexual harassment and discrimination.

Cf. Hutchison v. Amateur Elec. Supply, Inc., 42 F.3d 1037 (7th Cir. 1994). Plaintiff's counsel was entitled to be heard on the matter before a significant reduction in hours was made by the court.

Page 328, add to footnote 473:

Martin v. Cavalier Hotel Corp., 48 F.3d 1343 (4th Cir. 1995). An attorneys' fee award of approximately $100,000, less than half of the claimed fees, was proper when the plaintiff lost her sexual harassment, wrongful termination, and intentional infliction of emotional distress claims, but won her common-law assault and battery constructive discharge claims, and when some of the hours submitted were excessive.

Smith v. American Express Travel Servs., 179 Ariz. 131, 876 P.2d 1166 (Ariz. Ct. App. 1994) (attorneys' fees of $57,282 to defendant were improper when lower court should have held a hearing).

Attorney fees may be reduced for partial success. *See, e.g.*, Scheeler v. Crane Co., 21 F.3d 791 (8th Cir. 1994). The district court properly reduced attorneys' fees awarded in a sexual harassment action under the state civil rights act from $40,445 to $27,500 when the plaintiff recovered less than she sought and failed on her claims for disability, emotional injury, pain and suffering, and punitive damages.

§ 6.57 Appeals

Page 329, add to footnote 477:

Cf. Chambers v. American Trans Air, Inc., 17 F.3d 998 (7th Cir.), *reh'g & suggestion for reh'g denied, cert. denied*, 115 S. Ct. 512 (1994). Because there was evidence that female airline employees were routinely referred to in vulgar sexist language, in their absence, by the highest level of management, the plaintiff's claim of hostile environment might have survived a summary judgment motion, but she did not pursue this claim in her appeal in this discrimination suit. Although passing references on appeal to "overt hostility" could be viewed as an attempt to raise the issue, they were insufficient. The plaintiff's counsel never once cited *Meritor* or any other hostile environment case. "While the arguments below may have sufficed to preserve the issue for appeal, we will not reverse the entry of summary judgment based on skeletal snippets of argument without citation to authority." *Id.* at 1005.

CHAPTER 7

EMPLOYER DEFENSES

§ 7.2 Conduct Was Nondiscriminatory

Page 333, add to footnote 14:

Cox v. Phelps Dodge Corp., 43 F.3d 1345 (10th Cir. 1994). A female former employee's appeal from a judgment in favor of the employer on a sexual harassment claim under Title VII was moot when she did not appeal the ruling that she was discharged for valid nondiscriminatory reasons that were not related to her sex or to her prior complaints of sexual harassment.

§ 7.5 Employer Had No Notice of Harassment

Page 338, add to footnote 34:

Smith v. American Express Travel Servs., 179 Ariz. 131, 876 P.2d 1166 (Ct. App. 1994). An employer was not liable under respondeat superior for sexual assault and harassment in an action charging that a supervisory employee (though not the supervisor of the plaintiff) teased the plaintiff, grabbed and touched her breasts, rubbed up against her, threw a condom on her desk, on one occasion grabbed her and carried her out of the building, and on at least four occasions forced her to have sex with him at various locations in the building. "Nevertheless, Nally did not promise Smith any reward if she submitted to his advances or threaten her with any adverse consequences if she refused" (876 P.2d at 1169), and "no reasonable person could conclude that Nally acted within the scope of his employment in sexually harassing and assaulting Smith." *Id.* at 1168. The plaintiff produced no evidence that the employer knew or should have known of the supervisor's conduct or that the employer failed to take action to prevent such conduct. The plaintiff did not report the supervisor's conduct to either of the two women who were her supervisors during the time she was being harassed. When the employer found out about the harassment during an exit interview of another employee, it immediately told the alleged harasser to call in sick and conducted an investigation. Two weeks later it gave the supervisor a choice of discharge or resignation, and the supervisor resigned.

§ 7.6 Employer Took Prompt and Appropriate Remedial Action

Page 339, add to footnote 37 following "Katz" citation:

First Circuit: Klessens v. United States Postal Serv., 66 Fair Empl. Prac. Cas. (BNA) 1630 (1st Cir. 1994). A female employee who alleged that her coworkers made explicit remarks about her body, made comments like, "If I don't get laid I'm going to take hostages," that she was "a nice piece of ass," that she had "small tits," and that she should "go fuck herself," and spoke of their sexual exploits did not prove a hostile environment. After she complained and management investigated, management offered the plaintiff a transfer that would take her away from one of the coworkers. She declined at first but later in the summer accepted the transfer; ultimately, the alleged harasser was also transferred to another post office. Before the transfers, however, the plaintiff and her alleged harasser regularly sat together in the plaintiff's car during breaks. The court noted that the sexual harassment issue was close, but that the lower court's finding that the post office responded appropriately to the plaintiff's complaints was insurmountable. With respect to a retaliation claim, the court properly found that the plaintiff was discharged because she had given false answers on her employment application, not because she had complained of sexual harassment.

Page 340, add to footnote 37 following "Fifth Circuit":

Carmon v. Lubrizol Corp., 17 F.3d 791 (5th Cir. 1994). The district court properly determined that an employer took prompt and remedial action in response to a female employee's two sexual harassment complaints, when the employer sprang into action immediately. It met with the plaintiff on the same day as her first complaint, questioned the alleged harasser, interviewed six witnesses, found that the alleged harasser and the plaintiff had used foul language, reprimanded the alleged harasser, and transferred him to another shift. A similar investigation was conducted the next year following another complaint of sexual harassment. The plaintiff's attorney was assessed with sanctions for a frivolous appeal.

Fishel v. Farley, 64 Empl. Prac. Dec. (CCH) ¶ 43,092 (E.D. La. 1994). A state licensing board was not liable for the alleged sexual harassment of a former contract compliance officer when the day after the board became aware of the woman's complaint, it placed the alleged harasser on leave, and then conducted an investigation into the allegations.

Page 340, update "Landgraf" citation in footnote 37, under "Fifth Circuit":

aff'd on other grounds, 114 S. Ct. 1483 (1994).

Page 340, add to footnote 37 following "Seventh Circuit":

Baskerville v. Culligan Int'l Co., 50 F.3d 428 (7th Cir. 1995). The employer reasonably responded to the plaintiff's complaints of sexual harassment in the form of suggestive comments when it promptly investigated the matter, the supervisor was told that his offensive behavior must stop immediately, he was placed on probation, and a salary increase was held up for several months.

Page 340, add to end of footnote 37:

Eighth Circuit: Fred v. Wackenhut Corp., 860 F. Supp. 1401 (D. Neb. 1994), *aff'd without op.*, 53 F.3d 335 (8th Cir. 1995). The employer responded properly to a female former nuclear security officer's complaints that among other things a coworker presented her with a styrofoam cup upon which was written the words "Suck my dick Ma-donna," and that sexist remarks were made over the intercom system. Once it became aware of the charges, it called a meeting of employees and circulated a memorandum that admonished the employees to cease any harassment. No additional harassment was reported.

Ninth Circuit: Nash v. Electrospace Sys., Inc., 9 F.3d 401 (5th Cir. 1993). The defendant employer adequately responded to an employee's claim of sexual harassment by a supervisor, thus precluding liability under Title VII, when the employer immediately began an investigation of the supervisor. When the charges could not be corroborated, because the supervisor denied them and coworkers had not experienced offensive behavior by him, the plaintiff was transferred to another department with no loss of pay or benefits. The investigation and transfer occurred within one week of the plaintiff's first complaint, and the record indicated that the transfer was successful, as the plaintiff got along well with her new boss and soon was eligible for a raise. A sexual harassment policy was conveyed to all newly hired employees. The plaintiff also had produced no evidence that the employer knew or should have known of the conduct before her first complaint.

*   Pereira v. Schlage Electronics, 902 F. Supp. 1095 (N.D. Cal. 1995). Genuine issues of material fact as to whether a former employer's investigation, counseling, and warnings were sufficient under Title VII precluded summary judgment in an action for former employee sex discrimination and retaliation under Title VII and state law. The plaintiff alleged that throughout her employment at Schlage three of her coworkers, Ban "Tony" Nguyen, Dung Tran, and Sum Diep, harassed her with abusive, vulgar, and offensive language spoken in Vietnamese. Plaintiff alleged in her declaration that she was subjected to foul, offensive, and sexually explicit language on a daily basis for over 10 months. This declaration was supported by her notes and the tape transcript of conversations between her coworkers in which such language is used repeatedly. On the tape, Pereira's coworkers engage in strange sexual conversations and sing lewd songs in Vietnamese. At one point, one of the coworkers said, "Mother Fucker, when it's fully aroused it looks like a boa . . . a boa head . . . the boa head rises fearfully . . . she will cry of pleasure." At another point, the same person said, "Fuck a man today, fuck another tomorrow. In the beginning, talk sweet, after the fucking, then things will be OK?" *Id.* at 1102. Pereira also alleged that on several occasions sexual comments were directed specifically at her, including remarks by her coworkers about wanting to have sex with a prostitute who looks like Pereira, and a request by one of these men that Pereira "go to bed" with him. When she complained to her supervisor, he allegedly responded that unless the offensive language was spoken in English there was nothing he could do about it. The plaintiff alleged that Tran and Nguyen confronted her and angrily threatened to kill her and her family if she continued to complain about their language.

Tenth Circuit: Besso v. Cummins Intermountain, Inc., 885 F. Supp. 1516 (D. Wyo. 1995). A female employee who was discharged when her position of credit manager was eliminated failed to state a prima facie case of hostile work environment when twice during one week a coworker harassed her by flipping file folders against her chest and pulling her bra strap and supervisory personnel took action to stop the behavior and it was not repeated.

Ball v. City of Cheyenne, 64 Fair Empl. Prac. Cas. (BNA) 286 (D. Wyo. 1993). In an action by a female police dispatcher alleging that a police officer engaged in sexually harassing behavior, including touching her, pushing his crotch into her leg, and an alleged attack in a utility closet, the city's motion for summary judgment on the plaintiff's Title VII claim was denied, because the inquiry into whether the city adequately responded to charges of sexual harassment involved disputed facts. The plaintiff alleged that the city failed to adequately respond to her charges of sexual harassment; although the city conducted an internal affairs investigation, the plaintiff claimed that it ignored or gave little or no weight to eyewitness testimony and suggested that her past participation in sexual comments affected her credibility. The city argued that the Police Department responded immediately by providing the plaintiff a hearing, officially reprimanding the alleged harasser, and ordering him to avoid contact with the plaintiff.

Arizona: Smith v. American Express Travel Servs., 179 Ariz. 131, 876 P.2d 1166 (Ct. App. 1994).

The fact that an employer has knowledge that some of its employees are having sexual affairs with one another does not give an employer knowledge that a hostile work environment exists; sexual advances must be unwelcome to trigger a duty on the employer to act to prevent them. Ulrich v. K-Mart Corp., 858 F. Supp. 1087 (D. Kan. 1994). An employer who warned an alleged harasser to have no further contact with the complainant as soon as it was notified of the offensive conduct, took written statements from the complainant and the alleged harasser, and one month after taking the plaintiff's complaint, discharged the alleged harasser, was not negligent in failing to remedy a hostile work environment. Nor was the employer liable under the theory that an authority or agency relationship aids the harasser. While the alleged harasser had the title of manager, he did not hire, fire, or discipline anyone or control employees' wages or schedules. Although the alleged harasser appeared to have exercised some nonsupervisory authority over the plaintiff, this did not render the employer liable. "Significantly, there is nothing in the excerpts of Ulrich's deposition which indicates that Denney used any supervisory authority to facilitate his sexual harassment of Ulrich." *Id.* at 1093.

Page 341, add to footnote 39:

See also Young v. Mariner Corp., 65 Fair Empl. Prac. Cas. (BNA) 555 (N.D. Ala. 1991). One isolated incident, in which a supervisor made a few "mild" advances for a few minutes to a hotel's director of catering, after which he purportedly apologized with apparent embarrassment, was not sufficiently severe or pervasive to create a hostile environment. The employer promptly investigated the complaint, notified appropriate officials of their headquarters, instructed the alleged harasser not to deal with the plaintiff directly, and instructed all concerned that anyone guilty of sexually harassing the plaintiff would be terminated immediately. The employer was not directly liable for the alleged harassment because the supervisor neither invoked nor was otherwise aided by his position in allegedly attempting to entice the plaintiff into a relationship. Moreover, the employer had a policy against sexual harassment and an effective grievance procedure in the form of its fair treatment policy, which encouraged employees to come forward with complaints about any problem. The plaintiff was aware of these facts.

Page 341, update "Foster" citation in footnote 40:

aff'd, 977 F.2d 567 (3d Cir. 1992).

Page 342, add to footnote 43:

The Seventh Circuit affirmed, Saxton v. American Tel. & Tel. Co., 10 F.3d 526 (7th Cir. 1993), noting that the alleged harasser's offensive behavior was relatively limited, presumably because the plaintiff "was forthright and persistent in making clear that the advances were unwelcome." *Id.* at 534. Management began an investigation the day after it was advised of the plaintiff's complaint; a detailed report was completed two weeks later and the alleged harasser was transferred to another department within five weeks after management learned that the plaintiff was not interested in a transfer herself. In light of the fact that nearly a year had passed since the principal events underlying the sexual harassment claim had occurred, the employer "acted with considerable alacrity." *Id.* at 535 (footnote omitted).

Page 343, add to footnote 49:

Carr v. Allison Gas Turbine Div., 32 F.3d 1007 (7th Cir. 1994). The district court improperly ruled in favor of the defendant former employer, in a sexual harassment action by a female tinsmith, on the bases that the plaintiff welcomed the conduct by participating in it herself, the alleged conduct had no effect on the conditions of her employment, and she did not show that the defendants had failed to take appropriate responsive action. The plaintiff was the first woman to work in the tinsmith shop and her male coworkers were not happy about working with a woman, making derogatory sexual comments on a daily basis, such as "I won't work with any cunt," referring to the plaintiff in her presence as "whore," "cunt," and "split tail," painting "cunt" on her toolbox, cutting the seat out of her overalls, hiding and stealing her tools, stripping down to their underwear in her presence when changing in and out of their workclothes, exposing themselves, and making other vulgar and racist statements. With respect to the adequacy of the defendant's response to complaints of harassment, the trial court's opinion depicted General Motors as the victim of silence among the tinsmiths. The responses were in fact limited to several meetings that the company arranged between the plaintiff and her "tormentor"; no disciplinary action was undertaken against any of the plaintiff's coworkers, and no one was reprimanded for the harassment:

> General Motors was astonishingly unprepared to deal with problems of sexual harassment, foreseeable though they are when a woman is introduced into a formerly all-male workplace. Supervisor Roth testified that if he encountered a problem of sexual harassment he would have to ask the personnel department what to do. His supervisor's recipe for solving problems of sexual harassment was to recommend that the woman work harder than the men to prove that she could do the job.

Id. at 1012.

Page 345, add to footnote 58 following "Fifth Circuit":

Carmon v. Lubrizol Corp., 17 F.3d 791 (5th Cir. 1994). The district court properly found for the employer, in a hostile environment action by a female former employee, because the plaintiff did not establish the employer's failure to take remedial steps. During her 10-year tenure with the company, the plaintiff twice claimed that she had been subjected to a hostile environment caused by sexual harassment: once for an argument regarding her failure to complete a work assignment, during which she and a coworker traded insults and the coworker allegedly asked her questions about her sexual activities, and once in a 10-page letter sent to the company (but not detailed in the opinion). Both times the employer "sprang into action," *id.* at 793, conducting a prompt investigation during which it interviewed witnesses, and, as a result of the first complaint, reprimanded the coworker and transferred him to another shift. For the second complaint, having found only horseplay, it distributed a memorandum to all employees about inappropriate conduct.

Page 346, add to footnote 58 following "Seventh Circuit":

Cf. Stefanski v. R.A. Zahetner & Assocs., 855 F. Supp. 1030 (E.D. Wis. 1994). A female receptionist alleged that her supervisor, after drinking at a bar with the plaintiff and other employees, touched her breast, attempted to staple it, compared his sexual prowess to that of the plaintiff's husband, offered to provide her with oral sexual services, demanded that the plaintiff provide him with sexual favors, sprayed the contents of a fire extinguisher at her waist, and sexually assaulted another employee. The plaintiff complained to supervisors and filed a criminal complaint against the alleged harasser; the supervisor was suspended without pay for three weeks and pleaded no contest to a charge of fourth degree sexual assault. Despite the plea and sentence, the supervisor retained his supervisory status. The plaintiff's claim that the terms and conditions of her employment were adversely affected by sexual harassment was not conclusory and unsupported by the factual allegations in the complaint. The complaint alleged three specific actions that the plaintiff claimed amounted to adverse employment action: her supervisor sprayed her with a fire extinguisher; other employees repeatedly asked her to meet with the supervisor so that he could apologize, notwithstanding her objections to such a meeting; and the employer forced her to work with the supervisor after his reinstatement, despite her wish to avoid contact with him.

Page 347, add to footnote 62:

Steiner v. Showboat Operating Co., 25 F.3d 1459 (9th Cir. 1994), *cert. denied,* 115 S. Ct. 733 (1995). A former casino employee, the first female "floorperson," established a prima facie case of hostile environment sexual harassment in an action alleging sexual harassment, retaliation, constructive discharge, and intentional infliction of emotional distress. She proved without contradiction that her supervisor habitually referred to her and other female employees in a derogatory fashion, using sexual explicit and offensive terms such as "dumb fucking broad," "cunt," and "fucking cunt." The evidence suggested that the defendant was consistently slow to react to the plaintiff's claims, and did not seriously investigate them or strongly reprimand the supervisor until after the plaintiff filed a formal complaint. Moreover, the defendant twice changed the plaintiff's shift to get her away from the supervisor, rather than changing his shift or work area within the casino "or indeed, firing him outright and early on." *Id.* at 1464.

Page 348, add to footnote 65:

Buchanan v. Sherrill, 51 F.3d 227 (10th Cir. 1995). Plaintiff's claim that she was sexually harassed after filing a worker's compensation claim in order to force her to quit her job could not be sustained when it was undisputed that the defendant had arranged to transfer the plaintiff to another restaurant, thus ending the alleged harassment or discrimination, but she quit her job anyway. There was no evidence that the harassment would have continued at the plaintiff's new place of employment.

§ 7.7   Company Policy and Grievance Procedures

Page 349, add to footnote 71:

* Gary v. Long, 59 F.3d 1391 (D.C. Cir. 1995). A supervisor's alleged sexual harassment of a female employee was sufficiently severe and pervasive to create a hostile environment under Title VII, but the employer would not be held liable. Plaintiff's second-level supervisor, Long, allegedly first attempted to entice Gary into having sexual relations with him through promises that he could make her job easier. "After this carrot proved unsuccessful, Long tried using a stick." *Id.* at 1393. He repeatedly threatened Gary with adverse employment consequences, including termination of employment, if she did not submit to his advances, made crude references to her body, regularly expressed his desire to have sex with her, threatened to "get" her for refusing to meet with him, and indicated that he would have her fired if she told anybody of his sexual advances. Gary repeatedly rejected Long's overtures and made him aware that they were unwelcome. Under the pretext of conducting an inspection of a WMATA construction site, Long drove her to a secluded storage facility and, while driving, fondled her breasts and rubbed his hands between her legs. Upon their arrival at the storage facility, he raped her. Thereafter, Long threatened reprisals if Gary told anyone what had happened. Gary was subsequently in an automobile accident and when she returned to work, Long resumed his verbal harassment.

EMPLOYER DEFENSES

[A]n employer may not be held liable for a supervisor's hostile work environment harassment if the employer is able to establish that it had adopted policies and implemented measures such that the victimized employee either knew or should have known that the employer did not tolerate such conduct and that she could report it to the employer without fear of adverse consequences. . . . While a supervisor might purport to act or speak on behalf of the employer, there can be no liability if the victim could not reasonably rely on the supervisor's representations.

*   *   *

[W]hen . . . an employer has taken energetic measures to discourage sexual harassment in the workplace and has established, advertised, and enforced effective procedures to deal with it when it does occur, it must be absolved of Title VII liability under a hostile work environment theory of sexual harassment.

Id. at 1398. Here the employer had pursued an active and firm policy against sexual harassment throughout the period of Gary's alleged mistreatment. It also had a detailed grievance procedure for the formal and informal internal processing and review of discrimination complaints. As a result of Gary's complaint, an attorney met with Gary's attorney and interviewed all persons concerned; although he determined that there was no corroborating evidence to support her claim, defendant's general counsel granted Gary's request to be transferred to another facility to avoid contact with Long.

Although Long qualified as an "employer" under Title VII because he served in a supervisory position, he could not be held liable in his personal capacity, and the plaintiff's claim against him essentially merged with her claim against the employer.

The Third Circuit held that an effective grievance procedure—"one that is known to the victim and that timely stops the harassment"—shields the employer from Title VII liability for a hostile environment. *Bouton v. BMW of N. Am.*, 29 F.3d 103, 110 (3d Cir. 1994). The lack of a separate, written grievance policy for sexual harassment was not dispositive in this sexual harassment action, as it was clear that sexual harassment complaints could be pursued through the general grievance procedures.

Although rarely explicitly recognized, the choice whether to permit a grievance procedure to alleviate liability under § 219(2)(d) is a policy decision based on the appropriate amount of deterrence. If employers are liable whenever supervisors harass their subordinates, they have an economic incentive in the amount of the potential judgments to recruit, train, and supervise their managers to prevent sexual harassment. . . . The marginal reduction in the incentive that occurs if employers can rely on an internal grievance procedure may be justified by the concomitant decrease in litigation. This rationale is supported by the statutory policy that requires complaint to the EEOC and a conciliation process before a complainant has a right to sue.

Id. at 110.

Cuesta v. Texas Dep't of Criminal Justice, 805 F. Supp. 451 (W.D. Tex. 1991). The court found sexual harassment in an action by a female parole case worker against the parole officer and parole board. The court also concluded that the defendant board did have a working grievance policy against sexual harassment, but that it was unclear whether a timely complaint would have resolved the issue:

> Plaintiff asserted throughout the trial that this grievance procedure was ineffective, and was perceived as such by the members of the Board. . . . The Board grievance procedure . . . directs the employee to report harassment to the immediate supervisor, or any member of management, on up the chain of command to the Division Director. But unlike the discrimination policy discussed in *Meritor*, the Board's employee manual specifically addressed sexual harassment. The policy also gave the aggrieved employee the avenue of pursuing a complaint in the personnel department, or with any member of management.
>
> In Ms. Cuesta's case, the harasser was the supervisor in charge of the regional office. Ms. Cuesta also perceived Ms. Gonzales, her immediate supervisor, to be in league with [the parole officer] so that any complaint to Ms. Gonzalez would fall on deaf ears, or result in retaliation. Ms. Cuesta and other employees testified that they did not believe the grievance procedure [could] provide an effective remedy to their complaints. Although Plaintiff's failure to involve the grievance procedure works against her constructive discharge claim, it does not insulate the Board from liability. . . . Nor does it reflect poorly on her credibility. Soon after resigning, Ms. Cuesta filed her complaints with the EEOC and the Texas Department of Human Rights.
>
> But the Board should be given some credit for making an effort to deal with the problem of sexual harassment. The Board's policy provided that the entire echelon of upper management would be receptive to a sexual

harassment complaint. . . . We are not prepared to say that Ms. Cuesta was
without a receptive audience anywhere in the management of the Board.

Further, the policy [allowed] the employee to lodge a complaint with
the personnel office. . . .

It is not enough, however, for an employer to pay lip service to a
sexual harassment policy by setting up a grievance procedure that is inef-
fective or which the employees regard as an empty promise. Some of Ms.
Cuesta's witnesses indicated that they did not trust the Board's grievance
procedure.

* * *

The Court concludes that the Board did have a working policy against
sexual harassment, but that it is unclear whether a timely complaint would
have provided a remedy in Ms. Cuesta's case. It is not always easy for a
woman to report sexual abuse when the abuser occupies a position of
authority over the target. . . . And we are not convinced that the Board
acted swiftly and effectively on her claim. Yet the Board does deserve
some consideration for the policy that was in place and its effort to
enforce it. If we were to disregard the anti-harassment policy, then
employers might see little incentive to develop such a policy, and employees would suffer no penalty for ignoring the grievance procedure in favor
of immediate resort to litigation.

Id. at 460–61.

Page 350, add to footnote 73:

See also Cross v. Alabama, 65 Fair Empl. Prac. Cas. (BNA) 1290
(11th Cir. 1994). Female former and present state employees established
that the commissioner of the state department of mental health and mental retardation and the associate director of the mental illness division
knew or should have known that the facility director harassed women,
and they failed to take prompt remedial action to remedy the hostile
environment. The district court's questioning of defense witnesses, such
as asking the facility director whether his style could have a different
effect on female employees than on male employees, was not improper.
The court's instruction to the jury—that it was not necessary, to prevail
on their claims, that the plaintiffs file a grievance under agency or facility policies or that they exhaust or complete any administrative remedies
available to them under state law—did not mislead the jury and prevent

the jury from evaluating relevant evidence in determining employer liability, such as the defendant's anti-harassment policy. *Meritor* does not require the trial court to charge the jury that a grievance procedure exists and that the plaintiffs failed to utilize the grievance procedure, if such are the facts. "The district court need not instruct the jury on each and every piece of evidence." *Id.* at 1303.

Page 350, add to footnote 74:

Cf. also Cross v. Alabama, 49 F.3d 1490 (11th Cir. 1995). Evidence supported Title VII liability against a state department, state officials, and a supervisor in a § 1983 sexual harassment action by female employees of a state mental health facility. The employer was not prejudiced by any error that occurred when the trial court failed to instruct the jury that it could take into account the fact that the employer had a well-defined and publicized sexual harassment policy and that none of the plaintiffs made a formal grievance. The jury had heard testimony from several employees regarding their failure to use the grievance procedure, and the employer had argued to the jury that the employees' failure to use the procedure was important to the jury's determination of whether the employer knew or should have known of harassment.

§ 7.9   —Poor Work Performance

Page 352, add to footnote 79 after Ninth Circuit case:

Tenth Circuit: Sauers v. Salt Lake County, 1 F.3d 1122 (10th Cir. 1993). See § **6.45.**

Page 352, add to footnote 79 following "Eleventh Circuit":

Fishel v. Farley, 64 Empl. Prac. Dec. (CCH) ¶ 43,092 (E.D. La. 1994). There was no causal connection between a former contract compliance officer's sexual harassment complaint and her discharge when the state licensing board's decision to terminate her was based on her falsification of her employment applications, her poor work performance, and her insubordination.

EMPLOYER DEFENSES

§ 7.10 —Tardiness or Absenteeism

Page 355, update "Foster" citation in footnote 92:

aff'd, 977 F.2d 567 (3d Cir. 1992).

§ 7.12 —Failure to Follow Company Policy

Page 357, add to footnote 102:

See also Bookman v. Shakespeare Co., 442 S.E.2d 183 (S.C. Ct. App. 1994). A female employee who got involved in an altercation with a coworker could properly be terminated for violating the company's policy against physical violence and fighting, despite the plaintiff's claim that had the company properly investigated the incident, it would have discovered that the altercation resulted from sexual harassment by the coworker and that pursuant to the employee handbook, the employer had an obligation to investigate the claim. Although the employer may have breached the policy's promise to carefully investigate sexual harassment claims, when the plaintiff was interviewed, she denied any fighting and claimed sexual harassment for the first time. "Even if Shakespeare had conducted a careful investigation, and had discovered the altercation was the result of sexual harassment by the fellow employee, it could have fired Bookman anyhow" under the at-will employment doctrine. *Id.* at 184. The only limitation on the defendant's right to terminate the plaintiff was a prohibition against retaliatory discharge for filing a sexual harassment complaint, and the plaintiff here did not claim a violation of that prohibition.

§ 7.13 —Employee's Misconduct

Page 357, add to footnote 104 following "Eleventh Circuit":

Cooper v. Housing Auth. of Birmingham Dist., 67 Fair Empl. Prac. Cas. (BNA) 617 (N.D. Ala. 1995). An employer properly terminated a female employee for insubordination six weeks after she went to the EEOC office to try to file a sexual harassment complaint (but was told that the relevant incident did not constitute sexual harassment), when she did not negate the legitimacy of the other reasons for which she was

240

discharged. Those reasons included the failure to get authorization to be absent from her work station and attend a board meeting. Her refusal to change her time card to reflect hours that she believed were false was not a legitimate nondiscriminatory reason for discharge as the request by her supervisor to change her time card violated the Fair Labor Standards Act. Nevertheless, by plaintiff's own admission, she was guilty of insubordination, and she failed to show that a similarly situated employee who had not engaged in statutorily protected activity was treated differently.

Page 358, add to footnote 108:

Johnson v. Merry-Go-Round Enters., 67 Fair Empl. Prac. Cas. (BNA) 1456 (N.D. Ill. 1995). A female former employee who alleged that she was discharged from a retail clothing store because she resisted the advances of another employee did not state a claim for relief when there was no evidence that the alleged harasser played any role in her termination and evidence showed that the plaintiff violated store policy by issuing credits to credit cards not matching the original purchases.

See also Conaway v. Auto Zone, Inc., 866 F. Supp. 351 (N.D. Ohio 1994). Misrepresentations on the plaintiff's application for employment precluded her state sexual harassment claims under the "after-acquired evidence" doctrine.

Page 358, add to footnote 110:

Churchman v. Pinkerton's, Inc., 756 F. Supp. 515 (D. Kan. 1991) (application falsehoods prevented any relief under Title VII). *Accord* Mathis v. Boeing Military Airplane Co., 719 F. Supp. 991 (D. Kan. 1991).

§ 7.14   —Lack of Work

Page 359, add to footnote 111:

Koelsch v. Beltone Elec. Corp., 46 F.3d 705 (7th Cir. 1995). A former employee failed to prove hostile environment sexual harassment even under the continuing violation theory or retaliation. The alleged harasser's conduct, while offensive, was composed of two seemingly isolated incidents, one involving the stroking of the plaintiff's leg during a company meeting, and the other, the grabbing of her buttocks in a soundproof room during a plant tour after which he kept his distance from the plaintiff. The plaintiff's amorphous allegations of an atmosphere of sexually suggestive joking carry no weight in the totality of circumstances analysis because the record was completely "barren of so much as a sliver of substantiation." *Id.* at 708. Even viewing the evidence in the light most favorable to the plaintiff, evidence showed that the company required significant downsizing to remain profitable, and the plaintiff's position and one other were the most easily eliminated.

§ 7.16   Retaliation

Page 360, add to footnote 117:

Goeffert v. Beech Aircraft Corp., 64 Fair Empl. Prac. Cas. (BNA) 1387 (D. Kan. 1994). Summary judgment on a retaliation claim was granted to an employer that discharged the employee for allegedly assaulting another employee within a week of her reporting incidents of alleged sexual harassment; the charge against her was substantiated by all witnesses and there was nothing in the record indicating that the investigation into the assault was not conducted in good faith.

Cf. Gleason v. Callahan Indus. Inc., 610 N.Y.S.2d 671 (1994). Evidence supported a jury's finding that the defendant employer discharged the plaintiff for making a sexual harassment complaint; the record revealed that the plaintiff received regular and intermittent raises, was scheduled to receive another raise after the date of her complaint, and had never had a poor job review, but was fired shortly after submitting her complaint of sexual harassment.

Page 360, add to footnote 118:

Marquart v. McDonnell Douglas Corp., 859 F. Supp. 366 (E.D. Mo.), *aff'd without op.*, 56 F.3d 69 (8th Cir. 1994). A terminated female custodian alleged that she had been called a whore by coworkers; a bag of horehound candy had been placed near her locker; photographs of coworkers' wives and girlfriends in swimsuits were displayed in the workplace and other pictures of other women in swimsuits were in the work area; she had seen a male employee simulate sexual intercourse using a tool; there was howling and whistling in the workplace; on a single occasion a man's name had been placed over hers on a union campaign-for-office poster; an American Cancer Society brochure on testicular cancer had been placed in her locker; and some *Playboy* pictures and cartoons were in trash containers she was required to empty. Nevertheless, she did not make out a claim of retaliation when the plaintiff repeatedly displayed abnormal behavior at work and failed to comply with the employer's direct order that she obtain psychiatric diagnosis and treatment.

Strickland v. Hillsborough County, 65 Fair Empl. Prac. Cas. (BNA) 255 (M.D. Fla. 1994). A discharged county veterinary assistant probationary employee, who had filed a formal sexual harassment complaint against a coworker, established a prima facie case of retaliation when she was terminated about two months after she filed her complaint and her work-related performance problems were not documented until after she filed the complaint. The defendant rebutted the presumption, though, by showing that the plaintiff did not properly lock cabinets containing drugs, failed to clean up blood after performing a procedure, left styrofoam bowls in animal cages, and clocked in to work only to leave and deal with her car. The plaintiff did not show that the defendant's proffered explanation was unbelievable or pretextual; in fact, she failed to present any feasible discriminatory motive on the part of the defendant to discriminate. The court found the plaintiff's argument—that it was easier for the county to terminate her as an employee in her initial probationary period than to terminate the coworker as a tenured employee—"unpersuasive and irrelevant." *Id.* at 260.

Johnson v. Tower Air, Inc., 149 F.R.D. 461 (E.D.N.Y. 1993). A former flight attendant trainee did not proffer evidence sufficient to support a claim of retaliatory discharge when a letter responding to a report indicating that the plaintiff did not follow FAA procedure did not mention allegations of sexual harassment.

Young v. Mariner Corp., 65 Fair Empl. Prac. Cas. (BNA) 555 (N.D. Ala. 1991). One isolated incident, in which a supervisor made a few "mild" advances for a few minutes to a hotel's director of catering, after which he stopped and purportedly apologized with apparent embarrassment, was not sufficiently severe or pervasive to create a hostile environment. The court rejected the plaintiff's claim that she suffered retaliation after she filed a discrimination charge, despite evidence that the company started documenting communications with her after she filed her charges:

> Such documentation served to protect both her and the hotel in light of the possibility of litigation, a possibility that Young and her attorney quickly

[and] pointedly brought to Mariner's attention. Now that Young has sued and brought all concerned before the Court, the benefit of clearly documented communication is all the more obvious. Where communication between the parties was documented, the Court can readily resolve conflicting testimony about who said what to whom.

[Also], documentation was necessary to facilitate Mariner's investigation of Young's allegation of sexual harassment. An essential part of such an investigation requires scrutiny of the hotel management's response to the allegation. The hotel management's response raised questions about performance and attitude problems on the part of Young, and a lack of documentation of such problems hampered the investigation. Mariner's need and desire to thoroughly investigate the matter made it essential that further communications and performance or attitude problems be documented.

* * *

A corporation can hardly investigate a female employee's allegations of sexual harassment and the response of her superiors, who complain of performance and attitude problems on her part, without insisting that future problems be documented as they should have been in the past. Mariner insisted on proper documentation as to the plaintiff and all other managers. Such insistence does not amount to retaliation.

Id. at 575–76.

§ 7.17   Constructive Discharge

Page 361, add to footnote 120:

Cuesta v. Texas Dep't of Criminal Justice, 805 F. Supp. 451 (W.D. Tex. 1991). The court found sexual harassment in an action by a female parole case worker against the parole officer and parole board. Although a reasonable person would have considered the working conditions to be intolerable because of sexual harassment, the court would not find constructive discharge because the plaintiff's resignation did not result solely from the harassment. Although the plaintiff stated that the main reason for leaving was that she perceived that her immediate supervisor acted as a go-between for the parole officer and thereby cooperated in the harassment, the court was not convinced that the plaintiff did not have other alternatives to resignation.

CHAPTER 8

SEXUAL HARASSMENT CLAIMS UNDER OTHER CIVIL RIGHTS LAWS

§ 8.1   Section 1983

Page 364, add to footnote 1:

Cross v. Alabama, 65 Fair Empl. Prac. Cas. (BNA) 1290 (11th Cir. 1994). Plaintiff employees proved a violation of § 1983 when a supervisor's sexually harassing conduct was obvious, flagrant, rampant, and continuing.

Page 364, add to footnote 4:

Annis v. County of Westchester, 36 F.3d 251 (2d Cir. 1994). "While we do not subscribe to a categorical view that sexual harassment equals sex discrimination, we do agree that harassment that transcends coarse, hostile and boorish behavior can rise to the level of a constitutional tort." *Id.* at 254. In this action by a police lieutenant alleging harassment by her supervisor, conduct including vulgar sexual references, harsh and unfounded criticism, and other conduct singling out the plaintiff was evidently calculated to drive her out of the workplace. Irrespective of whether the plaintiff was pleading sexual harassment or discrimination, she pleaded a claim under § 1983.

Page 365, add to footnote 7:

The Civil Rights Act of 1991 does not supplant § 1983 as a federal discrimination statute by adding compensatory damages and a jury trial to Title VII; Title VII still does not yet provide all of the relief available under § 1983 to victims of discrimination, such as the absence of administrative filing requirements and the statute of limitations of a personal injury action. Beardsley v. Isom, 828 F. Supp. 397 (E.D. Va. 1993).

See also Annis v. County of Westchester, 36 F.3d 251 (2d Cir. 1994). Title VII is not intended to be the exclusive remedy for workplace discrimination; here, the district court improperly dismissed a complaint on the ground that a plaintiff alleging sex discrimination may not bring an action solely under § 1983 but must at least concurrently plead a violation of Title VII and follow that statute's procedures. *Accord* Beardsley v. Webb, Nos. 93-1732, 93-1747, 1994 WL 386866 (4th Cir. July 26, 1994); Bowen v. City of E. Chicago, 799 F.2d 1180, 1185 (7th Cir. 1986).

Page 366, add to footnote 10:

Annis v. County of Westchester, 36 F.3d 251 (2d Cir. 1994). In an action by a female police lieutenant under § 1983, alleging that she was subjected by supervisors to vulgar sexual references, harsh and unfounded criticism, and singled out for treatment different from that given male officers, the court rejected the defendants' argument that the plaintiff's complaint really pleaded sexual harassment, and that such a claim is distinct from sex discrimination and is purely a creation of Title VII.

> While we do not subscribe to a categorical view that sexual harassment equals sex discrimination, we do agree that harassment that transcends coarse, hostile and boorish behavior can rise to the level of a constitutional tort. . . . When—as alleged here, sexual harassment includes conduct evidently calculated to drive someone out of the workplace, the harassment is tantamount to sex discrimination.

Id. at 254.

§ 8.2   States or State Officials

Page 367, add to footnote 14:

Cf. Verde v. City of Phila., 862 F. Supp. 1329 (E.D. Pa. 1994) (Title VII does not authorize suits against officials in their official capacity).

§ 8.3   Local Government Entities

Page 367, add to footnote 16:

Sauers v. Salt Lake County, 1 F.3d 1122 (10th Cir. 1993) (§ 1983). The district court properly found no basis for liability by the county in a sexual harassment action by a former secretary with the county attorney's office, when there was no indication in the record that the alleged harasser's individual acts were officially sanctioned or ordered, and the specific acts alleged, including nonsexual bizarre conduct and comments about the plaintiff's breasts and her attire, did not rise to the level of a policy or custom within the division.

Page 368, add to footnote 20:

Dirksen v. City of Springfield, 842 F. Supp. 1117 (C.D. Ill. 1994). The plaintiff stated a cause of action for municipal liability under § 1983 against the city when she alleged a custom or practice of discrimination at the highest level of police department policymaking. The mayor was allegedly slow to take action against the alleged harasser, who allegedly still supervised women at the police department.

Page 368, add to footnote 21:

Howard v. Board of Educ. Sycamore Dist., 876 F. Supp. 959 (N.D. Ill. 1995). A female former director of music and band director stated claims for hostile environment sexual harassment and retaliation when she alleged that during her employment, notes referring to the plaintiff in a sexually offensive manner were posted, a male teacher made offensive comments about a female teacher, and male students made offensive comments. The principal in his official capacity and the Board of Education could not be held liable under § 1983 when the plaintiff did not allege any official policy or custom that resulted in any of the acts or omissions directed toward the plaintiff. Nor were there allegations that the principal was a person with final policy-making authority sufficient to bind the Board.

Page 368, add to footnote 25:

Webb v. Hyman, 861 F. Supp. 1094 (D.D.C. 1994). The District of Columbia failed to prove that no reasonable person, viewing the evidence in the light most favorable to the plaintiff, could find that the district was liable for the plaintiff's hostile work environment; the supervisor used his position to aid in his harassment, by, for example, attacking the plaintiff in a limited-access strip search room. There was also evidence that the district should have been on notice, in light of testimony that the district's procedures designed to eliminate sexual harassment had not been properly implemented; the supervisor had been scheduled three times for sexual harassment training but had attended none of the training sessions. There was also considerable evidence that the district was on notice of a hostile work environment under the supervisor because of previous complaints against him.

* *Page 369, add to footnote 28:*

Faragher v. City of Boca Raton, 76 F.3d 1155 (11th Cir. 1996). In an action by former city lifeguards against the city and supervisors for sexual harassment under § 1983, the district court erred in holding that the supervisors acted as the city's agents in harassing this plaintiff. The plaintiff did not contend that the supervisors were acting within the scope of their employment when they made offensive remarks and gestures and touched her, and the court of appeals found no record evidence suggesting that they were acting within the scope of their employment when they harassed Faragher. Here, the district court mechanically applied the factors listed in *Vance v. Southern Bell Tel. & Tel. Co.,* 863 F.2d 1503 (11th Cir. 1989), *overruled on other grounds,* 491 U.S. 164 (1989), without determining their relevance to whether the supervisors were acting within the scope of their employment in harassing Faragher.

> The harassment here consisted of offensive comments, gestures, and touching. If the supervisors had constructed something offensive and intimidating to women under the guise of trying to improve lifeguard performance, then their supervisory and disciplinary authority would support a finding that they acted as the City's agents in violating Title VII.

76 F.3d 1155, 1166.

Neither the district court nor Faragher asserted any factual basis for concluding that the city should have known of their conduct. The lifeguards were stationed at a remote location and had little contact with city officials. The district court clearly erred in finding that the city's knowledge may be inferred solely from the fact that the conduct was pervasive enough to create an abusive work environment.

*

§ 8.4 Supervisors

Page 371, add to footnote 37:

McWilliams v. Fairfax County Bd. of Supervisors, 72 F.3d 1191 (4th Cir. 1996). Supervisors were not liable under § 1983 for deprivation of employee's substantive due process rights resulting from an actual physical assault that occurred during the course of harassment. Liability could be imposed upon the supervisor-defendants only by proof of their direct culpability in causing the injury either by directly authorizing it or by expressly or tacitly condoning by inaction a known pattern of comparable coworker conduct. There was no evidence that either supervisor directly authorized the physical assaults or expressly condoned a known pattern of comparable conduct. To establish culpability by tacit condonation, the only remaining possibility, the plaintiff must have proffered evidence that the supervisors knew or reasonably should have known of a comparable pattern of coworker conduct that was sufficiently widespread to pose a pervasive and unreasonable risk of constitutional injury to McWilliams, and that in the face of that knowledge they took no action to stop it but remained deliberately indifferent to it. But here the plaintiff conceded that he never spoke to anyone about the harassment.

For the same reasons, the plaintiff's substantive due process claim against the county could not withstand summary judgment. The plaintiff sought to invoke a "policy-as-effective-cause" theory of municipal liability by pointing to deficiencies amounting to "policy" in the county's training program for employees such as the alleged harassment. Although this was a viable theory, the evidence proffered to support it was missing the critical requirement that a direct causal connection between specific deficiencies and specific injury be demonstrated. The only possible evidence of any such causal connection was that this injury did occur and that whatever training had or had not been provided did not serve to prevent it. McWilliams's attempt to invoke the "condoned-custom-as-effective-cause" theory of municipal liability was also lacking in even minimal evidentiary support.

§ 8.5 Coworkers

Page 372, add to footnote 46:

Cf. Anthony v. County of Sacramento, Sheriff's Dep't, 845 F. Supp. 1396 (E.D. Cal. 1994). In a § 1983 action by an African-American female deputy sheriff against the county, the sheriff's department, coworkers, and a civilian jail employee, alleging that for five years she suffered sexual and racial harassment as well as retaliation for defending the rights of African-American inmates and employees, the court noted that a state official may be liable for coworker harassment under § 1983 when the abuse is related to state-conferred authorities or duties, the same test that is applied when the victim is not a state employee:

> The complaint depicts a work environment made racially and sexually hostile by related attacks on plaintiff individually, on the abilities of African-American law enforcement personnel generally, and on inmates of color. The consistent theme linking these forms of abuse is that of African-American inferiority and criminality, in the context of law enforcement effectiveness.
>
> Such harassment is not independent of the powers and duties conferred on defendants by the state. Rather, the alleged pattern of harassment directly involves the discriminatory assertion of law enforcement authority. The connection between the specific acts of harassment alleged and the law enforcement duties and functions of defendants is accordingly sufficient to state a claim of constitutional violations "under color of law."

Id. at 1401–02.

Page 372, update "Woodward" citation in footnote 46:

cert. denied, 113 S. Ct. 3038 (1993).

§ 8.8   Immunities

* *Page 373, add at end of first paragraph:*

In *Jones v. Clinton,* 72 F.3d 1354 (8th Cir. 1996), a female former employee of the state of Arkansas charged President Bill Clinton with sexual harassment for conduct alleged to have occurred during his tenure as governor. Jones alleged that Bill Clinton, under color of state law, violated her constitutional rights to equal protection and due process by sexually harassing and assaulting her and that Mr. Clinton and a state trooper conspired to violate those rights under 42 U.S.C. § 1985. Her complaint also alleged intentional infliction of emotional distress by Clinton and defamation by Clinton and the state trooper. The district court rejected the application of absolute immunity but found that for separation of powers reasons Clinton was entitled to a "temporary or limited immunity from trial," and thus granted his request to stay the trial for the duration of Clinton's service as president. *Jones v. Clinton,* 869 F.Supp. 690, 699 (E.D. Ark. 1994). The court also stayed the trial against the state trooper for as long as Clinton is president because the claims against the trooper were factually and legally intertwined with the claims against Clinton, but permitted discovery on Jones's claims against both Mr. Clinton and Trooper Ferguson to go forward. The court of appeals held that the president is not entitled to immunity from civil suits alleging actionable behavior by him in his private capacity rather than in his official capacity as president, for as long as he is president:

> Article II of the Constitution, which vests the executive power of the federal government in the President, did not create a monarchy. The President is cloaked with none of the attributes of sovereign immunity. To the contrary, the President, like all other government officials, is subject to the same laws that apply to all other members of our society. . . . The list of those entitled to absolute immunity from civil liability includes the President of the United States for his official acts, *Nixon v. Fitzgerald,* 457 U.S. 731, 756. (1982); members of Congress for their legislative acts, regardless of motive, under the Speech and Debate Clause; . . . judges in courts of general jurisdiction for judicial acts; . . . prosecutors for prosecutorial functions; . . . and certain executive officials performing certain judicial and prosecutorial functions in their official capacities. . . . In addition, witnesses are entitled to absolute immunity from civil suit for testimony given in judicial proceedings, . . . and even government officials whose special functions do not require a full exemption from liability may have a more limited qualified immunity for their official acts . . . .

Id. at 1358. The parties and the court agreed that the fundamental authority on the subject of presidential immunity is the plurality opinion in *Fitzgerald,* where the issue was whether the president is entitled to absolute immunity from personal civil liability for his official acts. By only a five-to-four majority, the Court held that "[i]n view of the special nature of the President's constitutional office and functions, we think it appropriate to recognize absolute Presidential immunity from damages liability for acts within the 'outer perimeter' of his official responsibility." *Id.* at 756. By definition, unofficial acts are not within the perimeter of the president's official responsibility at all, even the outer perimeter. It was undisputed in this case that most of the acts alleged by Jones clearly fell outside the zone of official presidential responsibility, given that they occurred while Clinton was still governor of Arkansas.

> The rationale of the *Fitzgerald* majority is that, without protection from civil liability for his official acts, the President would make (or refrain from making) official decisions, not in the best interests of the nation, but in an effort to avoid lawsuits and personal liability. This rationale is inapposite where only personal, private conduct by a President is at issue.

72 F.3d 1354, 1360. The court concluded that if the trial preliminaries of the trial itself became barriers to the effective performance of his official duties, Clinton's remedy was to pursue motions for rescheduling, additional time, or continuances. The court had

> every confidence that the District Court will discharge its responsibility to protect the President's role as our government's chief executive officer, without impeding Mrs. Jones's right to have her claims heard without undue delay. If either party believes the court is failing to discharge that responsibility, the proper course is to petition this Court for a writ of mandamus or prohibition.

Id. at 1363. The dissent argued that the majority's decision left as many questions unanswered as it answered:

> Must a President seek judicial approval each time a scheduled deposition or trial date interferes with the performance of his constitutional duties? Is it appropriate for a court to decide, upon the President's motion, whether the nation's interest in the unfettered performance of a presidential duty is sufficiently weighty to delay trial proceedings? Once a conflict arises between the court and the President as to the gravity of an intrusion on presidential duties, does a court have the authority to ignore the President's request to delay proceedings? Finally, can a court dictate a President's activities as they relate to national and international interests of the United States without creating a separation of powers conflict? While the majority would encourage other courts to exercise "judicial case management sensitive to the burdens of the presidency," *ante* at

1361, only a stay of civil litigation during a President's term in office will ensure the performance of Executive duties unencumbered by the judiciary and thereby avoid separation of powers conflict.

*   *   *

The well-known travail of litigation and its effect on the ability of the President to perform his duties, as well as the subjection of the President to the ongoing jurisdiction of the court and the attendant impact on the separation of powers, dictate the postponement of non-exigent, private civil damages litigation until the President leaves office.

In my opinion, the stay should include pretrial discovery, as well as the trial proceedings, because discovery is likely to pose even more intrusive and burdensome demands on the President's time and attention than the eventual trial itself. Similarly, I would grant a stay of proceedings against a co-defendant of a sitting President where, given all the circumstances, the claims against the co-defendant cannot proceed without materially diminishing the effectiveness of a stay of proceedings against the President. I agree with the district court's conclusion here that a stay of the claims against Trooper Ferguson is essential if the President is to be fully protected.

Id. at 1369–70 (Ross, J., dissenting).

Page 374, update "Foster" citation in footnote 57:
aff'd, 977 F.2d 567 (3d Cir. 1992).

Page 374, update "Woodward" citation in footnote 58:
cert. denied, 113 S. Ct. 3038 (1993).

Page 374, add to footnote 59:

* Howard v. Board of Educ., 893 F. Supp. 808 (N.D. Ill. 1995). A former band director brought an action under Title VII, Title IX, and § 1983 against the board of education for the school district that employed her, the high school principal, and the assistant superintendent for a second school district alleging sex discrimination, sexual harassment, and retaliatory discharge. The plaintiff alleged that she was intentionally discriminated against based on her being a female and as a result of the sexual harassment directed at her and the failure to eliminate that harassment after she complained. She also alleged that the board's widespread

practice of ignoring sexual harassment in the schools was so permanent and well settled as to constitute a custom or usage with the force of law within the school district. Moreover, she alleged that the principal knew of the plaintiff's complaints and took no action against the students to stop the harassment, thereby intentionally permitting the harassment to continue.

The principal was not entitled to dismissal, based on qualified immunity, of the plaintiff's § 1983 action alleging violation of the equal protection clause. The plaintiff alleged that the principal knew of her complaints of sexual harassment by students and intentionally took no action against students to stop harassment, and, given clearly established law that sexual harassment in the workplace is actionable as a denial of equal protection if intentional, combined with the unique role the principal plays in school administration, it was objectively unreasonable to believe that the alleged conduct did not violate the plaintiff's equal protection rights.

Nor were the principal and the nonschool official entitled to dismissal, based on the intracorporate immunity doctrine, of the plaintiff's civil rights conspiracy claim. A conspiracy allegedly manifested itself through a meeting among the principal, other school officials, and the nonschool official regarding the plaintiff's complaints about the nonschool official's son, and about the removal of the plaintiff from her job. It could not be determined whether the nonschool official's participation defeated the intracorporate immunity defense, and it was not possible to determine whether the individual conspirators were motivated by personal animus against the plaintiff.

Faragher v. City of Boca Raton, 864 F. Supp. 1552 (S.D. Fla. 1994). Supervisors were deemed agents of the city in an action by female former city lifeguards, alleging that among other things, the supervisors touched them on the waist, neck, breasts and buttocks, made sexual comments such as "There are a lot of tits on the beach today," and referred to women as "cunts" and "bitches." The workplace structure had a paramilitary configuration and through a chain of command, the employers vested in the supervisors both administrative and disciplinary authority over the lifeguards. With respect to her § 1983 claim, the court found no merit in one supervisor's qualified immunity defense when he did not show that he acted within the scope of his discretionary authority when he sexually harassed the plaintiff; it was difficult for the court to conceive of a situation where a supervisor's discretionary authority includes the uninvited touching of subordinates. Moreover, the statutory right to be free of discrimination based on sex in the workplace is embodied in the civil rights act and since 1986, a § 1983 cause of action of sexual harassment, as violative of the equal protection clause, has been recognized by the Seventh Circuit.

Dirksen v. City of Springfield, 842 F. Supp. 1117 (C.D. Ill. 1994). Two supervisors, whom a demoted female secretary for the city police department claimed failed to report her harassment complaint in violation of her constitutional rights, were protected by qualified immunity when the plaintiff failed to meet her burden of showing a clearly established constitutional right. Although the Seventh Circuit had not yet articulated the proper constitutional response to a sexual harassment claim, other courts had found that the failure to respond to a sexual harassment complaint did not at this time have constitutional implications. Other defendants did not enjoy qualified immunity when they allegedly either harassed the plaintiff or retaliated against her for filing her EEOC complaint.

* *Page 374, add to footnote 60:*

Nicks v. Missouri, 67 F.3d 699 (8th Cir. 1995). Evidence of sexual harassment was sufficient to sustain a verdict for the plaintiff in a § 1983 sexual harassment action by a former employee of a state-run mental health facility, alleging that supervisors failed to prevent her harassment by a coworker. The court rejected the facility's argument that they were entitled to qualified immunity from damage claims based on the evidence in question because Nicks had no clearly established right to be free from sexual harassment by a fellow facility employee following her dismissal. The defendants did not contend that Nicks did not have a clearly established constitutional right to have her supervisors take reasonable steps to protect her from sexual harassment by a fellow employee in her public-sector workplace. The appellants' liability to Nicks was based on events that occurred during her employment. Her theory of the case was that Little, never cautioned and disciplined by the appellants during Nick's employment, continued to harass her after she was dismissed, thereby adding to the injuries that flowed from the appellants' failure to fulfill their duty to her prior to her dismissal. Thus whether the defendants were entitled to qualified immunity from suit on the basis of Little's postdismissal harassment of Nicks was irrelevant.

Two supervisors argued they were entitled to judgment as a matter of law because the evidence was insufficient to show that they had the authority or control over Little necessary to find them liable for their failure to intervene. They argued they could not be liable for Little's actions because they were not his supervisors. The court found that because of their positions Nicks was entitled to look to them for protection from Little. They could have taken action to produce an appropriate response by the facility to Nicks's complaints, "and they were totally remiss in not doing so." *Id.* at 704.

In *Jones v. Clinton,* 72 F.3d 1354 (8th Cir. 1996), a female former employee of the state of Arkansas charged President Bill Clinton with sexual harassment for conduct alleged to have occurred during his tenure as governor. Jones alleged that Bill Clinton, under color of state law, violated her constitutional rights to equal protection and due process by sexually harassing and assaulting her and that Mr. Clinton and a state trooper conspired to violate those rights under 42 U.S.C. § 1985. Her complaint also alleged intentional infliction of emotional distress by Clinton and defamation by Clinton and the state trooper. The district court rejected the application of absolute immunity but found that for separation of powers reasons Clinton was entitled to a "temporary or limited immunity from trial," and thus granted his request to stay the trial for the duration of Clinton's service as president. *Jones v. Clinton,* 869 F.Supp. 690, 699 (E.D. Ark. 1994). The court also stayed the trial against the state trooper for as long as Clinton is president because the claims against the trooper were factually and legally intertwined with the claims against Clinton, but permitted discovery on Jones's claims against both Mr. Clinton and Trooper Ferguson to go forward. The court of appeals held that the president is not entitled to immunity from civil suits alleging actionable behavior by him in his private capacity rather than in his official capacity as president, for as long as he is president.

> Article II of the Constitution, which vests the executive power of the federal government in the President, did not create a monarchy. The President is cloaked with none of the attributes of sovereign immunity. To the contrary, the President, like all other government officials, is subject to the same laws that apply to all other members of our society. . . . The list of those entitled to absolute immunity from civil liability includes the President of the United States for his official acts, *Nixon v. Fitzgerald,* 457 U.S. 731, 756. (1982); members of Congress for their legislative acts, regardless of motive, under the Speech and Debate Clause; . . . judges in

> courts of general jurisdiction for judicial acts; . . . prosecutors for prosecutorial functions; . . . and certain executive officials performing certain judicial and prosecutorial functions in their official capacities . . . . In addition, witnesses are entitled to absolute immunity from civil suit for testimony given in judicial proceedings, . . . and even government officials whose special functions do not require a full exemption from liability may have a more limited qualified immunity for their official acts . . . .

72 F.3d 1354, 1358. The parties and the court agreed that the fundamental authority on the subject of presidential immunity is the plurality opinion in *Fitzgerald,* where the issue was whether the president is entitled to absolute immunity from personal civil liability for his official acts. By only a five-to-four majority, the Court held that "[i]n view of the special nature of the President's constitutional office and functions, we think it appropriate to recognize absolute Presidential immunity from damages liability for acts within the 'outer perimeter' of his official responsibility." *Id.* at 756. By definition, unofficial acts are not within the perimeter of the president's official responsibility at all, even the outer perimeter. It was undisputed in this case that most of the acts alleged by Jones clearly fell outside the zone of official presidential responsibility, given that they occurred while Clinton was still governor of Arkansas.

> The rationale of the *Fitzgerald* majority is that, without protection from civil liability for his official acts, the President would make (or refrain from making) official decisions, not in the best interests of the nation, but in an effort to avoid lawsuits and personal liability. This rationale is inapposite where only personal, private conduct by a President is at issue.

*   *   *

> If the trial preliminaries of the trial itself become barriers to the effective performance of his official duties, Mr. Clinton's remedy is to pursue motions for rescheduling, additional time, or continuances. Again, we have every confidence that the District Court will discharge its responsibility to protect the President's role as our government's chief executive officer, without impending Mrs. Jones's right to have her claims heard without undue delay. If either party believes the court is failing to discharge that responsibility, the proper course is to petition this Court for a writ of mandamus or prohibition.

CLAIMS UNDER OTHER CIVIL RIGHTS LAWS

72 F.3d 1354, 1360, 1362–63. The dissent argued the the majority's decision left as many questions unanswered as it answered:

> Must a President seek judicial approval each time a scheduled deposition or trial date interferes with the performance of his constitutional duties? Is it appropriate for a court to decide, upon the President's motion, whether the nation's interest in the unfettered performance of a presidential duty is sufficiently weighty to delay trial proceedings? Once a conflict arises between the court and the President as to the gravity of an intrusion on presidential duties, does a court have the authority to ignore the President's request to delay proceedings? Finally, can a court dictate a President's activities as they relate to national and international interests of the United States without creating a separation of powers conflict? While the majority would encourage other courts to exercise "judicial case management sensitive to the burdens of the presidency," ante at 1361, only a stay of civil litigation during a President's term in office will ensure the performance of Executive duties unencumbered by the judiciary and thereby avoid separation of powers conflict.

$$*\qquad*\qquad*$$

The well-known travail of litigation and its effect on the ability of the President to perform his duties, as well as the subjection of the President to the ongoing jurisdiction of the court and the attendant impact on the separation of powers, dictate the postponement of non-exigent, private civil damages litigation until the President leaves office.

In my opinion, the stay should include pretrial discovery, as well as the trial proceedings, because discovery is likely to pose even more intrusive and burdensome demands on the President's time and attention than the eventual trial itself. Similarly, I would grant a stay of proceedings against a co-defendant of a sitting President where, given all the circumstances, the claims against the co-defendant cannot proceed without materially diminishing the effectiveness of a stay of proceedings against the President. I agree with the district court's conclusion here that a stay of the claims against Trooper Ferguson is essential if the President is to be fully protected.

72 F.3d 1354, 1369–70 (Ross, J., dissenting).

§ 8.12 Pleading § 1983 Claims

Page 377, add to footnote 77:

Gierlinger v. New York State Police, 15 F.3d 32 (2d Cir. 1994). The district court erred in its instructions to the jury with respect to individual liability, when it was not possible to determine from the instructions whether the jury found a supervisor liable on the theory of respondeat superior, which is not available in a § 1983 claim, or liable for his own performance as a commanding officer. A Title VII plaintiff is not precluded from bringing a concurrent § 1983 cause of action as long as the § 1983 claim is based on a distinct violation of a constitutional right, such as the Fourteenth Amendment. Section 1983 liability can be imposed upon an individual employer or responsible supervisors for failing to properly investigate and remedy complaints of sexual harassment when, through this practice, the conduct becomes an accepted custom or practice of the employer. So, although it was proper for the district court to instruct the jury on this claim, the instructions must have permitted the jury to understand the requisite showing of involvement on the part of the particular defendant in order to sustain liability.

§ 8.15 —Equal Protection

Page 379, add to footnote 89:

Cf. Howard v. Board of Educ. Sycamore Dist., 876 F. Supp. 959 (N.D. Ill. 1995). A female former director of music and band director stated claims for hostile environment sexual harassment and retaliation when she alleged that during her employment, notes referring to the plaintiff in a sexually offensive manner were posted, a male teacher made offensive comments about a female teacher, and male students made offensive comments. With respect to a claim that she was denied equal protection, the plaintiff failed to specifically identify what the basis of her equal protection claim was; although she did not need to engage in fact pleading, at the very least she should have identified the basis upon which her legal theory was premised so that the defendants could prepare a defense. Moreover, the principal could not be sued in his individual capacity when the plaintiff did not allege that the principal intentionally sought to harass her by failing to take action against the students who allegedly made the sexually offensive comments.

Page 380, add to footnote 91 following "Sixth Circuit":

Bremiller v. Cleveland Psychiatric Inst., 879 F. Supp. 762 (N.D. Ohio 1995). A defendant coworker was not immune from plaintiff's equal protection claims in an action charging sexual harassment and retaliation against a psychiatric institution. The plaintiff alleged that the male employees subjected the plaintiffs to verbal threats, physical intimidation, sexual jokes, and unwanted touching and groping and that although nurses constantly reported this behavior to their supervisors and the female acting CEO, no one took any action to stop the harassment. The plaintiff alleged that the defendant continually harassed her by, among other things, stalking her, repeatedly asking her for sex, and finally holding her at gunpoint for 1 1/2 hours, during which he fondled her and masturbated in front of her, and thus acted with discriminatory purpose. Another defendant, the acting CEO, also was not immune from plaintiff's claims when instead of addressing the plaintiff's claims of sexual harassment, she instructed another employee not to discuss sexual harassment during nurse orientation.

Page 380, add to footnote 91 following "Tenth Circuit":

Lankford v. City of Hobart, 27 F.3d 477 (10th Cir. 1994). A city police chief was not immune from liability under § 1983 for allegedly sexually harassing two female police dispatchers. It was clearly established at that time that sexual harassment can violate the equal protection clause even if the alleged victim is not terminated. The plaintiffs alleged that the police chief fondled them, requested sexual favors, and made obscene gestures and unwelcome advances. When they rejected him, the police chief began spying on them while they were off duty and spreading rumors that one of the plaintiffs was a lesbian. He also allegedly used his authority to obtain this plaintiff's medical records without her consent to discredit her. Starrett v. Wadley, 876 F.2d 808 (10th Cir. 1989) does not require a discharge for sexual harassment to be actionable.

Page 381, add to footnote 95:

Bator v. Hawaii, 39 F.3d 1021 (9th Cir. 1994). In an action against the state by a female former employee claiming racial and sexual harassment, the court rejected the defendants' argument that they were entitled to qualified immunity because the plaintiff did not proffer any evidence that her race or gender motivated their acts. The plaintiff showed that she suffered purposeful, invidious harassment in violation of the equal protection clause with evidence that she was harassed when she refused to go on a date with a married man, was hit intentionally many times on her breasts, buttocks, and other areas of her body, and was rammed with a file folder between her legs.

Sauers v. Salt Lake County, 1 F.3d 1122 (10th Cir. 1993) (§ 1983). Evidence of mental illness of an alleged harasser was relevant to the plaintiff former employee's § 1983 sexual harassment claim, when such evidence went to the intent necessary to violate the Fourteenth Amendment.

§ 8.16   —Due Process

Page 383, add to footnote 103:

Saulpaugh v. Monroe Community Hosp., 4 F.3d 134 (2d Cir. 1993), *cert. denied*, 114 S. Ct. 1189 (1994). The district court properly found that a public hospital employee, who was subjected to sexual advances by her supervisor and then was threatened and berated by him when she complained, was subjected to quid pro quo sexual harassment under Title VII. The court properly dismissed her First Amendment claim because the plaintiff's complaints were personal in nature and generally related to her own situation rather than matters of public concern. However, the plaintiff's assertions that the defendant deprived her of both a property and a liberty interest without due process were sufficient to survive the defendants' motion to dismiss.

Bremiller v. Cleveland Psychiatric Inst., 879 F. Supp. 762 (N.D. Ohio 1995). The plaintiff stated a substantive due process claim when she alleged that the defendants conspired to destroy documents relevant to her claim.

§ 8.18   —First Amendment

Page 385, add to footnote 111:

Morgan v. Ford, 6 F.3d 750 (11th Cir. 1993), *cert. denied*, 114 S. Ct. 2708 (1994). In a civil rights action by a former employee correctional officer against the state department of corrections and supervisory personnel, alleging First Amendment and Title VII violations, the employee's complaints of sexual harassment did not constitute speech of "public concern" for purposes of a First Amendment violation:

> A court must . . . discern the purpose of the employee's speech—that is, whether she spoke on behalf of the public as a citizen, or whether the employee spoke for herself as an employee. . . . To accomplish this, a court considers "the content, form and context of a given statement, as revealed by the whole record." *Deremo v. Watkins*, 939 F.2d 908, 910 (11th Cir. 1991) . . . . A court may consider the employee's attempts to make the concerns public, along with "the employee's motivation in speaking." *Id.* at 911.
>
> While we heartily agree with Morgan that sexual harassment in the workplace is a matter of important social interest, "'the mere fact that the topic of the employee's speech was one in which the public might or would have had an interest is of little moment.'" *Kurtz v.* [*Vickrey*, 855 F.2d 723 (11th Cir. 1988)] at 727 . . . . Rather, we must determine whether the purpose of Morgan's speech was to raise issues of public concern, on the one hand, or to further her own public interest, on the other. . . .
>
> In the case at hand, Morgan's speech largely focused upon how Ford behaved toward her and how that conduct affected her work. The speech that Morgan cites is in the form of complaints to official bodies—the Superintendent of ACMI, Internal Affairs, and the Office of Fair Employment Practices. She did not relate her concerns about sexual harassment to the public, or attempt to involve the public in any manner. . . . The record shows that Morgan's speech was driven by her own entirely rational self-interest in improving the conditions of her employment. Her complaints about Ford's behavior, as serious as they were, centered around her private matters, not matters of social interest. As an employee grievance, Morgan's speech was not a matter of public concern. . . .
>
> That Morgan spoke on behalf of Sheila Parrish does not change the outcome. An employee's speech will rarely be entirely private or entirely

public. . . . Considering the entire record, we conclude that Morgan primarily spoke as an employee to improve her work environment.

6 F.3d at 754–55 (footnotes omitted).

Saulpaugh v. Monroe Community Hosp., 4 F.3d 134 (2d Cir. 1993), *cert. denied*, 114 S. Ct. 1189 (1994). The district court properly found that a public hospital employee, who was subjected to sexual advances by her supervisor and then was threatened and berated by him when she complained, was subjected to quid pro quo sexual harassment under Title VII. The court properly dismissed her First Amendment claim because the plaintiff's complaints were personal in nature and generally related to her own situation rather than matters of public concern. However, the plaintiff's assertions that the defendant deprived her of both a property and a liberty interest without due process were sufficient to survive defendants' motion to dismiss.

* A former band director alleged sexual harassment by students in Howard v. Board of Educ., 893 F. Supp. 808 (N.D. Ill. 1995), an action brought under Title VII, Title IX, and § 1983 against the board of education for the school district that employed her, the high school principal, and the assistant superintendent for a second school district alleging sex discrimination, sexual harassment, and retaliatory discharge. The plaintiff alleged that she was intentionally discriminated against based on her being a female and as a result of the sexual harassment directed at her and the failure to eliminate that harassment after she complained. She also alleged that the board's widespread practice of ignoring sexual harassment in the schools was so permanent and well settled as to constitute a custom or usage with the force of law within the school district. Moreover, she alleged that the principal knew of the plaintiff's complaints and took no action against the students to stop the harassment, thereby intentionally permitting the harassment to continue.

With respect to her First Amendment claim, the plaintiff generally alleged that her complaints of sexual harassment were on "an issue of public concern." However, such conclusion was belied by the more specific allegations of the amended complaint, which made it clear that it was plaintiff personally who was offended and that she was not speaking for other teachers at the school when she voiced her complaints. The plaintiff failed to allege, other than in a generalized and conclusionary fashion, that her complaints were driven by her motivation to remedy sexually offensive conduct at the school for the benefit of others or the public at large.

§ 8.19   Remedies for § 1983 Claims

Page 386, add to footnote 118:

Nicks v. Missouri, 67 F.3d 699 (8th Cir. 1995). Evidence of sexual harassment was sufficient to sustain a verdict for the plaintiff in a § 1983 sexual harassment action by a former employee of a state-run mental health facility, alleging that supervisors failed to prevent her harassment by a coworker, Little, whose unwanted attention included purposeless visits, some of several hours duration, to the office Nicks shared with Karras, her immediate supervisor; Little's attempts to discuss his personal and marital problems with Nicks; statements of Little's desire to have a relationship with her; quests through the parking lot for her car; and attempts to follow her around at work. The court found the evidence of Little's harassing behavior to be substantial. During the plaintiff's 30-day sick leave, Little visited her apartment complex, posing as a concerned coworker, and convinced the apartment manager to let him into Nick's apartment. He telephoned Nicks at her apartment several times daily, calling back when Nicks would hang up on him. He sent a long personal note professing his "love" for Nicks in a package disguised to look as if it had been sent by a St. Louis University professor. He left notes for her at St. Louis University, where she was taking graduate courses, and, on one occasion, he left a single red rose and a note for Nicks at the psychology department office. A jury reasonably could conclude that Little's conduct during the period following Nick's dismissal flowed from the previous inaction of the appellants that Nicks argues violated her rights. "Thus, evidence that tended to prove that Little continued to harass Nicks after her dismissal by their common employer, her superiors never having lifted a finger to discourage Little's offensive conduct prior to Nick's dismissal, is clearly relevant to the jury's assessment of Nick's damages." *Id.* at 703.

§ 8.21   Section 1985(3)

Page 388, add to footnote 131:

Bremiller v. Cleveland Psychiatric Inst., 879 F. Supp. 762 (N.D. Ohio 1995). The plaintiff could properly maintain an action under § 1985 in an action charging sexual harassment and retaliation against a

psychiatric institution. The plaintiff alleged that the male employees subjected the plaintiffs to verbal threats, physical intimidation, sexual jokes,
and unwanted touching and groping and that although nurses constantly
reported this behavior to their supervisors and the female acting CEO, no
one took any action to stop the harassment. The court rejected the defendant's contention that the plaintiff could not maintain such an action
because of the "intracorporate conspiracy" doctrine:

> The Sixth Circuit recently created an exception to this doctrine. The court
> said "when employees act outside the course of their employment, they
> and the corporation may form a conspiracy under 42 U.S.C. §1985(3)."
> *Johnson v. Hills & Dales Gen. Hosp. et al.,* 40 F.3d 837 (6th Cir. 1994).
>
> Taking the plaintiff's allegations as true, the court finds that plaintiff
> pleads facts sufficient to show that defendants acted outside of their scope
> of employment. Typically actions such as managerial decisions and the
> implementation or ratification thereof are protected within the scope of
> employment. Yet, if the decision was part of a conspiratorial plan to limit
> access to documents, related to plaintiff's complaint, to the co-conspira-
> tors and then those documents are destroyed by the co-conspirators, those
> activities fall outside the scope of employment and thereby provide an
> exception to the intracorporate conspiracy doctrine.

Id. at 789. The court also rejected the argument that the plaintiff's claims
did not amount to more than mere Title VII allegations and so the plaintiff could not use § 1985 to pursue those claims when the plaintiff
alleged a right not created by Title VII: an equal protection clause right
to be free from sex-based governmental discrimination.

Page 388, add to footnote 133:

Bedford v. Southeastern Pa. Transp. Auth., 867 F. Supp. 288 (E.D. Pa.
1994). Gender-based animus is encompassed by § 1985(3). "Sex is an
immutable characteristic resulting from a fortuity of birth and women
historically have been victims of discrimination." *Id.* at 294.

Page 388, add at end of section:

In *Russell v. City of Overland Police Department,* 838 F. Supp. 1350
(E.D. Mo. 1993), a former employee alleged sexual harassment and
discrimination that started before but continued into the period after
enactment of the Civil Rights Act of 1991. She thus stated a continuing
violation and so was entitled to a jury trial on all of her claims; the

plaintiff could also seek punitive damages. A claim of conspiracy under § 1985 was dismissed because the plaintiff's complaint lacked material facts demonstrating an agreement reached by the defendants and because allegations of a conspiracy to violate Title VII will not support a claim under § 1985(3).

§ 8.26 Claims Under the Constitution

Page 390, add to footnote 148:

* *Cf.* United States v. Lanier, 73 F.3d 1380 (6th Cir. 1996). A state judge was convicted under a federal statute criminalizing the willful deprivation of a constitutional right by a person acting under color of any law, for the sexual harassment and assault of state judicial employees and litigants. The court of appeals held that sexual assault could not be prosecuted as a violation of a constitutional substantive due process right to bodily integrity.

> After consideration of the legislative history of this statute, the case law, the long established tradition of judicial restraint in the extension of criminal statutes, and the lack of any notice to the public that this ambiguous criminal statute includes simple or sexual assault crimes within its coverage, we conclude that the sexual harassment and assault indictment brought under § 242 should have been dismissed by the District Court upon motion of the defendant. . . .
>
> . . . The prosecution . . . neither articulated nor proposed the recognition of a gender-based crime for sexual assault involving discrimination against or oppression of women in violation of the Equal Protection Clause. Nor did the prosecution allege in the indictment, or attempt to prove as an element of the offense, that the state criminal process in Tennessee was incapable of enforcing its own criminal statutes prohibiting sexual assault, nor did the prosecution allege as an element of the § 242 offense that state law enforcement officials have laws, customs, policies or practices that discriminate against or oppress women as a class. There is no claim that state law enforcement officials and state prosecutors, judges or jurors are any less concerned about such crimes than their federal counterparts. Therefore, our opinion addresses only the substantive due process, "shock-the-conscience" crime alleged by the prosecution, not a crime based on equal protection, state-sanctioned abuse, or some other legal theory.

Id. at 1384.

Cf. Davis v. Ector County, Texas, 40 F.3d 777 (5th Cir. 1994). The plaintiff, a former investigator with the county drug task force, whose wife had filed a sexual harassment suit against her employer, the county sheriff's office, was discharged when he defied an admonishment by his superior to keep the task force out of his wife's lawsuit by writing a letter to the county commissioners' court underscoring the seriousness of his wife's allegations and attempting to squelch rumors that his wife's complaint was fabricated as a means of causing the current sheriff to resign or tarnishing his image. A jury awarded compensatory and punitive damages for violations of the First Amendment and the Texas Whistle Blower Act. The court of appeals reversed the verdict for the plaintiff on the whistleblower claim, finding that the jury instruction was sufficiently vague to make the correctness of the verdict uncertain, but affirmed the verdict for plaintiff on the First Amendment claim, concluding that the letter was on a matter of public concern, despite the fact that the plaintiff may have sought to strengthen the credibility of his wife by writing the letter. The plaintiff wrote the letter in his capacity as a citizen, not as a public employee, and the value of the speech outweighed the threat that the speech posed to efficiency.

CHAPTER 9

COMMON LAW LIABILITY

§ 9.2 Effect of State Antidiscrimination Laws

Page 394, add to footnote 10 following "District of Columbia":

King v. Kidd, 640 A.2d 656 (D.C. 1993). The District of Columbia Comprehensive Merit Personnel Act did not preempt a district employee's claim of intentional infliction of emotional distress based on acts of sexual harassment and subsequent retaliation in light of the specific exclusion of sexual harassment claims from the Act; nor does the Act preempt tort claims in general or intentional infliction of emotional distress claims in particular. It implicitly preempts common law actions only if the employee claims wrongful treatment and injury cognizable as a "personal issue" under the Act's "performance ratings," "adverse actions," and employee "grievances" provisions.

Page 394, add to footnote 10 following "Illinois":

Augustin v. Mason, 65 Fair Empl. Prac. Cas. (BNA) 1513 (N.D. Ill. 1992). The state human rights act does not bar common law tort claims even if they arise in an employment context; it preempts only claims predicated on the policies or provisions of the state act, such as a claim for wrongful discharge based on a discriminatory classification. Plaintiff's claims of battery and intentional infliction of emotional distress were common law tort theories rather than civil rights violations and therefore were not dependent on the state act for viability; the elements of battery and intentional infliction of emotional distress are quite different from those necessary to establish a civil rights violation under the act, and may be present even when a civil rights violation based on sex discrimination cannot be shown.

Page 396, add to footnote 15:

See also Chester v. Northwest Iowa Youth Emergency Servs. Ctr., 869 F. Supp. 700 (N.D. Iowa 1994)

§ 9.5 Workers' Compensation Statutes

Page 399, add to footnote 26 following "District of Columbia::

Webb v. Hyman, 861 F. Supp. 1094 (D.D.C. 1994). Neither the workers' compensation act nor the Comprehensive Merit Personnel Act barred the plaintiff's claim for intentional infliction of emotional distress when that claim was intertwined with plaintiff's Title VII cause of action. "Regardless of whom the Defendant may be, a tort claim *fundamentally linked* to a sexual harassment claim is more than a mere 'personnel issue' under the CMPA, and therefore is not barred under that Act." *Id.* at 1101 (emphasis in the original).

Page 399, add to footnote 26 following "Coleman" case:

Pennsylvania: Barb v. Miles, Inc., 861 F. Supp. 356 (W.D. Pa. 1994) (claim of intentional infliction of emotional distress was not preempted by state workers' compensation law).

Gruver v. Ezon Prods., 763 F. Supp. 772 (M.D. Pa. 1991). The state workers' compensation act did not bar a sexual harassment-related claim for intentional infliction of emotional distress when the claim stemmed from alleged harassment from a third person who was acting from purely personal motivations.

Page 400, add to footnote 26 following "Hawaii":

Cf. Bator v. Hawaii, 39 F.3d 1021 (9th Cir. 1994). In an action against the state by a female former employee claiming racial and sexual harassment, a finding by the state workers' compensation board that a workplace injury was caused by unintentional contact with another employee's elbow did not bar the plaintiff from arguing, in the sexual harassment action, that she was injured when a coworker struck her from behind with a legal folder which he rammed up into her vaginal and rectal areas.

Page 400, add to footnote 26 following "Illinois:":

Dirksen v. City of Springfield, 842 F. Supp. 1117 (C.D. Ill. 1994). The plaintiff's claim of intentional infliction of emotional distress against the city and the mayor was barred by the state workers' compensation act.

Page 401, add to footnote 26 following "Virginia":

Middlekauff v. Allstate Ins. Co., 439 S.E.2d 394 (Va. 1994). An action by a former employee for intentional infliction of emotional distress arising out of sexual harassment was not barred by the exclusivity provision of the state workers' compensation act as she alleged a gradually incurred injury caused by cumulative events and did not allege an injury that could be construed as resulting from an obvious sudden mechanical or structural change in her body and thus did not allege an injury by accident under the law.

Page 401, add to footnote 26 following "Wisconsin":

Stefanski v. R.A. Zahetner & Assocs., 855 F. Supp. 1030 (E.D. Wis. 1994). A female receptionist alleged that her supervisor, after drinking at a bar with the plaintiff and other employees, touched her breast, attempted to staple it, compared his sexual prowess to that of the plaintiff's husband, offered to provide her with oral sexual services, demanded that the plaintiff provide him with sexual favors, sprayed the contents of a fire extinguisher at her waist, and sexually assaulted another employee. The plaintiff complained to supervisors and filed a criminal complaint against the alleged harasser; the supervisor was suspended without pay for three weeks and pleaded no contest to a charge of fourth degree sexual assault. Despite the plea and sentence, the supervisor retained his supervisory status. The plaintiff's claims of assault, battery, and loss of consortium were not barred by the state workers' compensation statute, as the allegations implied an intent on the supervisor's part to cause bodily harm.

Other state claims of failure to maintain a safe workplace, conspiracy, and loss of consortium were barred, however, either because they were not against a co-employee or because they were not claims for assault intended to cause bodily harm.

Page 402, add to footnote 28, following "Illinois":

Al-Dabbagh v. Greenpeace Inc., 873 F. Supp. 1105 (N.D. Ill. 1994). See § **10.15.**

Page 405, add at end of section:

In *Herring v. F.N. Thompson, Inc.,* 866 F. Supp. 264 (W.D.N.C. 1994), a former employee brought a sexual harassment action against the employer corporation and two of its officers, alleging that both men told her of their sexual exploits, made sexually suggestive jokes, touched the plaintiff and other female employees on the breasts, and engaged in other conduct. With respect to the corporate defendant, a plaintiff charging sexual harassment was limited to recovery under the workers' compensation act when the court concluded that the individual defendants were not the alter ego of the corporate defendant. There was no evidence that the individual defendants acted with total autonomy in executing their duties as corporate officers, the complaint did not alleged the individuals to be the alter ego of the company, and the fact that the individual defendants were corporate officers did not show that they were indistinguishable from the corporation as an independent entity with its own structure.

§ 9.6   Intentional Infliction of Emotional Distress

Page 407, add to footnote 50:

Cf. Garcia v. Andrews, 867 S.W.2d 409 (Tex. Ct. App. 1993). A female employee who worked for one month, until her discharge, did not state a claim for intentional infliction of emotional distress by a supervisor who once observed her from top to bottom, once came into her office and flicked the lights on and off and asked if she did her best work in the dark, and once spoke to her through a plexiglass reception window and discussed a sexually oriented magazine article. There was no evidence that the conduct of the supervisor was either extreme or outrageous. The court refused to apply a reasonable woman standard to determine what constituted conduct that was extreme and outrageous. "Existing policy is concerned not only with safeguarding freedom of expression, but also with the even-handed disposition of all claims without regard to whether the plaintiff is a woman or a man, is young or old, or is a member of any one of numerous and varied sub-groups in our society, each, possibly, with its own standard of decency." *Id.* at 412.

Page 408, add to footnote 51 following Minnesota cases:

Nevada: Steiner v. Showboat Operating Co., 25 F.3d 1459 (9th Cir. 1994).

Page 409, in footnote 53, "Linebaugh" citation should read:

198 Mich. App. 335, 497 N.W.2d 585 (1993).

Page 409, add to footnote 54:

See also Steiner v. Showboat Operating Co., 25 F.3d 1459 (9th Cir. 1994), *cert. denied*, 115 S. Ct. 733 (1995). A former casino employee, the first female casino "floorperson," alleged sexual harassment, retaliation, constructive discharge, and intentional infliction of emotional distress by a supervisor. She did not establish constructive discharge when the supervisor was fired two and a half months before the plaintiff's resignation and for several months prior to her resignation she had been restored at her request to her favored shift. She also failed to establish retaliatory conduct by the employer. The court noted that although it had dismissed this claim, it did not mean to suggest that the fact that the plaintiff had quit her job could not weigh in to her proof of damages for sexual harassment and of the extent of her distress and other damages for the intentional infliction of emotional distress claim.

See also Lathrope-Olson v. Department of Transp., 128 Or. App. 405, 876 P.2d 345 (1994). The circuit court improperly entered summary judgment in favor of the defendant employer in an action by a female member of a highway crew against the State Department of Transportation for intentional infliction of emotional distress for sexual harassment by the crew chief and male crew members when there was a material issue of fact as to whether their conduct transgressed the bounds of socially tolerable conduct. Plaintiff alleged that the crew chief directed overtly racist and sexual comments to her and engaged in other acts of psychological and physical intimidation. "Such overt acts of racism and sexual harassment are not simply rude and boorish, but are more properly characterized as the kind of conduct that a jury could find was intended to inflict deep, stigmatizing and psychic wounds on another person." 876 P.2d at 347.

Page 409, add to footnote 55:

Piech v. Arthur Andersen & Co., 841 F. Supp. 825 (N.D. Ill. 1994). A claim for intentional infliction of emotional distress requires more than what is required for sexual harassment. Here the plaintiff's "most extreme allegation is that she was subjected to one isolated proposition or 'advance' over four years"; other allegations included being subjected to sexual humor, references to female anatomy, and general discriminatory conduct. Such allegations lacked the required systematic and intentional actions designed to humiliate the plaintiff.

Page 410, add to footnote 57:

See also Chester v. Northwest Iowa Youth Emergency Servs. Ctr., 869 F. Supp. 700 (N.D. Iowa 1994). Although plaintiff's emotional distress claim was preempted by the state civil rights act, the court discussed at length the fact that despite the state courts' reluctance to find conduct sufficiently outrageous to support a claim of intentional infliction of emotional distress, such conduct was presented here. Plaintiff juvenile detention center employee alleged that her supervisor, among other things:

1. Directly questioned her about her sex life
2. Demanded that she accompany him to a video about pap smears
3. Subjected her to sexually suggestive drawings and comics
4. Discussed his own sexual practices and preferences
5. Made sexually explicit comments about coworkers, employees, and suppliers
6. Used vulgar expletives in everyday vocabulary
7. Referred to female employees as bitches
8. Discussed the length of a client's penis, which he observed during a strip search
9. Replied to news of the plaintiff's pregnancy that he didn't care as long as the baby wasn't his
10. Made repeated suggestions that the plaintiff accompany him to a convention and share his bed there
11. Discussed spraying a semen-like substance at an adult bookstore
12. Told plaintiff he hired her to have fun and for income
13. Attached a note saying "cute butt" to a female employee's clothed buttocks
14. Discussed how the plaintiff might have sexual intercourse with her husband during pregnancy
15. Referred to the plaintiff as a "fucking bitch"

As a result of this conduct, the plaintiff alleged symptoms including anxiety attacks, headaches, sleeping difficulties, nightmares, loss of self-esteem, crying, loss of trust in males, marital stress, weight gain, depression, loss of appetite, panic disorder, a major depressive episode, and posttraumatic stress disorder.

Bintner v. Burlington N., Inc., 857 F. Supp. 1484 (D. Wyo. 1994). A former locomotive engineer who alleged that she was required to work in an environment that included propositions for sexual favors, physical attack, verbal catcalls and vulgarity, and written comments of a sexual and perverted nature, and that the work environment demeaned women with sexual cartoons and graffiti on engines and cabooses, pictures and sexual graffiti on the walls of the defendant's facilities, specifically using the plaintiff's name and suggesting that she participated in lewd and lascivious acts stated a claim for intentional infliction of emotional distress.

Page 410, line 15 should read:

The state supreme court held that, in an action for intentional infliction of

Page 410, add to footnote 60:

Thomason v. Prudential Ins. Co. of Am., 866 F. Supp. 1329 (D. Kan. 1994). An administrative assistant, who alleged that her supervisor bumped into her on two occasions, repeatedly used the word "fuck", repeatedly commented on the plaintiff's "copious" breasts, kissed her on two occasions, and grabbed her rear, did not state a claim for outrage when the court agreed that although the conduct was inappropriate, unprofessional, and had no place in the workplace, the conduct was not sufficiently egregious as to permit recovery under the tort of outrage.

Page 414, add to footnote 67:

Cf. Garcia v. Andrews, 867 S.W.2d 409 (Tex. Ct. App. 1993). The court rejected the plaintiff's attempt to use the reasonable woman standard to determine what constituted conduct that was extreme and outrageous in cases of intentional infliction of emotional distress:

> Existing policy is concerned not only with safeguarding freedom of expression, but also with the even-handed disposition of all claims without regard to whether the plaintiff is a woman or a man, is young or old,

or is a member of any one of numerous and varied sub-groups in our society, each, possibly, with its own standard of decency. Fairness dictates a general societal standard where liability is found only where the conduct goes "beyond all possible bounds of decency, and [is] to be regarded as atrocious and utterly intolerable in a *civilized community.*" *Wornick Co. v. Casas*, 856 S.W.2d 732, 736 (Tex. 1993).

867 S.W.2d at 412. Here the plaintiff alleged three acts: the observation by a supervisor of the plaintiff from top to bottom on her first day of work, and two sexual comments. Thus, the trial court properly found that the supervisor's conduct was not extreme or outrageous.

Page 414, add at beginning of footnote 70:

District of Columbia: Ryczek v. Guest Servs., Inc., 877 F. Supp 754 (D.D.C. 1995). See **§ 10.10.**

Page 418, add after carryover paragraph:

In *Meagher v. Lamb-Weston, Inc.*, 839 F. Supp. 1403 (D. Or. 1993), two female food processing plant employees failed to establish that their supervisor or employer intended to inflict severe emotional distress by telling off-color jokes, commenting on the attributes of female employees or his own perceived sexual prowess, engaging in offensive gestures and touching, and otherwise conducting himself inappropriately. His antics were obnoxious or immature but did not evidence an intent to inflict severe emotional distress. "At worst a jury might find Krug's antics were intended to make the listener uncomfortable." *Id.* at 1408. Although the employer should have confronted the situation more aggressively than it did, given the fact that a number of oral complaints were made about the supervisor, that by itself could not support a finding that the defendant intended for the supervisor to sexually harass female employees, or to inflict severe emotional distress on them. The supervisor's conduct toward others could be relevant from the standpoint of demonstrating intent to cause extreme emotional distress, or to show that management was aware of his conduct, but only the conduct experienced by the plaintiffs was actionable. The court rejected the plaintiffs' contention that an act directed at any female employee was an act directed at the plaintiffs, because the supervisor thereby created a hostile working environment; liability for intentional infliction of emotional distress cannot be predicated upon behavior toward a class.

Page 418, add to footnote 85:

Mains v. II Morrow, Inc., 128 Or. App. 625, 877 P.2d 88 (1994). The lower court improperly dismissed plaintiff's tort claim for intentional infliction of emotional distress. In order for an employer to be liable for an employee's tortious conduct, the employee must act within the scope of employment. Vicarious liability is imposed, regardless of whether the employer committed a morally wrongful act, as a policy of risk allocation. Here there was a factual question as to whether the employer condoned a supervisor's technique of controlling female employees with sexual harassment. The supervisor repeatedly made sexual comments and jokes, including referring to plaintiff as a "sex-atory" and "just another worthless woman" and often using the term "lick my balls." He physically harassed the plaintiff by touching her breast, shoving her, and grabbing her ankles.

> [I]n this case, a factfinder could infer from the record that sexual harassment was a characteristic of Berry's method of supervising and controlling female subordinate employees in the workplace, and that defendant condoned this supervisor technique. Berry created a pervasive atmosphere of sexual harassment, was the subject of an earlier sexual harassment claim that the Bureau of Labor and Industries investigated, and was notorious within the company for discriminating against women Despite the earlier complaint and his reputation, defendant retained Berry in a supervisory role. Berry told plaintiff that he harassed her because the male employees that he supervised expected the behavior. In a letter to the Employment Division after defendant fired him, Berry said that he "was discharged for something that my superiors condoned by participating in the same sort of conduct."

Id. at 92.

§ 9.7 Assault and Battery

Page 419, add at beginning of footnote 93:

Cf. Caprio v. American Airlines, Inc., 848 F. Supp. 1528 (M.D. Fla. 1994). Issues of material fact existed as to whether alleged battery resulting from the touching and slapping of a female reservation agent's buttocks by coworkers was conducted within the scope of employment; such issue is one best submitted to a jury.

Troutt v. Charcoal Steak House, Inc., 835 F. Supp. 899 (W.D. Va. 1993). An award of $50,000 as punitive damages for sexual battery was not excessive in an action for sexual harassment against a former employer and sexual assault. After the plaintiff's first month at work as a waitress, her supervisor began to make sexually suggestive remarks which escalated into physical contact, including putting his hands on her waist and breast, grabbing her buttocks, kissing her on the neck, reaching under her skirt, and grabbing her crotch. The supervisor's conduct caused the plaintiff to suffer extreme emotional distress, sleeplessness, and depression, and she quit her job.

§ 9.8 Tortious Interference with Contracts

Page 420, add to footnote 98:

Gruver v. Ezon Prods., 763 F. Supp. 772 (M.D. Pa. 1991). A female former employee—who alleged that during the course of her employment she was subjected to various forms of sexual harassment by her supervisor, which, though reported, went unpunished—could not argue that by allowing the harassment to go unpunished, the defendant breached a provision of an employment contract established by the anti-harassment terms of the employee handbook. Common law requires that for a policy to become part of an employment contract, it must be part of the offer of employment—an inducement to join the company. Nowhere in the complaint did the plaintiff state that she accepted employment by the defendant because of the anti-harassment section of the handbook or that the definite terms of the policy were made known to her prior to her acceptance.

§ 9.9 Defamation, Libel, and Slander

Page 422, add to footnote 114:

Cf. Chrzanowski v. Lichtman, 884 F. Supp. 751 (W.D.N.Y. 1995). A male employee plaintiff alleged that he was discharged because, when notified by female employees that the defendant had installed a video camera that allowed him to view those employees in the bathroom, the plaintiff found the camera and reported it to the office and finance managers. However, the plaintiff could not sustain a claim of defamation for statements made at another employee's unemployment compensation hearing, in which the defendant surmised that the plaintiff hooked up the camera. The statement was not made in the context of the plaintiff's termination and not offered as a reason for the plaintiff's termination. There was no compulsion upon the plaintiff to republish what transpired at the unemployment compensation hearing, and the defendant could not have foreseen any compulsion on the plaintiff's part to repeat his statement from the unemployment compensation hearing.

Frederick v. Reed Smith Shaw & McClay, 63 Empl. Prac. Dec. (CCH) ¶ 42,864 (E.D. Pa. 1994). A law firm partner, accused of sexual harassment by a female attorney, was properly found liable by a jury for defamation and invasion of privacy when in response to questions about the case by the media, he made statements saying that the plaintiff was disturbed, had committed extortion, and made obscene phone calls to people, and was under psychiatric care. While it was not necessary for the jury to find that all of those statements were defamatory, the court determined that each was capable of a defamatory meaning. Which statement or statements were found to be defamatory was irrelevant; the fact was that they found at least one of the statements to be defamatory and that there was sufficient evidence to support such a finding. As for the invasion of privacy claim, the alleged harasser's statements were not merely opinions but were expressions of fact that they jury was capable of determining to place the plaintiff in a false light. The defense of truth was a question for the jury to answer.

Page 423, in footnote 115, Linebaugh citation should read:
198 Mich. App. 335, 497 N.W.2d 585 (1993).

§ 9.10   Invasion of Privacy

Page 424, add to footnote 122:

See also Coulter v. Bank of Am., 33 Cal. Rptr. 2d 766 (Ct. App. 1994). A male employee who covertly recorded conversations with coworkers and supervisors, including discussions regarding a coworker's claim that he was harassing her, violated the Privacy Act even though he did not reveal the recordings to any third party; it was sufficient that the bank employees who were secretly recorded expected the conversations to be private.

§ 9.13   Wrongful Discharge

Page 428, add to footnote 146:

Mains v. II Morrow, Inc., 128 Or. App. 625, 877 P.2d 88 (1994). The lower court properly dismissed a wrongful discharge claim of a female employee who rejected reinstatement offers after the supervisor allegedly responsible for her sexual harassment was terminated. Although the plaintiff argued that the intolerable working conditions remained despite the termination of the supervisor, she never explained what those were and did not identify other employees who would continue to harass her.

Page 428, add to footnote 148:

EEOC v. Farmer Bros. Co., 31 F.3d 891 (9th Cir. 1994). Evidence of sexual harassment was relevant to a claim of discriminatory discharge:

> Individuals who engage in sexual harassment may have different motives. Sometimes, an employer or supervisor may use his power within the company's hierarchy in order to gratify his sexual desires. When an employee becomes the victim of her boss'[s] unwanted sexual attention, she may be forced to tolerate his sexually harassing conduct for fear that her job or her advancement in the company are at risk. A woman in this circumstance may reasonably feel subordinated and belittled even though the harasser's primary motive is to seduce her rather than to demean her or cause her anguish and distress. . . . In other circumstances, however, sexual harassment may be symptomatic of gender-based hostility, the employer or supervisor using sexual harassment primarily to subordinate women, to remind them of their lower status in the workplace, and to demean them. In this latter circumstance, the "sexual" element of the harassment is only secondary. . . . Because hostility against women underlies decisions to discharge or refuse to hire women because of their gender, evidence of sexual harassment often will be relevant to claims of gender-based employment discrimination.
>
> Of course, in many cases the harasser will have a mixed motive for engaging in this type of conduct and, as with any overlapping categories,

definitional problems will arise. Nevertheless, the distinction between sexual harassment which arises out of sexual desire and that which reflects hatred of women retains its validity. . . . The finder of fact, presented with evidence of sexual harassment, will have to determine whether and to what extent the employer's or supervisor's harassing conduct is probative of his intent to discriminate against women in his employment decisions. In order to make such a determination, however, the factfinder must first have access to the evidence.

Id. at 897–98.

Cf. Bintner v. Burlington N., Inc., 857 F. Supp. 1484 (D. Wyo. 1994). The state sexual harassment claim of the tort of wrongful discharge was dismissed in an action by a former locomotive engineer who alleged that she was required to work in an environment that included propositions for sexual favors, physical attack, verbal catcalls and vulgarity, and written comments of a sexual and perverted nature, and that the work environment demeaned women with sexual cartoons and graffiti on engines and cabooses, and pictures and sexual graffiti on the walls of the defendant's facilities, specifically using the plaintiff's name and suggesting that she participated in lewd and lascivious acts, when the plaintiff had a remedy under Title VII.

Page 429, add to footnote 150:

Cf. Douglas v. Coca-Cola Bottling Co., 855 F. Supp. 518 (D.N.H. 1994) (state law claims for wrongful discharge are not preempted by Title VII).

§ 9.14 Negligent Hiring, Retention, and Supervision

Page 429, add to footnote 152:

Cf. Thompson v. Campbell, 845 F. Supp. 665 (D. Minn. 1994). An employer did not negligently retain a supervisor accused of sexual harassment when after the plaintiff complained the employer promptly investigated the supervisor, put him on probation, and monitored his conduct. The fact that the employer had additional reasons for placing the supervisor on probation did not undermine the propriety of its response.

Thompson v. Haskell Co., 65 Fair Empl. Prac. Cas. (BNA) 1088 (M.D. Fla. 1994). A discharged female marketing representative stated a cognizable claim for negligent retention stemming from alleged sexual harassment by a supervisor. The court rejected the employer's argument that tort claims based on negligent retention arise only when the employee poses an unreasonable risk of serious physical injury to a third person, and here the plaintiff alleged only sexual harassment and not physical injury.

Minnesota courts have not clearly defined the parameters of the duty or the type of claims arising out of the negligent retention of an employee, but have recognized that a claim for negligent retention may lie when an employee subjects another to sexual harassment. This plaintiff, however, was unable to make the required showing that the employer knew or should have known of the alleged harasser's conduct and failed to take timely action. On the contrary, once aware of the inappropriate behavior, the employer promptly investigated the supervisor, put him on probation, and monitored his conduct. The fact that the employer had additional reasons for placing the supervisor on probation did not undermine the propriety of the response. The plaintiff conceded that except for one isolated incident, the offensive conduct stopped after disciplinary action was taken.

Phillips v. J.P. Stevens & Co. was officially reported at 827 F. Supp. 349 (M.D.N.C. 1993).

Page 431, add to footnote 157:

Under Tennessee law, a negligent supervision claim will lie in a sexual harassment case if it is supported by a viable claim of tortious conduct by the alleged harasser. Hays v. Patton-Tully Transp. Co., 844 F. Supp. 1221 (W.D. Tenn. 1993)(action by female former employees against their employer and male coworkers, alleging sexual harassment and pendent state claims of unlawful discrimination, outrageous conduct or infliction of reckless or intentional emotional distress, and negligent supervision):

> A claim that an employer negligently supervised an employee who has sexually harassed a co-employee does not transmute sexual harassment into a common law tort. Sexual harassment has never been a common law tort; as a cause of action, it is a statutory creation. . . . A negligent supervision claim cannot be based solely upon an underlying claim of sexual harassment *per se*, because the effect would be to impose liability on

employers for failing to prevent a harm that is not a cognizable injury under the common law. Sexual harassment, however, may include misconduct by a co-employee that is independently actionable under the common law, such as battery or intentional infliction of emotional distress.

Id. at 1223.

Page 431, add to footnote 160:

Campbell v. Jackson Business Forms Co., 841 F. Supp. 772 (S.D. Miss. 1994). A state law claim of negligent supervision of employees was barred by the state workers' compensation law; moreover, the claim was in reality a recharacterization of plaintiff's time-barred Title VII claim, and one cannot circumvent time limitations by renaming claims. Other state claims were also time-barred.

§ 9.15 The Common Law Tort of Sexual Harassment

Page 432, add to footnote 164:

Cf. Bintner v. Burlington N., Inc., 857 F. Supp. 1484 (D. Wyo. 1994). A former locomotive engineer who alleged that she was required to work in an environment that included propositions for sexual favors, physical attack, verbal catcalls and vulgarity, and written comments of a sexual and perverted nature, and that the work environment demeaned women with sexual cartoons and graffiti on engines and cabooses, and pictures and sexual graffiti on the walls of the defendant's facilities, specifically using the plaintiff's name and suggesting that she participated in lewd and lascivious acts could not bring a claim for the tort of breach of public policy when she had Title VII available to protect her interests. The court rejected her argument that she had no other remedy available to her because some of the incidents of hostile work environment alleged occurred before the passage of the Civil Rights Act of 1991. The Act is not retroactive when prior to the enactment of the Act, the Wyoming Supreme Court had determined that the state antidiscrimination law provided a remedy for discharge based on sex discrimination and the allegations in the plaintiff's complaint were not such that the court heeded to fashion a public policy remedy when remedies were already available for vindications of the plaintiff's sex discrimination claims.

Page 432, add at end of section:

Geise v. Phoenix Co., 159 Ill. 2d 507, 639 N.E.2d 1273 (1994). Plaintiff's claims of negligent hiring and negligent retention were dismissed when they had to be construed as charging the employer with a civil rights violation within the meaning of the state human rights act. Unlike Title VII, the state act imposes strict liability on employers for sexual harassment by supervisory employees, and thus the other claims were "mere surplusage." *Id.* at 1278.